'Francophonie' in the 1990s

Problems and Opportunities

Dennis Ager

MULTILINGUAL MATTERS LTD
Clevedon • Philadelphia • Adelaide

Library of Congress Cataloging in Publication Data

Data available

British Library Cataloguing in Publication Data

A CIP catalogue record for this book is available from the British Library.

ISBN 1-85359-324-9 (hbk)
ISBN 1-85359-323-0 (pbk) ✔

Multilingual Matters Ltd

UK: Frankfurt Lodge, Clevedon Hall, Victoria Road, Clevedon, Avon BS21 7SJ.
USA: 1900 Frost Road, Suite 101, Bristol, PA 19007, USA.
Australia: P.O. Box 6025, 83 Gilles Street, Adelaide, SA 5000, Australia.

Printed and bound in Great Britain by WBC Book Manufacturers Ltd

'Francophonie' in the 1990s

Multilingual Matters

Culture and Language Learning in Higher Education
     MICHAEL BYRAM (ed.)
Distance Education for Language Teachers
     RON HOWARD and IAN McGRATH (eds)
Educational Research in Europe
     JAMES CALDERHEAD (ed.)
Ethnicity in Eastern Europe
     SUE WRIGHT (ed.)
French for Communication 1979–1990
     ROY DUNNING
Intercultural Communication
     ROBERT YOUNG
The Guided Construction of Knowledge
     NEIL MERCER
Language, Education and Society in a Changing World
     TINA HICKEY and JENNY WILLIAMS (eds)
Languages in Contact and Conflict
     SUE WRIGHT (ed.)
Language Reclamation
     HUBISI NWENMELY
Le ou La? The Gender of French Nouns
     MARIE SURRIDGE
Mission Incomprehensible: The Linguistic Barrier to Effective
Police Co-operation in Europe
     ROY D. INGLETON

Please contact us for the latest book information:
Multilingual Matters Ltd, Frankfurt Lodge, Clevedon Hall,
Victoria Road, Clevedon, Avon, England, BS21 7SJ

Contents

List of Tables

Figure

FOREWORD

This book examines some of the problems and opportunities facing French-speaking countries in the world in the mid-1990s. After considering the development of French influence and presence outside France, it investigates the nature and diversity of countries and areas of the world where French is spoken. 'Francophonie' can be defined in three ways: by the use of the French language; by membership of a formal, organised community of nations; or by the acceptance and promotion of a set of values and beliefs. The problems facing Francophonie in all three senses are discussed next: the identity and culture associated with French, threats from English and other languages, the opinion of many that France's continuing overseas possessions are little more than the world's last colonies, the disparity between North and South in economic terms, and the as yet unresolved problem of the ideal organisational structure for Francophonie. In a final section are reviewed opportunities open to Francophonie in three different parts of the globe: Africa, the Far East and Europe. Conclusions examine the interdependence of four factors: language, politics, economics and cultural values.

The book is divided into three parts:
• The development and distribution of Francophonie
• Problems
• Opportunities
and is supported by a statistical appendix. The book is intended to make up-to-date information and opinion about Francophonie accessible to English-speaking readers interested in a range of disciplines: French studies, comparative international studies, sociolinguistics, the sociology of language, politics and economics, those concerned with questions of language and identity, and interested general readers. It is also an assessment of how well Francophonie is placed to face the future.

ACKNOWLEDGEMENTS

The author acknowledges the help and advice of many people and organisations in the writing of this book. Much of the work was carried out during a period of sabbatical leave in Australia and France, and thanks are due to Aston University, to Michael Clyne and colleagues at Monash University and to Chris Candlin and colleagues at Macquarie University. Particular thanks go to Annis Ager, Sue Wright, and to colleagues and many generations of students at Aston. Any errors of fact or judgement remaining are the responsibility of the author. Translations throughout have been made by the author except where specifically mentioned.

INTRODUCTION

Francophonie

'Francophonie' is a term originally coined by the geographer Onésime Reclus in the 1880s to describe those countries throughout the world which used French, usually as an official language. In the 1990s, the word has come to be used in a number of different ways (L'Année Francophone, 1994, preface). The first meaning applies to those countries and areas of the world where the French language is used as a means of communication, whether officially or not. The second use of Francophonie is to describe an official organisation of countries and regions whose leaders meet regularly to exchange views and consider joint policies and projects. But Francophonie is also used to mean 'not exclusively a geographic, nor even linguistic, but also cultural' approach - an attitude, a belief in a spirit, an ideology and a way of doing things, inspired by French history, language and culture but not necessarily using French, aware of and responsive to the nature of the modern world.

The term 'Francophonie' has been kept here, untranslated. As in French, its use normally implies all three meanings, although the differences are distinguished when necessary. Indeed, it is impossible to investigate Francophonie without examining all three senses of the word, and doing so by using not one but a variety of investigative approaches and disciplines. Linguistics, sociolinguistics and the sociology of language are helpful, but are insufficient to identify the motivations of language speakers, the attractions they see in one means of communication rather than another, or the effect of political or social change. Political science alone often misses the point: democracy is not an absolute, and its definitions depend not merely on history, traditions and individuals, but also on how the traditions have been communicated and on the meaning that certain types of discourse give to institutions and to power. The economics of Francophonie, too, are both relevant to international politics and also to the way in which an apparently cultural community is brought together. Cultural traditions, the intangible values and the artistic life of nations and communities are necessarily communicated through language, but their continued existence may depend not so much on their internal force or quality as on the associated cultural industries, or even on the personal whims of a powerful individual. In this way, the present book investigates Francophonie not solely as a language phenomenon, as an example of international co-operation or as a set of values, but identifies problems and opportunities and their interaction, and draws conclusions which cut across disciplines.

Our purpose in the present book is hence to undertake an interdisciplinary investigation of contemporary Francophonie. The interrelation of disciplines, and the necessity to draw on a range of insights, becomes clear when one examines three often-debated problems, to which indeed we shall return at various points: the question of language and identity; the unity of an international organisation; and the way a specific country understands and represents itself.

Language and Identity

French is spoken as a first language by more than a hundred million people across the globe, and many more learn French as a second or foreign language: it is still the first foreign language of the English-speaking world. French is an official language in more than thirty countries, for diplomacy, for many international bodies and groups, and for the Olympic Games. French-speaking peoples are significant members of the European Union. The use of French is a strong unifying factor across the world.

For French speakers, the language is the main symbol of common identity. In the past, the unity of France itself in the 'Hexagon' was forged against the threat of disintegration symbolised by the regional languages. More recently, the existence of organised and official Francophonie is providing opportunities to create a new, international, identity and a new form of unity. The international Francophone community provides support for many countries of the Third World, for potentially isolated States, and for French-speaking communities within larger States. The defence of French by France and by other Francophone countries is often symptomatic of defence of what is specifically French in other domains: culture, the media, but also international trade, diplomacy, economic and political relationships, and it is this which may explain the strength of the concept of cultural exclusion in the 1993 GATT negotiations.

In different ways, French is also a language symbolising conflict. In Belgium and Canada it is a symbol of resistance to other groups, while in many African states its use symbolises continuing elitist exclusion of local cultures, languages and ways of life. The overseas French possessions - the *Départements* and *Territoires d'Outre-Mer* (*DOM* and *TOM*) seem to many to be the last remnants of colonialism, with all the word implies in terms of control over unwilling populations. In France itself, French continues to dominate regional - and now immigrant - languages and dialects. Yet, also in France itself, French seems to have to resist potential cultural and economic domination by English, and the

'Anglo-Saxon' threat has to be countered by defensive language laws, whose impact may be greater in social and economic fields than in cultural ones.

The unity of Francophonie

The diversity of geographical setting and of economies, and the range of social structures and problems of Francophone countries mean that French language reflects differing realities, and the universal values and approaches of the *espace francophone* may conflict with both the reality of difference and the need for it to be expressed. The battle for human rights and democracy, and at the same time for economic and political development is particularly acute within Francophonie, where the contrasts between wealthy North and poverty-racked South are sharp and sharply felt.

Yet Francophonie - in all three senses - serves to unify. The French-speaking countries are united - to a certain extent - by language, but also by the institutional and political organisation of contemporary Francophonie, and by common attitudes towards the importance and centrality of certain notions of humanism, universality and the purpose of political organisation. We are necessarily as much concerned with the social, economic and political setting within which French acts as a means of communication, and with the values it conveys, as we are with language itself.

The history of France, with its moments of glory and grandeur - the reigns of Louis XIV and XVI, the French Revolution, the Napoleonic Empires, the two World Wars - has profoundly marked French-speaking countries everywhere. The Revolutionary ideals - liberty, equality and brotherhood - although often breached in practice, affect the discourse, the framework of thought and the approach to problems of all French-speaking nations. A common philosophical humanism underlies political and even economic policies. Belief in the universal applicability of French political habits and methods has not been affected by their demonstrated inappropriateness in the African context, and the underlying concepts of justice and the Rights of Man form a universe of discourse which enables fellow-members of the 'club' to understand why policies are established and to criticise or approve them. Even French administrative organisation, as exemplified in State centralisation, the legal codes or the nature and style of the bureaucracy, has extensively marked most French-speaking countries.

Institutional and political links between the different countries and regions are more and more centred around the frequent summit meetings of Francophone Heads of State and Government. These provide the opportunity to meet and discuss matters of common interest, for North to meet South and rich to meet poor, for 'exploiters' to meet the 'exploited'. The meetings ensure that France does not forget the obligations of an ex-colonial power to her former colonies, and that the implications of the French point of view in international diplomacy are fully understood and their effect on her actual and potential friends are calculated and evaluated. Similarly, the problems facing the Third World are discussed and reviewed, and the meetings provide a forum for different parts of the world to present and explain their policies without the necessity to defend them before a decision-making body. Increasingly, the meeting is proving attractive to countries who have no large French-speaking minority and no history of colonialism.

Francophone institutions are not limited to political Summits, however: there is a wide range of 'decentralised' bilateral and multilateral points of contact, and although commerce between Francophone countries is not, for most, a strong factor in unity, there is no doubt that common roots, a common linguistic and philosophical, if not political and economic, identity, and the common language, facilitate understanding which bears its fruits in other fora such as the United Nations and its agencies.

France in Francophonie

France herself contains half the French speakers in the world: fifty-five million of a total of over one hundred million. Her economy is overwhelmingly the most powerful, although Canada, too, competes with France to influence others and to show that France does not have economic priority. It is inevitable that France should take the lead among French-speaking nations, in ways which contrast strongly with the Anglophone Commonwealth. There is no other single Francophone country whose economy, population or influence matches that of France, whereas the Commonwealth itself does not include all English-speaking nations, and even within the Commonwealth English-speaking Australia, Canada and India, each in their own way, are equal with or superior to Britain.

France has retained direct involvement, too, in many of her former colonial possessions, even though they may enjoy internal autonomy in the same way as, or even to a greater extent than, the regions of France itself. France's own Parliament has representatives of Pacific, Caribbean and Indian Ocean interests in its committees and internal groups, and Parliament is directly involved in the internal affairs of these regions - as when the *Commission des Lois* visits New Caledonia or Tahiti to see how laws made in France are implemented, and how appropriate they are. Most French speakers would agree that the French spoken in France, and particularly in Paris, represents a standard and a norm to which all should aspire, whatever the conditions of use and the specific circumstances of their own communicative environment. The languages and cultures of Africa, Tahiti, and Guadeloupe, and even the North American nature of Quebec, are regarded by some as a potential danger: Francophonie could suffer fragmentation and disintegration if the stability and quality of standard French is not accepted by all. Many, too, would give priority to the cultural norms of France over those of other countries.

Is Francophonie then nothing more than a sounding board for France, a way of ensuring that she retains a world-wide influence and plays a global role which other former colonial powers have surrendered? If this were the case, former enemies would not wish to be associated, as Vietnam is - even though Algeria is not, at least formally in Summit meetings. European and North American Francophone countries and regions would dispute French domination. New countries - Bulgaria and Romania - would not wish to be join the formal organisation. The problems and opportunities of Francophonie are not - only - problems and opportunities for France in her external policies and practices.

The agenda of the 1993 Francophone Summit meeting was 'Unity in Diversity'. In language and identity, in co-operation and organisation, and in spirit and ideology, there is a constant contrast between Francophonie as 'dialogue' and as 'solidarity', between unity and diversity, between similarity and difference. Throughout our discussion of problems and opportunities, the three meanings of Francophonie, and the implications of dialogue and solidarity for each of them, will be borne in mind, and we shall return to them in the concluding chapter.

PART ONE

Francophone countries are often divided into three groups. Those where French is the historic language - France itself, parts of Belgium, Switzerland, Luxembourg and Italy - form 'frontier Francophonie', situated in Europe and bordering France itself. Countries and regions where French is the result of emigration and settlement - Quebec, Haiti, Mauritius, and other areas settled principally before the eighteenth century - form a second group. The countries concerned are situated mainly in North America, the Caribbean and the Indian Ocean, and Francophonie here has had time to develop distinctive forms of language, including Creole in the Caribbean and the Indian Ocean. The populations are mainly French-speaking, and represent the whole of the local society - its workers as well as its elite. Where French is the result of the massive colonial expansion, mainly in the late nineteenth and early twentieth centuries, now independent countries, many of them in Africa, form a third group. For these, French, in general, has not become the normal language of all the population, and retains elitist connotations: it is an official, governmental and educational language. In this group, too, fall the continuing remnants of Empire - the *Départements* and *Territoires d'Outre-Mer*, where France herself continues to take responsibility for government. The development of Francophonie has therefore given very different connotations to the meaning of the term: for some countries, it is a natural and inevitable descriptive term, conveying a set of ideas which are rooted in history and tradition. For the second group, too, Francophonie is a part of the normal fabric of life, although there may be undercurrents of discrimination - racial, linguistic or social - in society. The third group may regard Francophonie in quite a different light: as a fairly recent imposition, accompanied by a history of oppression and exploitation, but offering also, in the contemporary world, access to modernity and development.

French-speaking countries are distributed throughout the contemporary world. There are French speakers in every continent, and their influence can be felt in every aspect of international life. In the second chapter of this Part, we examine the diversity of Francophonie from the point of view of the current situation, investigating both the linguistic and the social setting in which the language is used. Not all the present tensions, existing characteristics of the range of countries and regions where French is spoken, and similarities and differences between them, can be traced back to their origin or their first contacts with Francophonie. Nor, however, is it easy to identify what still unites these countries and regions.

1. THE DEVELOPMENT OF FRANCOPHONIE

Frontier Francophonie

European Francophonie - France and the French-speaking areas of Belgium, Switzerland, Luxembourg and Italy - developed from the Roman invasion and settlement of 100 to 1 BC. Latin - although not a monolithic language - was used as the common vehicle for conquest, trade and control throughout the Roman Empire ranging from North Africa to Britain, from Spain to Romania, and from the Bay of Biscay to the Rhine. The Roman Empire collapsed under a number of pressures, including invasion from Germanic tribes over the Rhine, one of which - the Franks - established political control in the North of Gaul from the fifth century, and by about the tenth century AD the Latin spoken throughout what is modern France had broken up into dialects. *Francien*, the dialect spoken around Paris and that used by the military and political power of the Kings of the *ancien régime* in medieval times, imposed itself between the thirteenth century and the eighteenth to become modern French, although the territory of contemporary France did not achieve its final frontiers until the late nineteenth century.

The driving force of early diplomacy and conquest by the Kings of France was to establish 'natural' and defensible frontiers for France, to create the 'hexagon' within which there could be linguistic, ethnic and political unity. As a result, the linguistic and cultural boundaries of contemporary France very nearly coincide with the political: only the inclusion of German-speaking Alsace-Lorraine and the non-inclusion of southern Belgium and the French-speaking cantons of Switzerland represent comparatively major remaining anomalies. The process of cultural unification within the territory of France itself is by no means complete even now: although French is used everywhere within France, regional languages - Breton, Basque, Catalan, Occitan, Flemish, dialects of German - and many dialects, accents and varieties of French itself, together with the cultural identities they symbolise, are still understood and fiercely defended. More recently, immigrants have brought with them languages such as Arabic and Turkish. The potential such languages and dialects have for breaking up the coherence of linguistic and geographical unity still represents a danger to contemporary France - a danger which remains present in the minds of politicians to this day, and mentioned as such during the 1992 debate on the insertion of the language clause into the Constitution (Wilcox, 1994). This clause - 'the language of the Republic is French' - is an indication, also, of the importance of language as a symbol of France.

Standard, Parisian French was imposed throughout modern France as part of the creation of the modern State (Lodge, 1993). It was legally enforceable in official uses after 1539, when its use was decreed in courts, tribunals and legal documents, although its dissemination in the spoken form and in uses other than the official had to wait until free compulsory education in the nineteenth century.

Outside France, the forms of French used in Belgium, Switzerland, Luxembourg and the Aosta Valley are subtly different from standard French. The origins of the language distribution in these areas must be sought in Roman Gaul, and particularly its provinces of Belgica and Lugdunensis, where the frontier relationship with German-speaking tribes to the East caused the point at which the Romance language gave way to the Germanic to be imprecise and uncertain, and the language actually used to be a form of pidgin or even Creole. Luxembourg is probably the best example of the point at which French must compete: in this case with both German and the local Franco-mosellan dialect, the most widely understood language in Luxembourg. The official language is French, but German is most widely used in the Press (Etat, 1993, 269).

A different cultural reality, different political, social and economic structures and history, mean that these frontier regions do not fully share the attitudes, vocabulary or preferences of the French of France. But the cultural predominance of Paris and the lack of significant alternative power centres (except in Switzerland, where both Lausanne and Geneva play this role) mean that standard (i.e. Parisian) French has a part to play in the sociolinguistics of each of the frontier areas. This part may be great, as in Belgium, or comparatively insignificant, as in Switzerland or more notably in Luxembourg. The attraction of France, and the possibility of political unification with it, has always been part of the agenda of some militants in southern Belgium, and the gradual reduction in the role of French in government and in official, public uses in the Belgian State since its formation in 1830 has occasionally strengthened this view. The recent federalisation of Belgium, and the creation of linguistic Regions and Communities there, show the continuing strength of language-based identity.

Settlement

Outside Europe, the principles of emigration and settlement were established early in the seventeenth century, although well before then French sailors, fishermen, settlers and pirates had spread French to North America, to the Caribbean, to India, to islands of the Indian Ocean, and to Africa. For King

Louis XIII's Minister Richelieu, the purpose of settlement was to produce greater glory for King and Country - and for the Church; for Louis XIV's Colbert, the settlement of some Frenchmen, and the exploitation of overseas resources, was a simple matter of improving the royal finances; for Richelieu, again, the priority was conversion of natives to Catholicism, which meant that settlement must be controlled and that neither Protestants nor Jews could be allowed access to *Nouvelle France* in North America - possibly the single most significant decision in the future of Francophonie. The vigorous, commercially minded French Protestants who were expelled in 1685, and who established themselves in Smithfield and Amsterdam contributed wealth, ideas and work to Britain and Holland, but they did so in English and Dutch.

Greater glory for the King meant constant wars with other expanding European powers, particularly Britain. Nonetheless, during the seventeenth and eighteenth centuries, French settlers and merchants moved to North America and the Caribbean, and their trade and the plantation economy provided tropical goods for metropolitan France, using African slave labour to work the fields. France also established trading posts in India, the Indian Ocean and West Africa, and the resultant commerce made fortunes for aristocrats and merchants alike. Motives were not all financial: France sent voyages of scientific as well as commercial exploration across the oceans.

Barely 150 years after Jacques Cartier first started exploring the banks of the St Lawrence, however, the treaty of Utrecht in 1713 followed a first major defeat at the hands of the English. The Treaty of Paris fifty years later, ending the Seven Years War, marked the end of the first colonial empire. France lost the right bank of Louisiana (to Spain, which surrendered Florida to England), Canada, the left bank of the Mississippi, Dominica, Tobago, Grenada, and Saint-Vincent; and most of the trading posts in India and West Africa. It retained a foothold in Madagascar, Mauritius, Réunion and the Caribbean (Martinique, Guadeloupe, Saint-Domingue (Haiti)) from which came much of the wealth of some leading members of the French government.

With Louis XVI on the throne in 1774, the American War of Independence offered one way of restoring French credibility in opposing the English, although French colonialism gained little from its support for the rebellious Americans. Exploring the Pacific Ocean in expeditions whose purpose was openly scientific, rather than colonial, as Bougainville and Lapérouse did in the 1760s, was another way of affirming French power. As he mounted the scaffold after the Revolution, Louis XVI is said to have asked if any news had yet been received of the great explorer Lapérouse, who had sailed again for the Pacific in 1785. Later, Napoleon conquered most of Europe and the Middle East, but without establishing lasting colonies. But the end of the Napoleonic period, in 1814, saw the collapse of the eighteenth century colonial expansion. Wars on the continent had taken their toll and the colonies and trading posts fell to the British one after the other: Martinique in 1809, the Indian trading posts in 1803, Senegal in 1809, Mauritius in 1810.

After the Restoration France was allowed to regain most of what she had possessed in 1789, although it took some time to convince local commanders, for example in the trading posts in Madagascar and in French Guyana, that the Congress of Vienna had in fact restored these areas to France. From this base, and during the whole of the nineteenth century until the defeat of 1871, France added to her colonial empire. Algeria was conquered in 1830, although battles continued until 1847; in the Pacific, Protectorates eventually became colonies from 1840 - Tahiti and French Polynesia, Wallis and Futuna, New Caledonia, although French settlement of New Zealand and Australia was prevented by prior claims and brute force by the British. From 1852 to 1865 French West Africa was being slowly explored and colonised from Senegal. Indochina became French, slowly, during the 1860s, after Protectorates had followed the activities of Catholic missionaries.

The financial motive for trade outside France, if not for settlement, was strong. By 1789, six million people in France were living on the colonial trade: the Atlantic and Channel ports had sugar refineries, trade in cotton was flourishing, as were the fisheries and, indeed slavery, which brought wealth both to the Caribbean and to Nantes, where the slave transport ships were based. By 1814, the effect of the loss of colonies was dramatic: the population of Bordeaux and Marseilles, 120,000 in 1789, fell to 75,000 in 1814. The commercial fleet, and foreign trade, practically ceased. The loss of Saint Domingue, which had been the crowning commercial glory of the early empire but which fell to a black revolutionary in 1797, and became finally independent as Haiti in 1803, was a major blow. But the wealth from the major colonial areas, from the Caribbean, from Africa, from the Far East, became significant again during the nineteenth century, even though colonists themselves were nowhere near as numerous as those from England.

Being a new settler was hard work. Compared to the productivity of France, agricultural production in many of the new possessions was low; products had to be transported to markets, and labour was always in short supply. With unwilling and occasionally hostile local inhabitants, settlers needed to clear land, plant, collect the crop and make sure that the following year would be equally profitable. It was small wonder that settlers only established themselves profitably where markets were guaranteed and where the cost of installation was comparatively low: fishing and furs were popular, but so were tropical and 'colonial' products such as sugar, coffee and spices. There was, after all, little financial motive to leave France permanently. Nineteenth century France was dominated by rural interests, concerned politically by the consequences of the

Revolution, comparatively sparsely populated, and wealthy. The equivalent of the social upheaval caused by the Industrial Revolution, by the Irish famines or by the Scottish clearances, did not take place in France until after defeat by the Prussians in 1871. Prisoners were deported to New Caledonia and forced to stay, but became unwilling settlers; fishing did not require permanent settlement; the small elite of administrators, priests and businessmen did not attract supporting mass settlement. Labour supply in the colonies, for work in the fields, was hence always a major difficulty, particularly after the end of slavery.

Conversion of the natives to Catholicism was a major principle for the first, and an even stronger one for the later period of colonial expansion. The missionaries spread the doctrine of (French) Catholicism far and wide: in Indochina from the 1760s - there were 80,000 Catholics in Indochina at the end of the 18th century, and the bishop, Pigneau de Béhaine, took an active part in the wars establishing Gia Long as emperor in 1802; in the south Pacific from 1840, where French naval forces tried to support missionaries, whalers and settlers in New Zealand until the English took over. Tahiti in particular was subject to religious conflict between the Protestant missionaries of the London Missionary Society - who had been there since 1797 - and the Catholics, provoking French military intervention in 1840 and the eventual conquest, which took until 1846.

Expansion

The aims and purposes of colonial expansion during the nineteenth and twentieth centuries are complex (Girardet, 1986). One may have been resentment at military defeat and a desire to re-establish French military credibility after 1871. The rapid restoration of order and calm in the French Republic, the equally rapid payment of the Prussian demands, and the desire of the two great powers - Germany and Britain - to restore France to peace, allowed them to encourage France to think of joining them in the colonial rush, provided she did so in ways which did not encroach on their preserves. A second aim was undoubtedly economic and commercial. The Mayors and notables of Nantes, Bordeaux and Marseilles - towns dependent on overseas trade - were major players in the colonial committees set up after 1880, and the Colonies were run - for a short period - from the Ministry of Commerce after being detached from the Navy in 1881. By 1894, they were established as a separate Ministry. Jules Ferry, 'the architect of the new empire and spokesman for imperial groups' (Aldrich and Connell, 1992, 38) in a major speech to the *Chambre des Députés* in 1885, claimed that

> Colonial policy depends on industrial policy. For wealthy States, where the manufacturing system is continually expanding...export is a fundamental factor in public prosperity, and the field for use of capital, as for the demand for labour, can be measured by the development of the overseas market.

Associated with the purely commercial interests were many idealists, religious groups, and others whose motivation was that of grandeur or the glory of France, or the conversion of the heathen, rather than private profit. The *parti colonial* of the Third Republic - not a political party in the modern sense of the term, but a grouping of like-minded individuals - described the non-commercial, non-military purposes of colonialism as *la mission civilisatrice de la France*. Jules Ferry, indeed, said in the *Chambre des Députés* that 'The superior race does not conquer for pleasure, with the intention of exploiting the weak, but in order to civilise him, to raise him to her own level'. The League of the Rights of Man said: 'We must be considered as having a mandate to instruct, to raise, to emancipate, to enrich and to help the peoples who are in need of our collaboration'. Freemasons, whose importance in the Third Republic and in its colonial activities is great, noted 'We affirm that the work of colonisation of the Third Republic is fundamentally one of civilisation'. Clubs and associations, for example the *Comité de l'Afrique française* and the Geographical Society supported explorers, expeditions, publicity and propaganda in favour of the colonial enterprise. Even Jean Jaurès, the major Socialist figure, supported the creation of the *Alliance Française* as an instrument of assimilation:

> Our colonies will not be French in mind and spirit until they understand French...Particularly for France, the language is the necessary instrument for colonisation...Many French schools, to which the native should be called, must help French settlers in their difficult task of moral conquest and assimilation (quotations in Montagnon, 1989, 1, 237- 44).

There were more obviously political motives for colonialism, as well. Gambetta, Prime Minister of the Republic, made it clear that one of the purposes of the colonial expansion was to compensate for the loss of Alsace-Lorraine. Another was to ensure that Britain and Germany did not get all the spoils. Strategic interests, and the protection of religious missions, were alone responsible for French expansion in the Pacific, where commercial exploitation - trading between the Francophone and the Anglophone Pacific and connecting Australia, New Zealand, Tahiti, New Caledonia, Fiji, Hawaii and California - was carried out by British and Australian interests on regional lines until very recent times. French colonialism aimed at assimilating the newly conquered territories and their populations to the centralised, French-speaking 'one and indivisible' Republic. It did not mean by this that all the conquered populations would have the same rights as French citizens, and the status of the 'natives' was clearly differentiated from that of the settler. But 'assimilation' was unworkable without full integration of the populations, and the theory of 'association' (i.e. separate development, led by France) soon replaced it - to be replaced by 'co-operation' (i.e. of equal but different territories) when decolonisation started after 1945.

While it is possible now, with the benefit of hindsight, to identify such motives and stages in the processes of colonialism, at the time there was little system, planning or forethought. Expeditions, often supported by private money, would explore a region, set up trade or make arrangements with local populations, leaving the political protectorate or annexation to follow. Whatever the reasons and processes, in less than 40 years, from 1880 to 1914, France was to establish her dominion over the major part of her empire: and this was to be principally in Africa. In 1880, the African continent was little known to Europeans, except for the South where the English and the Dutch had established themselves and there was a white population of 400,000. In the North and West, Islam had conquered the desert and converted most of the black population, particularly, in the West, in Futa Djallon located at the source of the Senegal river. Over the majority of the Continent, sparse populations, organised in tribal and family groups, offered little resistance to the invader, while organised empires and kingdoms in West Africa (Benin, Mali, Ghana), which might have resisted, had often fallen into the hands of bloodthirsty tyrants and had lost the support of their populations. Slavery had marked the continent for a century or more. Black populations had been decimated by the removal of slaves, variously estimated at 15 to 40 million people, who had enriched the Arab regions in the North of Africa and populated the Caribbean islands where they had made the fortunes of European planters. Their departure had left behind ruined African economies, deserted villages, and little in the way of organised agriculture. For the European colonialists, the continent was 'available'.

The 1885 Berlin Conference, where the European powers shared Africa out between themselves, marked the beginning of the growth of the second largest colonial empire in the world. Bismarck, opening the Conference, outlined the principles: 'associate the African native with civilisation by opening up the interior of the Continent to commerce; provide the inhabitants with the means of instruction and education by encouraging Missions and enterprises which will encourage useful knowledge; and ensure the suppression of slavery'. The key concepts: civilisation, commerce, education, useful knowledge - i.e. work rather than slavery - all found their echo as motives in French colonial expansion.

Before 1880, France was already present in Algeria, in Senegal, in a number of West African trading posts from Gorée to Libreville, and in Djibouti at the end of the Red Sea. She expanded from the North, from the South and from the West to conquer an immense empire, bigger in this continent than that of the British. Tactically, the intention may have been to connect the West to the East, to ensure a completely French West, Central and Saharan Africa; this intention directly contradicted British ideas of a North to South link from Egypt to South Africa. When the French attempted to establish themselves at Fachoda, the key point on both routes, in 1898, before the British got there, the political consequences of a possible war with Britain were such that the French had eventually to withdraw; but the subsequent treaty left them the possibility of action over Morocco. When the French got to the right bank of the Congo before the Belgian expedition, they were more successful in claiming territory ahead of their rivals. From Algeria in the North, France entered the Sahara and West Africa to Chad, to Congo and to Gabon. From the West, she took over *Soudan* (later Mali), Guinea, the Ivory Coast and Dahomey (now Benin). In the South, close to Réunion, Madagascar fell to her.

The method followed by such colonial soldiers as Gallieni was to establish protectorates with local rulers, to strengthen these with the creation of transport routes - railways, roads - and with commerce; and to convert the protectorate into simple annexation in due course. Often, the expansion took place at the initiative of local French commanders, to be confirmed later when Paris was informed. Paris provided budgets, and occasionally encouraged expansion in one direction or another, but without an overall master plan. The advance was not simply a matter of overcoming small dispersed bands of savages: some of the opponents were well armed, established rulers, such as Samory Touré, and Gallieni had to establish treaties to prevent them establishing links - particularly with the British - before any actual conquest was possible. The decisive year, for the area around Senegal and on the banks of the Niger, was 1898. Samory Touré was finally captured, and resistance crushed. For Guinea, the Ivory Coast and Dahomey, conquest was easier, although the tropical forest and guerrilla warfare meant that full control was not established until nearly twenty years after the first French expansion in 1880. In the Centre with the Congo, in the North with Chad and Morocco (1912), in the South with the island of Madagascar, annexed in 1896 after being a protectorate from 1883 to 1885, France established herself throughout Africa, creating two unified regions in the West and the Centre: *Afrique Occidentale Française (AOF)* and *Afrique Equatoriale Française (AEF)*.

Forty or fifty years previously, the Indochinese region had fallen to French influence. French aims, here as elsewhere over the century of the colonial expansion, were as much oriented towards preventing other colonial powers from gaining excessive power as towards expansion for its own sake, and the need to stop Britain expanding throughout China meant that France needed to control the Red River and the Mekong systems. In 1840 treaties were concluded with the Vietnamese Empire to modernise their armies, but the second and third opium wars of 1856-1860 led to easy military conquest of Saigon, followed by the establishment of protectorates over Cambodia and six Vietnamese provinces. In 1877, French military expansion continued, to culminate in treaties with China in 1885 - after the French had shown their muscle by sinking the 'new' Chinese fleet in one hour in Fuzhou harbour. At the turn of the century, with no Chinese 'interference', the *Union Indochinoise* was established: 740,000 square kilometres, 10 to 11 million inhabitants, covering present-day Vietnam,

Cambodia and Laos. Vietnam became the colony of Cochinchine and two protectorates (Annam and Tonkin), and a large area of southern China itself fell under French influence.

In the Indian Ocean, the Mascareignes - Ile Bourbon (now Réunion), and Ile de France (now Mauritius), and its dependency Rodriguez - had been French since 1638 and 1715 respectively, although Mauritius had become a British possession after 1810. The exploitation of the area (including the Seychelles and the Comoros) through the *Compagnie des Indes Orientales* ceased after 1764, when possession was transferred to the French Government, but the exploitation of Madagascar through settlement and control from 1895 enabled the whole region to become enormously productive in sugar, coffee, spices and in 'colonial' (i.e. tropical) products generally.

The Pacific Ocean, although the conquest of the islands there predated the African expansion, was another region in which the strategic world role France wished to play required settlement and stable bases. Heavily or thinly populated islands - Micronesia ('islands of exiguity'), Polynesia ('islands of the multitude'), and Melanesia ('islands of negritude') (Chesneaux and MacLellan, 1992, 15), populated by peoples who had learnt to conquer distance and space, could be colonised only if sea transport was effective and secure. The loss of Mauritius and its splendid harbour after 1810, the implantation of the British in New Zealand and Australia meant that France needed naval bases if she was to protect the Catholic missionaries in Tahiti, New Caledonia or Wallis, or indeed influence Latin America. Polynesia fell to French influence more or less by accident: the London Missionary Society Protestants, led by George Pritchard, influenced Queen Pomare to expel Catholic Missionaries and to seek a British Protectorate, but while Pritchard was in London Admiral Dupetit-Thouars annexed the Marquesas and 'persuaded' most of the Polynesian chiefs and the Regent to request French protection. The final French conquest did not take place until 1846, and the British government acquiesced in the eventual annexation in 1880. New Caledonia similarly became a naval base in 1853, while the islands of Wallis and Futuna were added in 1886. It was not until the late 1800s that the other colonial powers established themselves in the islands (Britain in Fiji in 1874, Tonga in 1885; Germany in New Guinea in 1885; America in Hawaii in 1898).

France had to overcome considerable resistance by the inhabitants to impose military conquest. In the Marquesas long guerrilla warfare from 1842 to 1880 was only ended by the virtual massacre of the inhabitants, whose number fell from 60,000 in 1840 to 3,500 in 1902 (Chesneaux and McLellan, 1992, 70). In Tahiti, resistance was fierce from 1844 to 1846, and eventual annexation was not possible until after the death of King Pomare in 1880. There was rebellion in the

Leeward Islands, in Tuamotu, in Rapa, and peace was only established in the early twentieth century.

France's interest in New Caledonia started in 1843 with treaties with the local chiefs, followed by annexation in 1853. From 1864 to 1897 the island was a penal colony, receiving 25,000 transported convicts, including 4,500 deportees from the Paris Commune and more than a thousand Algerian rebels in 1871. These and other convicts were not allowed to return to France, and while the free settlers farmed on land taken from the Melanesians, their approach and intentions contrasted with a mainly urban settlement composed of 'freed' convicts. After the start of the exploitation of nickel in 1879, workers came from China and Java (Indonesia). Revolts by the Melanesians were easily crushed in 1878 and 1917, their land confiscated and handed over to French settlers, so the original inhabitants were forced into mountains and remote valleys. By the 1930s the colony had become a quiet backwater where the indigenous peoples had little land, where only the missions - both Catholic and Protestant - provided any developed education for them, and where systematic exclusion meant that the Kanaks had 'neither political nor civil rights... an example, unique in the French Empire except in Algeria, of the civil death of a whole population' (Chesneaux and McLellan, 1992, 69).

In New Hebrides (Vanuatu), close to New Caledonia, French influence based in New Caledonia led to most land being held by French interests by 1882. Australia, concerned at the growth of French influence, put pressure on London to develop treaties in 1878 and 1888 imposing non-interference by each country, but private French colonisation continued. In 1906 improved relations between France and Great Britain led to dual rule by both powers in a condominium, which was often farcical yet also conflictual. Each Resident Commissioner had power over his own nationals and the 'natives', but constantly referred decisions each to his own Government and waited, often for months, for the reply. The French supported their planters, while the British, provoked by Protestant missionaries, criticised these same planters for their inhumane working conditions and their forced labour. The French Government, by contrast with the British, subsidised its settlers, allowing them to import labour from China and maintaining copra and cotton prices in the 1929 slump, yet both governments had legal equality and the resulting differences in profitability for each group became practically untenable. Independence was much harder for the local French to accept than for the British.

Decolonisation

If there were three principles to the creation of empire - assimilation, association and co-operation - decolonisation was equally complex, coming about through war, trade and constitutional change. Saint-Domingue (Haiti) was the first of the French colonies to free itself by war or revolt by the local population, although the Spanish recaptured the eastern part in 1814 to create, eventually, the Dominican Republic, and Haiti, through internal violence and a difficult history, has become one of the poorest countries in the world. After the second World War some colonies experienced local revolts: for example Madagascar in 1947, where the number of deaths may have been as high as 100,000 and there was much physical damage.

Vietnam had remained neutral on the surface through World War 2 in an uneasy truce with the Japanese until they attacked the (Vichy) French on 9 May 1945, and took over Vietnam, Laos and Cambodia, showing how Asian powers could defeat the Europeans. The Viet-Minh under Ho Chi Minh, set up in 1941 to fight against Japanese and French 'fascism' - but which openly represented itself as the only force which could unite all nationalist sentiment and groups - benefited from American 'neutrality' which preferred not to see the French return to colonial control after the war, and from more active American support when it started a small guerrilla war against the Japanese. When the Japanese surrendered after Nagasaki, the puppet Emperor Bao-Dai surrendered, not to the French or the Americans, but to the Viet-Minh which declared Vietnamese independence. At Potsdam, however, it had been decided that the British would liberate the South and the Chinese the North of the peninsula; while the British were happy to allow the French to return in the South, France had to surrender her Chinese concessions (Shanghai, Canton, Tonkin) before the Chinese troops allowed the French in. The return of French troops, at first accepted, was soon resisted and the war of independence which started seriously in 1946 lasted until 1954 and the French defeat at Dien Bien Phu. The French defeat was followed by a cease-fire, the division of Vietnam in two, the involvement of Americans under the flag of the United Nations, and, from 1975 and the defeat of the Americans, the creation of an independent Vietnam.

The bloodiest of the wars of independence for France, however, was that of Algeria, which started with dispersed attacks from the *Front de Libération Nationale (FLN)* on 1st November 1954 and did not end until the Evian agreements of 1962. The war still marks contemporary France, was responsible for the fall of the Fourth Republic, for (nearly) a civil war in France, and for the creation of the modern French Constitution in 1958.

French response to the *FLN* attacks was militarily strong, although many acts were dubious, matching terrorism with torture and worse. Algerian forces were supported from Tunisia and Morocco, provoking French attacks: Sakiet, in Tunisia, was bombed. Politically weak, the Fourth Republic, constantly changing governments, faced a divided France in which major politicians openly preached revolt: 'insurrection to keep Algeria French is legal insurrection...the abandonment of French sovereignty in Algeria is illegal'

(Michel Debré, quoted in Montagnon, 1990, 2, 361). There were strong economic and political reasons to keep Algeria, apart from the settlers and their investments: oil and the nuclear testing sites in the Sahara would all be forfeited if France withdrew. In May 1958 the army commander General Salan, approved by representatives of the Navy and the Air Force, made clear in a telegram that 'the French Army unanimously would consider the abandonment of this national possession (i.e. Algeria) as an outrage. It is impossible to predict what its reaction of despair would be' (Montagnon, 1990, 2, 374). On 13th May 1958 Algerian settlers set up *Comités de Salut Public* and there was a distinct possibility that paratroopers would land in Paris to take over the government. General Salan, on the balcony of the official residence in Algiers, shouted *Vive de Gaulle*, seeing him as the only saviour. The Fourth Republic collapsed ignominiously, President René Coty appealed to de Gaulle, and on 3rd June the *Assemblée Nationale*, by 350 votes to 161, gave de Gaulle liberty of action to reform the State. It was not until 1962, however, that Algeria gained its independence through the Evian agreements. Before this happened, de Gaulle had to face down the *quarteron de généraux à la retraite* - the foursome of retired generals - who had attempted to take over power in 1961, and impose his will on the *Organisation de l'Armée Secrète (OAS)* - which had attempted to kill him and committed many acts of terrorism in its support of *Algérie Française*.

A second route to independence was simple trade. The rest of Louisiana was sold to the United States in 1804 for 60 million francs, with a ten per cent discount to various intermediaries. 'Never was a continent sold off so cheaply' said Lavisse (Montagnon, 1989, 1, 85). In Africa, the 'ownership' of many areas was adjusted as part of the bargaining between the major colonial powers, and the eventual frontiers of colonies - which were to become those of newly independent states - were fixed on a haphazard basis, bearing no relationship to tribal or language boundaries or even to those of simple geography, but often coinciding with the commercial advantage of colonialists.

The third route to independence was through constitutional change. In de Gaulle's speech in February 1944 in Brazzaville he declared France to be the 'Nation whose genius it is to raise men, step by step, towards the heights of dignity and fraternity where all will be able to unite one day' (Kazadi, 1991, 18). De Gaulle maintained that Brazzaville declared the right of peoples to decide their own destiny (*disposer d'eux-mêmes*), although the historical record of the meeting of approximately 20 colonial governors, administrators and observers, together with 9 putative members of the Algerian consultative assembly (all Europeans, except for a small number, of whom the most significant was Eboué, governor general of the *AOF*) shows that any concept of autonomy, development outside the French imperial bloc or movement towards self-government was out of question (Montagnon, 1990, 2, 80). Nonetheless, the Brazzaville decisions, even though they were mainly administrative detail, reflected a new spirit aimed at closing the era of colonisation.

The 1939-45 war itself had had a major influence on thinking and on colonial practice. Both New Caledonia and New Hebrides (Vanuatu) had become advanced bases for the American offensive in the Pacific, while Tahiti was bombed and the nearby island of Bora-Bora, designated as a rest and recreation centre for American troops, found its future vocation as a tourist centre. Over a million GIs passed through New Caledonia, bringing equality between black and white, and unseen wealth.

The new spirit was confirmed by Marius Moutet, Minister for Overseas France in 1946: 'The brutal colonial fact, conquest, the imposition of one nation on other races, the maintenance of sovereignty through force alone is impossible today. This historical period of colonisation has gone' (quoted in Montagnon, 1990, 2:163). The new French Constitution of 1946 created a *Union Française*, in which colonies became Departments (Antilles, Guyane, Réunion; Algeria, whose full status was uncertain), associated States (Vietnam, Laos, Cambodia) or protected States (Morocco and Tunisia), Overseas Territories (mainly the African colonies and Madagascar), and associated territories (Togo and Cameroon, formerly under League of Nations mandate). The Departments became part of France, the associated or protected States were to move to independence, the territories remained under French administration pending clarification of their status at some future time. Significantly, the personal status of individuals also changed: notions of 'subject', of the 'native', and particular laws such as those concerning forced labour, special jurisdictions and other limiting statutes were removed; ex-colonial subjects became French citizens without having to renounce their personal status (i.e. Koranic or customary law), but with, however, a restricted right to vote in a second electoral college, the first being reserved for citizens of France or naturalised French. The new Assembly of the Union was still dominated by France (129 members from France itself, 75 from the Departments and Territories, 72 from the associated States), although the Departments and Territories also elected 64 members of the 586 in the French National Assembly, and some members to the *Conseil de la République* (i.e. today's Senate). This apparent acceptance of former subjects was however, restricted. The two colleges were very unequal: five to six thousand Europeans per Member as against more than a million Africans for each. Nonetheless, significant individuals, soon to be major African leaders, now entered the political world: Leopold Sedar Senghor from Senegal, Houphouët-Boigny from the Ivory Coast, Hamani Diori from Niger, Sékou Touré from Guinea.

The *Union Française* brought about the independence of Laos and Cambodia in 1949, but was destined to disappear before the majority of the French colonies found their independence. The trade outposts of India - Pondicherry, Mahé, Chandernagor, and Karikal, with about 325,000 inhabitants, following India's independence from Britain in 1947 and local referenda, joined the Indian Republic at different times between 1951 and 1954, not without considerable pressure from India and some local riots. 1956 saw the independence of the kingdom of Morocco, and Tunisia, with transfer of power in the latter case to a formal monarchy soon to be replaced by Bourguiba's one party state. The new Tunisian constitution made clear that Tunisia was 'a free State, independent and sovereign, having Islam as its religion and Arabic as its language'. Both Morocco and Tunisia soon saw the number of French and European settlers decrease as land was nationalised: Tunisia's 260,000 Europeans in 1954 dropped to 60,000 in 1960 and 15,000 (French) in 1980. 1956 saw also the independence of the associated territory of Togo. A new permissive law enabled internal self-government for the African colonies, but also prevented any federation or grouping, confirming the colonial frontiers for the potential new states, and defeating the hopes of some of the new politicians, particularly Senghor, who had wished for independence to be granted to a broad Franco-African federation of states, rather than to individual colonies.

The new Gaullist Constitution of 1958 was put to a referendum in France and throughout the remaining departments and territories. De Gaulle deliberately constructed the referendum as a plebiscite in favour of the new Constitution, with its Community: it was all or nothing. In France, the vote was 79% in favour. In Africa, the vote in favour was: Chad, Ivory Coast - 99%; Upper Volta, Oubangui-Chari - 98%; Dahomey, Senegal - 97%; Gabon, Mauritania - 93%; Madagascar - 83%; Niger - 77%. Guinea, where Sekou Touré had made clear his opposition, voted 93% against. Guinea declared itself independent on 2nd October. The French administrators, settlers, and soldiers left immediately; all French aid was stopped forthwith.

The Constitution created a Community to replace the Union. France retained control over external affairs, defence, finance, strategic raw materials, and higher education, and the official language was French. Individual countries obtained self-government in other areas. In accordance with article 83 of the Constitution and a further modification to it in 1960, most African colonies now demanded complete independence, which was accorded in 1960 to Madagascar, Dahomey (Benin from 1975), Niger, *Haute-Volta* (Burkina-Faso), the Ivory Coast, Chad, Oubangui-Chari (*République Centrafricaine*), *Moyen-Congo*, Gabon, Senegal, *Soudan* (Mali), and Mauritania. France retained military bases; in many cases the President or Government of the new country could call on French military support in times of trouble; and commercial and cultural co-operation agreements were signed.

In 1977 Djibouti, in East Africa, voted 96% for independence. The Comoro islands, self-governing since 1961, proclaimed their independence on 6th July 1975, although one island, Mayotte, did not join the movement to establishing an Islamic Sultanate, a decision which it reaffirmed in 1976 by 99.4%. Despite a United Nations vote in 1982 (110 to 1, with 22 abstentions) calling on France to leave, Mayotte is still a French *Collectivité d'Outre-Mer*. In the New Hebrides in 1978 and 1979 elections were held by the condominium, and won by a political party supported by Anglophone Protestants and discreetly by the British. The elections were followed by a revolt, led by an independence movement heavily supported by French and New Caledonian interests. Independence as the new country of Vanuatu was won only in 1980, after armed intervention by Papua New Guinea (approved by Australia). Two Pacific territories - New Caledonia and French Polynesia - have remained under direct French control as *Territoires d'Outre-Mer*.

At its largest, in 1918, the French Empire contained 55 million inhabitants and 12 million square kilometres of land. It is essentially this Empire, together with other French-speaking countries and regions such as Belgium and Quebec that forms the heart of modern Francophonie, and provides it with both its problems and its opportunities.

2. THE DISTRIBUTION OF CONTEMPORARY FRANCOPHONIE

In this chapter we examine the spread of Francophonie - the use of the French language - through the world, noting that not all countries or regions where French is spoken are members of organised Francophonie, nor indeed do they all subscribe to the values of Francophonie. We also give a brief analysis of the contemporary situation in a selected range of countries: Belgium, Lebanon, Algeria, Guinea, Mauritius, Quebec, Guadeloupe, and New Caledonia. The purpose of this selection, covering 'typical' countries and regions, is to investigate the diversity of Francophonie, rather than to describe exhaustively every country and region where the language is used. Statistics relating to French speakers - and indeed, speakers of any language - are notoriously unreliable, since few countries administer a language or language-related question as part of their census forms. Canada asks three: declared mother tongue, whether French is spoken at home, and 'French ethnic origin'. The differences for Ontario alone are significant: French is claimed as mother tongue by 475,450 people; French is spoken at home by 337,900 and people of French ethnic origin number 652,400 (Année Francophone, 1992, 33), so it is quite difficult to decide who is really a French speaker.

A number of distinctions are usually made when language-related statistics are collected. The main one is between the individual and society: in individual bilingualism an individual controls one or more languages, while in societal bilingualism a number of languages may be in use within the political community, although individuals may only use one or have only a smattering of others. Individual bilinguals are often distinguished by the chronology of language acquisition: they may be First Language (L1) speakers, where the language is acquired from birth (also known as speakers of a mother tongue, native language, main, vernacular or usual language); Second Language (L2) speakers, who have learned the language, usually at school where they have often learned some subjects through it (also known as users of a lingua franca or a vehicular language); and Foreign Language (FL) speakers, who have also learned the language, often at school but usually as a subject. Other ways of describing individual bilinguals is to measure their ability in each language, describe the skills they use, or the frequency of their use of it. Thus they may have mastery of a language, use all four skills (reading, writing, speaking and listening), and use it all the time; be competent in it, use it only for reading and use it frequently; or be poor at it and use it only to a small extent - speaking to visitors, on holiday or in a specific function such as market selling. The second set of distinctions applies to society: languages may be distinguished by geography, their domain of use or by sociolinguistic attitude. Geography distinguishes at least three levels: international, national and regional languages. Domains of use (functions) are reflected in terms such as official language, language of education, commercial language. Sociolinguistic attitude is reflected in terms like standard language and dialect; majority and minority languages; the languages of political, ethnic and speech communities; and processes such as diglossia, language shift and language loss (cf. Truchot, 1994).

In 1985 and 1990, the French Government Report *Etat de la Francophonie* attempted an overall count of French speakers across the world, obtaining a 'best-guess' set of figures from French Embassies and diplomatic representatives. 1985 statistics were based on societal bilingualism, and assumed for example that in a 'Francophone' country all or most of the speakers spoke French. The 1990 statistics, which form the basis for the present chapter, were based more on individual bilingualism and gave two figures for each country: 'real' French speakers were defined as those for whom French was first or second language, and for whom the use of the language was a daily practice. Second language users included, for example, 'authors, artists, teachers, scientists, international bureaucrats who have adopted French as their language of creation or work' (Etat, 1990, 28). 'Occasional' French speakers were defined as those living in societal bilingualism - Belgium, Switzerland and Canada, or developing countries. These figures are given for each country in the review below, in the form NN + NN, where the first figure is that for 'real', and the second that for 'occasional' speakers of French. If only one figure is given it is followed by R (real) or O (occasional). The Appendix (Table A2) gives the proportion of Francophones in each country. Overall, it was estimated in 1990 that some 104,612,000 'real' Francophones are present in all the continents, together with 54,225,000 'occasional' speakers of French. In addition, about 100 million learners of French as a foreign language fall outside these statistics altogether, a grand total of more than 250 million.

Europe

French-speaking countries in Europe include France itself (57,000,000 R), Belgium (4,500,000 + 3,200,000), Luxembourg (300,000 R), Monaco (27,000 R), Switzerland (1,200,000 + 2,000,000) and part of Italy (the Aosta Valley (12,000 R)), although this latter area, after massive immigration from the South and from tourism, is rapidly losing its French-speaking character. Many European countries in addition to these contain small populations of French speakers: Romania (1,000,000 + 4,000,000), Poland (30,000 R), Bulgaria with a similar number, Spain, Greece, Italy and Portugal, with a total of 1,300,000 R,

Andorra with 13,000 R, and unknown numbers in Britain, Ireland, Germany and elsewhere.

Belgium is the site of a fierce linguistic battle between Flemish speakers, in the North of the country, and the French speakers of Wallonia (see McRae, 1986; Lemaire, J., 1989; Etat, 1993 and 1994; Francard, 1993; Verdoodt and Sonntag, 1993). Three semi-autonomous language-based 'Communities' - French (approximately 4.5 million speakers), Flemish (5.7 million), and German (68,000) - coexist with three geographical 'Regions' - Flanders, Wallonia and Brussels. The capital, Brussels, is 89% French-speaking but is situated in the Flemish-speaking part of the country. The term 'Flemish' (vlaams, *flamand*) is used here in preference to 'Dutch', which refers to the standard form of the language spoken in Holland.

The country became independent in 1830, with French as the official language and the de-facto language of the ruling elite. Bilingualism (French and Flemish) was introduced in 1892, and spread to all levels of official life in 1921; during the thirties, the two main regions became in practice monolingual, and their frontiers were fixed in 1962. Prior to that time they were supposedly adjusted every ten years in line with a linguistic census - which, because of its sensitivity, has not taken place since 1947. The Constitution was revised in 1970, creating the Communities and Regions; Assemblies and Executives were established in these in 1980; the Region of Bruxelles-Capitale was created in 1988 at the same time as financial autonomy for what had become to all intents and purposes a federation rather than a unitary State. One might summarise the 150 years of independence as representing three movements: linguistically, in greater recognition for Flemish; politically, in the increased firmness of conviction of the two main groups leading even to violence in the pursuit of identity symbolised through language; and constitutionally, in the recognition that separation - although in a Federal State - was the only workable situation.

In 1993, the fourth Constitutional amendment since World War Two ratified the creation of the Federal State. The Communities are competent in people-oriented matters (health, education, culture...), while the Regions were intended to administer matters based on geography. The six bodies are co-ordinated through a Co-ordination Committee, and each has had freedom since 1993 to organise its Parliament, Government and administration in its own way, while the Federal State organisations (Government and Parliament) retain some overall rights and duties in defence, foreign policy, social security, justice and public order, economic and monetary union. Social security, in particular, is still the focus of conflict, with the wealthy Flemish North more and more unwilling to support the burden of the poorer Francophone South. Both Communities and Regions can however sign international treaties, be represented abroad and conduct separate foreign policies: it is for this reason that both the French Community and the

Kingdom of Belgium have representation within the Francophone Summit meetings. The Flemish Community and Region have fused, while the French Community has delegated some of its competencies to the Regions of Wallonia and Brussels. But the 'territorial principle' of language-based separation (without complete autonomy) is not the only dichotomy present in contemporary Belgium, and social and religious divisions often parallel the linguistic: the archetype of the 'Flamand' is 'conservative, catholic and small businessman', while that of the 'Wallon' is lay, socialist and worker' (Miroir, 1990; Beaugé, 1994). The French Community is vigilant on legislation affecting French: there is both a *Conseil Supérieur de la Langue Française*, with responsibility for advising on Francophonie and on any matter affecting the use of French in Belgium, and a surveillance *Commission* with the particular duty of ensuring that language legislation is implemented. While *wallon*, the local dialect of French, has practically disappeared, many *belgicismes* - in pronunciation, vocabulary and syntax - remain, and the debate in Belgium over whether to decry or glorify these differences with standard French seems now to have resulted in acceptance of, but not yet pride in, a Belgian form of French. The discussion has not gone so far as accepting a new norm of Belgian French different from the norm of Paris, and standard international French is still accepted as the prestigious variety (Hanse, J., in Lemaire, J., 1989, 79; Francard, 1993). Etat (1993, 46), reporting on the language situation in Belgium, noted, too, a growing tendency to use English: 'publication in French or Dutch is conflictual and too limited, bilingual publication is expensive, and English enables outdated language conflicts to be bypassed'.

Near East

Lebanon (894,000 + 800,000) has long-standing contacts with France, going back to the time of the Crusades. Syria (12,000 R), also a former French Protectorate, Iran (50,000 R), Israel (500,000 R) and Turkey (10,000 R) have maintained a French-speaking tradition, mainly among emigrant families.

Lebanon (Gueunier, 1993; Abou and Haddad, 1994) became a French Protectorate under the League of Nations Mandate from 1920 to 1943. Lebanon was part of the Roman Empire from 64 BC to 640 AD, under Arab control until 1299 when it fell to the Ottoman Empire, was autonomous from 1861 to 1920 and independent after 1943, so its formal connections with France were fairly brief. Lebanon is situated at the heart of the Middle East, the central point of contacts between Europe, Turkey and the Arab countries. From the eleventh to the thirteenth centuries, Lebanon was the object of Christian attention during the Crusades, which had little linguistic effect, except on the Crusaders; and from missionaries, traders and educationalists from the sixteenth - two Universities, St-Joseph using French and the American University in Beirut using English, were founded in the mid-nineteenth century. Commerce was and always has been central to Lebanon's contacts with Europe, so that the country has for centuries had contact with French, as an important commercial, cultural and political language. As a result, contemporary Lebanon is a multilingual country of ethnic and religious communities - Druze, Maronite, Shiite, and Sunnite - where spoken Arabic is the mother tongue. Armenian and some Turkish are spoken by the families of the 1915 wave of refugees from Turkey, while French is widely used as a (second, prestigious) spoken language in the bourgeoisie and in education, where its use is (theoretically) compulsory both in private and public schools. English is also widespread, mainly for commerce, and is growing in use.

The use of French is mainly noted among older inhabitants, the bourgeoisie, women and girls, those in private education and among Christian groups. French is in no sense an official language: indeed, the proposal by some, mainly Christian groups in the 1940s that it should be so was opposed by Muslims, who did not see that Lebanon should have a different linguistic status from other Arab countries. The Constitution declared Arabic as the official language and left the status of French unclear. Although it would be going too far to say that French and Arabic symbolise the underlying conflicts between the West and the Middle East, Abou (in Abou and Haddad, 1994, 419) makes a distinction between an essentially ethnic view of the nation as 'culturally homogeneous, specified by its language, religion or both' leading to chauvinism and isolation, and another, promoting openness and co-operation, which sees the nation as made up of 'reasonably free individuals, resolved to live together and share their destiny'. The first, according to him 'can often be found in Arab nationalism', while language diversity in society, and particularly the use of French, guarantees freedom. Different conceptions of the State, of the necessity and nature of cultural homogeneity for all, and of the role of affective links such as language and religion, lay at the heart of the wars in Lebanon which have so marked recent years.

Lebanon is still suffering from the effects of the disastrous wars of the last twenty years, from invasions and occupation from Syria and Israel, from waves of refugees from Palestine and from occasional incursions by others. The effects include the massive departure of refugees - nearly a million were living abroad in 1993 and the world counts nearly 18 million people of Lebanese origin - and a complete lack of accurate data, although the current estimate is that the 51.6% of Christians of 1970 has probably changed to an Islamic majority of 62% (Gueunier, 1993, 269). Internal population movements include a shift from the countryside to the towns, the departure of the middle classes and the educated, and the arrival of poor refugees, many from Palestine, while 'nearby' emigrants who went to France, Africa or the Gulf are said to be returning (Etat, 1994, 499). Since the end of the wars, however, Francophonie 'has made a spectacular return' (Etat, 1993, 51): book sales are up from 19 million francs in 1991 to 36 in 1993; sales were made of two French-language films to the Lebanon in 1991 and of 28 in 1993; two French-language magazines saw their sales increase to 20,000 in 1993. Gueunier (1993, 271) is rather more cautious, noting that French 'is more and more in competition with English, under the triple effect of Francophone emigration, subsidies for English-language activities, reduction in monies from France and the political orientation of the government established by the Taëf Agreements of 1989'. In secondary education, Etat (1993, 302) claims 75% of children using French as vehicular language (25% in English), although this drops to 58% in Higher Education, where 30% of lectures are given in English and 20% in Arabic. Etat 1994 (311) notes that three French-speaking Universities still attract large numbers of students: 30,000 in the *Université Libanaise*, 6,000 in St-Joseph and 4,000 in Saint-Esprit de Kaslik. Gueunier (1993, 266) warily notes however that education is in such a bad state after the wars that younger pupils have notably poorer French language skills than their elders.

The conflicts facing Lebanese Francophonie are clear: with Islam, with English, with economics and with social and cultural values. The Lebanese Minister of Culture and Higher Education, speaking in May 1993, defined what, for Lebanon, was associated with Francophonie:

> If Lebanese maintain French as second language, while English is the world economic language and has become practically universal, it is because Francophonie is a social choice: a choice for freedom, justice, fraternity and democracy...This experiment, between Muslims and Christians, in living together must be pursued...(Abou and Haddad, 1994, 560).

North Africa

The three Maghreb countries Algeria (7,470,000 + 7,470,000), Tunisia (2,370,000 + 3,160,000) and Morocco (4,610,000 + 6,400,000) have been French colonies or protectorates, and have retained many aspects of French culture including for example much of the educational system. Egypt (215,000 + 1,700,000) retains the use of French in some fields, particularly in education, where it is associated with Christian sects and schools.

Algeria was conquered in 1830, and became politically an integral part of France, with numerous *Départements* (see Benrabah, 1992 and 1995; Cherrad-Benchefra, 1989; Harbi, 1994; Kepel, 1994). The fiction of assimilation came to an end in 1962 when the Evian agreements between the French Government and the *Front de Libération Nationale (FLN)* brought complete independence after a bitter, expensive and savage war lasting from 1954. France relocated its atomic testing facility to the Pacific but retained commercial links for oil and natural gas. Many French settlers - *pieds noirs* - a number of whom were in fact of

Italian, Maltese, and Spanish origins, rather than French - left the territory to install themselves first in France, and then, for many, in Corsica, New Caledonia and French Polynesia. French nationality was offered to Algerians, whether of French origin or not, who had been born while the territory was in French hands. The new Government of Algeria also, in seeking a new Algerian identity, established a Code of Nationality differentiating 'original', Muslim and 'acquired', lay or non-Muslim nationality, and gave State approval to a role for religion and the mosques in education and justice.

The *FLN* and the Algerian Governments which succeeded it during the period of one-party rule from 1962 to 1989 were in effect - or have been portrayed as such - a French-inspired, military, lay, 'Socialist' movement, looking forward to the modernisation of the country but within the Western tradition of growth and economic prosperity. They had used Islam as a symbol: development would come from Marxism. In 1965 Ben Bella was replaced as President by Boumediene, whose control used a mixture of authoritarian military force, the elitist eastern Arab families rather than those of the Centre and the West, ignoring Berber groups and reducing the French influence, removing the 'democratic' Marxists, but also much of the Islamic motivation for the freedom fight, characterising this as 'reactionary clericalism'. The Arabisation of the country in administration and education, however, supported by the *FLN* from 1968, was a pan-Arab notion, bringing Algeria closer to the Egypt of Nasser. In 1978 Boumediene died, to be replaced by President Chadli Benjedid.

By 1982 protests took on a more Islamic character: the *Mouvement Islamique Armé (MIA)* was created to take the struggle to the *maquis* in a deliberate imitation of the *FLN*'s anti-French guerrilla war. The popular uprising in 1988 provoked a new, multiparty Constitution in 1989, and the *Front Islamique du Salut (FIS)* was proclaimed in the same year. After taking most of the vote in the June 1990 municipal elections, the overwhelming victory of the *FIS* in the December 1991 first round legislative elections gave it 188 seats against the *FLN*'s 15, with 28 for the two other parties. The Army and traditional *FLN* authorities were not prepared to let the *FIS* take over, and the abandonment of the second round of elections, the removal of President Chadli Benjedid and his replacement by Mohamed Boudiaf in January 1992, the subsequent banning of the *FIS* in March 1992, the murder of the new President Boudiaf in June 1992, and the choice of General Zéroual as President in 1994, all stress the continuing role of the Army in determining Algeria's political future. Authoritarianism has met intransigence: deaths through terrorism reached more than 10,000 by September 1994, with 36 foreigners killed in the 6 months to March 1994, and many since, and reported executions by the authorities in reprisals are numbered in their hundreds. Etat (1994, 61) lists 37 Algerian intellectuals killed in 1993 and 1994; teachers, particularly of French, and women not wearing the veil have frequently been fundamentalist targets. In December 1994, the *Groupe*

Islamique Armé (*GIA*)   seized an Air France Boeing on the tarmac at Algiers airport, reportedly because it was taking Algerians to France for Christmas; passengers were released unharmed in the attack by French gendarmes on the ground in Marseilles.

Islamic fundamentalism achieved its success in Algeria through clandestine activity, taking advantage of poor economic circumstances, but also by making France and Western values the target of its attack. *FIS* proclaimed that the original purpose of the movement from 1954 to 1962 - the removal of colonial France and its values by Arab nationalism and by Islam - had been betrayed. The Islamic party's return to basic values, its pan-Arab (but non-racial) approach, its roots in a rejection of Western values and culture, was attractive to the poor and poses a major threat to Western influence, particularly to French culture and economic interests.

On independence in 1962, policy was to use both French and Arabic. With Boumediene, however, Arabisation was increased, and in 1968 it was announced that public administration would take place totally in Arabic by 1971 - even though newly appointed Civil Servants in 1969 generally lacked adequate, or indeed any, skills in the appropriate kind and level of Arabic. Partly, this refusal to support French was caused as a reaction to French boycotts of Algerian petrol and gas. Early education hence used Arabic, and by 1977 'it was too late; when Arabisation of the Universities started in 1980 (secondary school) monitors became (fully fledged) teachers in the human sciences...The generations coming from our schools now no longer master any language' (Benrabah, 1995, 39). But the difficulty of fusing Francophone and Arab-speaking elements and roles in society and government meant that in effect the elites were divided, with economic and social modernisation, the army and commerce generally being Francophone, and French being supported by satellite television and increases in education, while education, justice and culture were dominated by Arabic - and by Islam (Harbi, 1994). The symbolism of French as the obligatory second language for Algerian education was further complicated in April 1993 when English became the required foreign language, potentially a major blow for Francophonie throughout the country.

> Is this a concession towards fundamentalists in a secret dialogue?...Is it
> a response to pressure from without? Clearly, the complex of the
> colonised and the neo-colonised has never completely left Algerians.
> Isn't the Government mistaking the target by continuing to criticise the
> 'secular assimilationists' (Belaïd Abdeslem, Prime Minister)...Isn't he
> condemning French-speaking intellectuals to fundamentalist
> vindictiveness? (Année Francophone Internationale, 1994, 236).

In Algeria, the linguistic situation is complex and the use of each language has political, social and religious connotations. French remains widely used, even though the official language of the 1989 Constitution is Arabic, and bi- or even multi-lingualism is necessary for social progression (Cherrad-Benchefra, 1989; Benrabah, 1992). French retains a double role - as the language of the oppressor and the colonialist, and of the continuing elite, but also as the language of scientific and economic progress, of opening towards the wider world, and of daily life in shops and in town, where language mix is the norm.   Classical Arabic is the language particularly of religion, and its prestige is high, particularly among the Islamic fundamentalists who are now fighting for political power.   The Algerian form of spoken Arabic is the language of daily intercourse and of the home, of rural life, while standardised modern Arabic is the written and formal language and is more used in the cities.   Berber (Tamazghit) and other languages are spoken by well-established groups - the original inhabitants before the Arab invasion of the seventh century - although the prestige of these languages is low and they are mainly confined to rural and deprived urban groups, and to the Kabylie area. Nonetheless, a demonstration in favour of Berber was allowed in Algiers in April 1994, and in Kabylie schools were on strike for the academic year 1994-1995. Berber, indeed, may be used by the political authorities to oppose the increasing power of (Arabic-using) Islam, while Berber speakers see their struggle as 'at the core of democracy throughout the Maghreb...Were the government to solve the Berber problem, it would be a positive signal for Algerian democracy' (Said Sadi in Guardian, 6.2.1995). For a number of reasons - the historical context, continuing opposition to French policy, the language-based tensions - Algeria has never been a member of organised Francophonie.

Many Arabic-speaking immigrants have installed themselves in France, to an extent where estimates can count up to a potential total of 14 million migrants and descendants of migrants living there, most of whom will be regarded as Maghrebin, Islamic and a social if not criminal problem (Silverman, 1992; Ager, 1995). Although many of these immigrants have brought with them their native language - Berber, Hebrew, Italian and Spanish, not merely Arabic - the strength of assimilationist tradition in metropolitan France means that it is highly unlikely that languages other than French will survive the third generation. Contacts between Algeria and France, however, will continue for a long time to come, and each country is likely to affect the political and linguistic situation of the other.

West, East and Central Africa

18 countries, mainly in West and Central sub-Saharan Africa, have French as their official language, sometimes in conjunction with one or more national languages, and sometimes by itself: Benin (470,000 + 940,000), Burkina-Faso (610,000 + 1,300,000), Burundi (165,000 + 550,000), Cameroon (1,940,000 + 2,160,000), Central African Republic (140,000 + 365,000), Chad

(150,000 + 980,000), Congo (770,000 + 660,000), Djibouti (29,000 + 100,000), Gabon (300,000 + 400,000), Guinea (355,000 + 710,000), the Ivory Coast (3,630,000 + 3,630,000), Mali (890,000 + 890,000), Mauritania (120,000 R), Niger (520,000 + 1,110,000), Rwanda (210,000 + 350,000), Senegal (720,000 + 1,100,000), Togo (680,000 + 1,020,000) and Zaïre (1,740,000 + 3,500,000). The Cape Verde Islands (Cabo Verde, Cap-Vert) (500 R), Guinea-Bissau (1,000 R), and Equatorial Guinea (500 R) have Portuguese or Spanish as official language. Ethiopia (4,000 R) has retained some use of French, despite its chequered history of colonialism and more recent wars.

Francophone Africa is multilingual, and each language often has defined functions and particular uses: Swahili or English are widely used linguae francae, Classical Arabic is the language of Islam, local languages are used in the market. French is the language of education, particularly higher education, and French plays the role of the language of social advance (see for example Manessy and Wald, 1984; Juilliard 1990; Gueunier 1992; Ka, 1993). Hence French is an elitist, minority language, a vehicle for science, technology, commerce and diplomacy. Depending on the country and its history and situation, a version of French may however be in popular use - for example in the Ivory Coast and Senegal. French is in any case part of the multilingual mix of Africa, confronting not merely local languages but other exogenous languages as well, particularly English. In Cameroon, for example, where the former federation of the Francophone and Anglophone sections of the country joined in 1972,

> The Francophones, who are in a majority of five to one and who now run Cameroon, changed the name of (the coastal town Victoria to Limbe) in 1983 in an attempt to extend "la Francophonie" desired by France, which ruled the rest of the country until independence. Anglophone resentment at what is regarded as systematic discrimination in education, employment and political representation has surfaced in the form of vociferous political opposition to the authoritarian regime of President Paul Biya (Guardian, 2.5.1991).

Guinea, an independent Republic situated on the West Coast of Africa, has a population of some 6 million (Slowe, 1991; Diallo, 1993). Between 1720 and 1830, Guinea had formed part of the Islamic empire of Futa Djallon. Guinea became a French colony in 1899. In order to reduce the power of Muslim officials, the role of tribal chiefs was emphasised by the French in a 'divide and rule' policy whose consequences included the breakdown of social structures and established hierarchies of power. Led at the time by Sekou Touré, it was the only country that chose independence from France in the series of referenda conducted in 1958 and 1959. The French reaction was to withdraw all administrators and aid immediately, the French Press accused Sekou Touré and the country of domination by the Soviet Union, and the country was targeted as an example of the incompetence and disaster rejection of France necessarily entailed. A difficult period followed for Guinea as an independent Republic trying to find an 'African' solution rejecting the West.

Although on independence no more than 10% of children had received any education and there was a mere handful of graduates, a number of technicians, of teachers and of other potential supporting trades and professions was available. Sekou Touré, the independence leader, determined that policies of integration and nation-building must precede economic progress. External threats also determined this policy: in 1960 French mercenaries helped in an attempt to force the country back into the French African Community; the Soviets were involved in a teachers' plot in 1961; Americans mishandled the arrest of Guinean Ministers in Ghana in 1966; and an invasion by Portuguese troops from Guinea-Bissau in 1970 aimed at releasing Portuguese prisoners held by independence movements on Guinean territory.

During the colonial period, the economy was oriented around the export of cash crops (coffee and bananas) and minerals (gold, bauxite and diamonds). Capital investment was limited to the port of Conakry and a handful of other towns, together with the connecting railways and roads. From independence to 1985 however all economic development was accorded second priority to ethnic integration. Thus, in 1959, bauxite production in the Foulah area was cut until iron ore production in the Kissi region could be developed; rice prices were held stable at Conakry despite greater transport costs from the Malinké region inland. Infrastructure policies were deliberately oriented away from export and towards ensuring internal equality between regions. The policy of ethnic integration also led to decision-making at village level and to power being accorded to village assemblies, with no intermediate (regional) organisation, on matters of local investment. But the policy was implemented through a one-party state, with the *Parti Démocratique* completely dominant: the *Parti* was intended to be the agent of social equalisation, its leaders doing four months of compulsory rural labour each year and occasionally excluding capitalists, including small businessmen, from its elite. Among other consequences, such measures also had the result that no competing cadre could easily become established.

In 1984 Sekou Touré died. A coup d'état followed his burial, giving power to Colonel Lansana Conté. Policies changed drastically, to prioritise economic growth. The *Parti Démocratique* was disbanded, along with the village-level organisations. Investment was encouraged from large-scale international organisations; inevitably, it was concentrated in mining and the extractive industries, and in Conakry. 10,000 civil servants were dismissed at the insistence of the International Monetary Fund. Since the government was principally Soussou, the dismissals were concentrated on people of other ethnic origins, mainly Malinké. Close connections were established with international organisations and with France, and Guinea joined the Francophone summit meetings when these were established in 1986.

Since 1987, with privatisation and the use of IMF money for infrastructure projects in transport, exploitation of the immense mineral resources of the country has increased. The country has 25% of the world's known bauxite reserves, 6.5 billion tonnes of high-grade iron ore reserves, 400m carats of diamonds of great purity, and potential for further exploitation of gold. These reserves are spatially dispersed, and it is likely that their exploitation will counter some of the effects of the abandonment of Sekou Touré's ethnic and spatial integration policies. Nonetheless, balance of commercial trade with France in 1992 still showed 611 million francs deficit for Guinea, almost exactly balancing the 600m FF in direct aid from France in 1986 paid as part of the IMF agreement.

Since independence, Guinea's language policy has given priority to national languages. French is the official language since 1990, and (Classical) Arabic the religious language for 95% of the population. Three main national languages and five minor ones are used as teaching media (all teaching is in national languages up to the second secondary year), and in youth organisations, giving a literacy rate of 41.6% in national languages as against about 30% in French in 1983. Overall, however, the literacy rate in that year was only 19% of the age group (this figure has since risen to 32%). Since 1984 French is regaining a role in education, and the return from exile of political leaders has also brought about the return of French as a political language.

Indian Ocean

Mayotte (20,000 + 20,000) is a *Collectivité Territoriale Française*, having been allowed to vote separately from the rest of the Comoro archipelago in the referendum for independence in 1960. Réunion (460,000 + 87,000) is a *Département d'Outre-Mer*. The Comoros Republic is an Islamic Republic (35,000 + 120,000). Mauritius (270,000 + 600,000) and the Seychelles (5,000 + 15,000) have two official languages, English and French. Madagascar (1,060,000 + 1,300,000) is a former French colony.

Mauritius , with a population of approximately one million, is an independent State discovered in 1513 by the Portuguese, occupied by the Dutch from 1638 to 1710, by the French from 1721 to 1810, and under British administration from 1810 to 1968 (Baggioni and Robillard, 1990; Robillard, 1992; North, 1994). It has a multiracial population of 966,863 (1983 census), with, in the categories of that census, 500,833 'Hindus', 160,500 'Muslims', 28,040 of 'Chinese' origin, and 277,490 of the 'General Population'. Mauritius is an ethnically and linguistically mixed society. The prestige of individual languages follows a recognised pattern, with (standard) English and French, followed by standardised oriental languages, then Creole, with the Indian language Bhojpuri (non-standardised) at the base (Robillard, 1992, 1993). The only language which is in common use everywhere is Creole, while English is used in formal written situations (Parliament, the law, administration), and standard French is also used in Parliament and the law, and orally in administration. The use of other languages is a marker of the situation, and can have political, economic or social implications as well as personal ones connected with the nature of the interaction. Many social problems are said to be associated with the sociolinguistic status and prestige of languages and ethnic origins. The labels applied to different ethnic origins often indicate mutual evaluations of prestige for example, rather than any ethnic reality, and a range of Creole and French terms such as *franco-mauricien, blanc, blanc-bec, lérat-blanc, frontière, gens de couleur, mulâtre, créole, Afro-mauricien, indien baptisé, tamoul, télégou, indo-mauricien, musulman, lascar, sino-mauricien* offers a number of possibilities for self-evaluation and for 'placing' others.

The education system suffers from language problems (Baggioni and Robillard, 1990; Etat, 1993, 82). Creole and French are used in the 1,400 kindergarten schools, Creole, French and some English in 283 primary schools, 60 of which are private, and a mixture of all three in 125 secondary schools, of which 103 are private. Officially, English is the language of education, and French is a school subject. About half the 40,000 children entering primary education fail to complete the Certificate of Primary Education, with about 25% achieving a satisfactory pass level; 10% of the age group succeeds in School Certificate and 2.5% in Higher School certificate. Among the reasons for the poor level of achievement is said to be the fact that some mother tongues (particularly Indian languages and Chinese) are not used in education, that education is often multilingual and that much time is spent in language education (60% of primary school time, where both French and English are officially taught), and that language competence is not taken into account in progression through the school. Education is nonetheless a priority for the budget, accounting for 12.3% of expenditure, follows a ten-year master plan set up in 1991, and is subsidised by external aid from the World Bank and the Bank for African Development, with France the principal bilateral aid source.

Mauritius is in a fairly healthy economic situation by comparison both with most African countries and with other Indian and Pacific Ocean islands: a GDP per person of around US$ 3,000 in 1994, by comparison with the 480$ of the Comoros or the 1900$ of Fiji, although it does not reach the Réunion figure of over 4,000$. The rate of population increase is low; manufacturing is booming, passing the value added by agriculture for the first time in 1993. Product specialisation - in clothing (80% of manufacturing), flowers, electronic assembly - associated with (respectable) offshore banking and tourism, together with political stability and healthy democracy, have ensured continuing rises in incomes. The lack of a pampered social elite, no indigenous population before immigration, and racial harmony combine to make Mauritius' future reasonably secure (North, 1994).

North America

Canada (6,580,000 + 3,000,000) is officially bilingual in English and French, while the Province of Quebec (5,620,000 R) is officially monolingual in French. New Brunswick has 245,000 'real' Francophones, Ontario 337,900, and even the United States of America has large French-speaking populations in Louisiana (100,000 + 200,000) and New England (200,000 R). St Pierre et Miquelon (total population 6,100 R), a *Collectivité Territoriale* situated just off the New Brunswick coast and officially a part of France since 1534 (without interruption since 1816) has a convenient location near rich fishing grounds which enables France to claim a useful Exclusive Economic Zone.

Quebec has suffered rejection from a number of possible solutions to the Constitutional crisis which have dogged its relations with the rest of Canada since the 'repatriation' of the Canadian Constitution in 1982. In 1980 Quebec had rejected complete independence from the rest of Canada by 60%-40%. Pierre Trudeau, Prime Minister of Canada at the time, worked to retain the Federation and he and his successors through the 1980s have generally attempted to make concessions to Quebec's sense of difference, in both its culture and its insistence on the continuing use of French, particularly in education, commerce and public life, in an attempt to avoid the disintegration of the Federation. The 1990 failure of the Lake Meech accord between the Federal and Provincial Prime Ministers to resolve Quebec's demands (it was rejected by 2 Provinces), and of the 1992 referendum on the Charlottetown agreement on the Constitution - which had been carefully prepared by numerous Commissions and a massive public relations exercise, but which was nonetheless rejected by 54.4% of the electorate and by six of the ten Provinces - led to a hardening of the attitudes of the autonomy movements, both in French-speaking Quebec and also in the Anglophone Provinces of the West. Canadian legislative elections in October 1993 replaced the Conservatives, in power since 1988, in a dramatic rejection of the new leader Kim Campbell and the previous Premier, Brian Mulroney, who had resigned in August (from 153 seats, the Conservatives dropped to 2). Jean Chrétien, leader of the Liberals and Canadian Premier, is unlikely to be able to persuade either Quebec or the increasingly impatient Anglophone western Provinces to retain federalism: in fact, economic contacts are now stronger with the USA on North-South 'vertical' links, one in the West and the other in the East, than they are 'horizontally' across Canada from East to West. Economically, there is not much doubt that Quebec, whose Gross Domestic Product is bigger than that of Denmark and as big as Belgium's, coul l exist independently, particularly since the North American Free Trade Area would presumably allow few tariff barriers to continue. Politically, the internal problems - with the native peoples, immigrants and other groups, and particularly the nature of the relationship with the rest of Canada - that independence would bring are not resolved.

Jean Charest, new leader of the Conservative Party and also a Quebecker, was certain that Quebec would refuse independence (Lacroix, 1993; L'Express, 13.1.1994). But the largest opposition party in the Canadian parliament after 1993 was the *Bloc Québecois*, which held 54 of the 75 seats allocated to Quebec, became the largest opposition party and hence the formal opposition in the Canadian Parliament.   Led by Lucien Bouchard, whose aim is to pursue independence for Quebec, the *Bloc* feels that the rejection of Charlottetown was the last possibility that federalism could survive, and that the only possible solution is now independence. Quebec's Liberals, who had been in power since 1985 and were led by Daniel Johnson since the retirement of Robert Bourassa at the beginning of 1994, are determined federalists and do not wish to see Quebec follow the route of independence proposed by the *PQ* led by Jacques Parizeau. The *PQ*'s proposed referendum on autonomy, now planned for October 1995, is not expected to convincingly support independence, mainly since despite the *PQ*'s winning 77 of the 125 Quebec Parliament seats in September 1994, it achieved only a narrow percentage victory (44.7 to 44.3%) and opinion polls showed that autonomy would be rejected, again, by about 60 - 40.

Quebec has affirmed its language, and political, rights to be different from the rest of Canada in increasingly strong terms since the *Révolution Tranquille* of the 1960s. The passage of Law 101, the Charter of the French Language, the official monolingualism of the Province, and the range of language defence mechanisms placed in position to defend Quebec's right to use French represent the most complete legal mechanism for the protection of a language minority in Francophonie, and have often served as a model to France in developing its language laws. The laws now confer rights on French-speakers: to receive, in French, any communication from the public administration, health services, public utilities, professional orders, unions and enterprises; to express oneself in French in political assemblies; to work in French; as a consumer, to be informed and served in French; and to receive education in French (Maurais, 1993, 81). The laws do not apply to Federal institutions (which are bilingual, in English and French), nor to certain businesses (e.g. export). The purpose of the legislation is 'to ensure that immigrants integrate more with the French majority than with the English minority; otherwise, Montreal, the Province's metropolis, would lose its character of a town in majority French-speaking' (Maurais, 1993, 80). The results of this language planning are notable: in 1971 47.2% of 'Allophones' (i.e. speakers of languages other than French) said they used French, while in 1986 the figure was 67.2%. Obligatory attendance of allophones at French-speaking schools has meant that French, rather than English, is now the normal language in use at home. The proportion of Anglophones capable of holding a conversation in French increased to 53% in the 1980s and has stabilised there (Mougeon, 1994). In business, Francophones went from 30% in managerial posts in 1959 to 58% in 1988. 76.4% of businesses have received certificates showing that they use French internally. Judgements by Quebeckers on the characteristics of English-speakers as against French speakers showed that whereas, in the 1960s, Francophones had a poor opinion of themselves, in the 1980s positive views were held of their psycho-social characteristics such as honesty, trustworthiness, loyalty (Mougeon, 1994).

Nonetheless, the danger of being swamped by English is still present: if 67.2% of 'allophones' used French, 72.4% of them used English in 1986. French speakers 'converge' more towards English than English speakers do towards French, and 'the behaviour of English speakers is more characteristic of a high status dominant minority...French speakers' behaviour is more like that of a low status dominated majority than that of a high status dominating majority' (reported in Maurais, 1993, 83).

Caribbean

Haiti (570,000 + 250,000) has been independent since 1804. Dominica (1,000 R), Grenada, Saint-Vincent, Trinidad and Tobago (7,000 R), Costa Rica (1,000 R), Saint Lucia (2,000 R) have small Francophone populations. The three Caribbean *Départements d'Outre-Mer* - Guyane (55,000 + 15,000) on the South American mainland, and the base for French space exploration, Martinique (270,000 + 50,000), and Guadeloupe (270,000 + 50,000) - are considered integral parts of France, despite the existence of small autonomy movements in each.

Guadeloupe is a good example of an area in which the sociolinguistic situation assigns different roles to standard French, to Creole and to other languages (Bebel-Gisler, 1981; Aldrich and Connell, 1992; Hazaël-Massieux, 1993; Belorgey and Bertrand, 1994). It is a *DOM* with a total area of 1,780 square kilometres, formed of seven islands in an archipelago, and with a total population of 330,000. The islands have been settled by the French since 1635, became sugar plantations with imported slaves from 1650, were officially annexed by France in 1674, lost in the Napoleonic Wars, and after restoration to France in 1816, have remained in French possession. Slavery was abolished in 1848. Separated from Martinique by (English-speaking) independent Dominica, Guadeloupe's local politics and economy are dependent on its status as *DOM*, with the consequential problems of managing the European Union connection and the advantages of continuing subsidies from France and Europe.

As in Martinique, Guadeloupe's economy has been developed around sugar and bananas. Sugar production, heavily supported by France and Europe (about 16% of planters' receipts derives from subsidies), is subject to weather - the four refineries were rebuilt as two in 1989 after Cyclone Hugo - and is in decline, despite the production of rum. For bananas - after riots and pressure on France - a managed European market was agreed in April 1993 guaranteeing preference - and higher prices - for banana exports to the Union, which has caused protests particularly from Germany, where prices have increased by 30% since 1991 (Le Monde Diplomatique, July 1994). Banana exports to Europe from Latin America have increased despite the managed market's taxes, and competition for Guadeloupe and Martinique means that hope of these French dependencies achieving economic independence on this basis remains precarious: less than a third of Guadeloupe's GDP derives from agricultural exports. The contrast between the surrounding Third World economies of other Caribbean islands and the protected, subsidised falsity of the local economy remains evident.

As both *DOM* and Region, Guadeloupe has both a *Conseil Général* to manage its departmental affairs and a *Conseil Régional*, with considerable devolved budgetary and administrative responsibilities, for its role as a region. The 1992 elections to the *Conseil Régional* saw the return of Lucette Michaux-Chevry (RPR) as President, and of Dominique Larifla as President of the *Conseil Général*. Local management of the regional finances had produced a deficit of 411 million francs in 1992; unemployment is high and the popularity of the independence movement said to be growing. Both Martinique and Guadeloupe returned Lionel Jospin as their preferred Presidential candidate in the 1995 elections. In Guadeloupe, increased participation between the first and the second rounds of the election - up from 35% to 45% of the electorate - favoured Jospin, showed the traditional left-wing orientation of party politics, and also dealt a blow to the active campaigning of Michaux-Chevry on behalf of Jacques Chirac. Independence has been on the agenda in Guadeloupe for a considerable period, starting in 1956 with student protests. In 1967 a strike was put down with excessive severity. As the prosperity of the sugar trade diminished, Trade Union groups became more and more politicised, provoking a move of the Communist Party to support independence and the creation in 1978 of a *Union populaire pour la libération de la Guadeloupe (UPLG)* and an armed *Groupe de Libération Armée (GLA)*. Successive bombings in the early 1980s, and a policy of rejection of elections did little to make the movement more acceptable to the general population, despite widespread agreement on the need for greater use of Creole and recognition of Creole-based Guadeloupean identity. Nonetheless the *UPLG*, opposed to violence, does have some support (Aldrich and Connell, 1992, 217).

Linguistically, Creole is the normal language of Guadeloupe, with standard French in the official role, in education and the administration. The ethnic mix of the population is 80% descendants of slaves, 10% originating in south-east Asia, 5% 'Creole Whites' and 5% from France, mainly administrators posted for a tour of duty. As elsewhere in France, recognition of language rights to the use of Creole was non-existent until the early 1980s and, slowly, has since developed. Bebel-Gisler (1981), in a strongly-worded attack on French attitudes, showed how domination and forced assimilation had produced a sense of alienation in her, and how the sense of shock at her reception in France provoked her to study how 'the colonial system succeeded in producing the internalisation, in the dominated population, of its own structure of dominance, to the point of creating an indigenous demand for the reproduction of the dominant system'. The Toubon law insisting that French alone be used by public servants was criticised by Camille Darsières from Martinique in the National Assembly on 3rd May 1994, pointing out his fear that

> bureaucrats and other executives, behind the times, may make bad use of the law to confuse workers, tax-payers, those accused of crimes, by speaking French, imposed as an official language and as a superior one, whose use could be an obstacle for the masses, who do not master it as a normal vehicle for their thought and their mentality' (*Journal Officiel*, 26, AN (CR), 1397).

Demands that Creole be used, and that '*Créolité*' be respected have followed rejection of dominant French culture by writers and intellectuals such as Aimé Césaire of Martinique (aged 80 in 1993), who developed the idea of Caribbean *Négritude* developing from Senghor's African ideas. More recent attempts to define *Créolité* by writers and intellectuals such as Barnabé, Confiant, Chamoiseau, with more established authors such as Maryse Condé and Edouard Glissant, have oriented the concept more towards the expression of a unique identity, but the word's political and ideological meaning is more important than its literary one, and the regional impact of the concept of *Créolité* is unclear. Although in literary terms it might be possible to unite Guadeloupe and Martinique, the development of one official French-based Creole for use everywhere in the Caribbean, including independent countries like Haiti, remains problematic. Chamoiseau's novel 'Texaco' obtained the Goncourt prize in 1992, showing perhaps a degree of acceptance by France itself of change. 'Texaco' was not written in Creole itself, as is much poetry and 'insignificant' writing such as advertisements, or speech-oriented writing such as theatre. Nonetheless, writing in Creole - as opposed to writing in standard French but using the occasional Creole expression and with a Caribbean setting - suffers from a number of problems, ranging from the economic one of finding an adequate readership to the linguistic one of the absence of standardised Creole (in spelling and sentence structure for example) or of formal registers of the language (cf. Hazaël-Massieux, 1993).

Asia and Oceania

Since the visit of Alain Decaux, *Ministre de la Francophonie* in 1989, and the 1992 visit of François Mitterrand, Vietnam (70,000 R) has been the subject of intense pressure to re-establish commercial, cultural and other links with the West - not just with Francophonie (see also Chapter 9). Cambodia (10,000 R) and Laos (4,000 R) have retained small Francophone populations, as indeed have some of the Indian trading posts such as Pondicherry (2,000 + 10,000). In Oceania, apart from Vanuatu (45,000 R), the former Anglo-French condominium of the New Hebrides, French presence in the Pacific is strong and shows every sign of continuing in the three *TOM* - Wallis and Futuna (7,000 + 2,000), French Polynesia (128,000 + 16,000) and New Caledonia (120,000 + 15,000).

New Caledonia (total population 164,173 (1989 census)), with an electorate of 94, 639 for the two National Assembly seats in 1993 (see Christnacht, 1987 and 1990; Aldrich, R., 1991, 1993; Aldrich and Connell, 1992; Chesneaux and McLellan, 1992; Chand, 1993), has had a chequered history. 22,315 convicts were transported to New Caledonia between 1864 and 1897: 40% died in the jails, but 12,000 were released to form the nucleus of French colonisation. It is indeed to this origin that the 'Kanaks' (Melanesians) allude when they consider the 'Caldoches' (mainly descendants of these French inhabitants) to be 'victims of history'. The colony was also intended to be an agricultural settlement supplying France with its surplus - 13,000 free settlers had arrived by 1902 - although transport and marketing problems defeated this aim. The discovery of nickel on the islands in 1863 has led to a series of booms, the latest in 1960, as the metal was needed by different industries, particularly armaments, in the treatment of steel. 40% of the world's nickel resources lie in New Caledonia; the production of raw ore amounted to 3,385,000 tonnes in 1988. Many of the permanent installations which used to represent investment outside the capital, Nouméa, have however been abandoned since the violence of the early 1980s, and the largest industrialist concerned, Jacques Lafleur, has sold his northern interests to the local government. While nickel is still smelted in Nouméa, much of the raw ore is shipped direct to Japan and elsewhere for processing: the ore is simply scraped from the Thio plateau, dumped on the foreshore and conveyed direct into ore carrying ships.

In 1981 the independence leader Pierre Declerq was assassinated. Massive demonstrations by Kanaks caused immense surprise in metropolitan France, where the normal assumption had been that the Melanesian population was not interested in autonomy. In 1984 the *Front de Libération Kanak, National et Socialiste (FLNKS)*, formed from organisations and groups supporting autonomy, and led by Eloi Machoro, Jean Tjibao, and Yeiwené Yeiwené, not convinced that the message had been understood,   violently opposed the

November elections, and 20 people were killed in subsequent confrontations. Edgar Pisani, formerly a Minister and a highly regarded senior politician, proposed a peace and development plan; shortly after its release, Yves Tual, teenage son of a European settler, was shot and killed by Kanaks; Eloi Machoro, a leading member of the *FLNKS*, was shot by French gendarmes during protests in Nouméa. The incoming French government of 1986, led by Jacques Chirac as Prime Minister, rejected the Pisani plan and favoured a harder line. Commentators foresaw nothing but further violence as a result of such an approach:

> Contemporary French policies (1986-88) which aim only at satisfying the short-term demands of the Caldoche community alone, led by its rich extremists, are leading the territory to an impasse which renders any economic development illusory, badly affects French influence among Pacific powers and can only lead ... to a rupture between a Melanesian Caledonia and France, which might keep a corner of the island after a catastrophic disaster (Mathieu, 1988, 149).

In April 1988, further violent protests indeed occurred, leaving thirty dead. The Matignon Agreements of June 1988 were accepted by the *FLNKS* (Jean-Marie Tjibao), the *Ralliement pour la Calédonie dans la République (RPCR)* (Jacques Lafleur). The proposals were to create three provinces overall, two of which (the North and the Loyalty Islands) would be likely to be controlled by the independence movement, a number of economic and social reforms, and a ten-year period of preparation for a referendum on independence to be held in 1998. The independence leader, Jean-Marie Tjibaou, was assassinated with Yeiwéné Yeiwéné in 1989 by Kanaks opposed to independence.

But by 1990 France had made notable investments in training programmes, tourism, fisheries and infrastructure. The review of progress in February 1994 concluded that France had kept her side of the bargain struck in 1988. For *FLNKS* President Néaoutyine the situation in the mid-1990s is closer to that of a truce than of a permanent peace, and the outcome of the 1998 referendum is by no means assured: 'The Matignon agreements are not a declared decolonisation process, and the Kanak community, preparing the country for independence, cannot consider the New Caledonia situation as settled' (Néaoutyine in Nouvelles Calédoniennes, 21.6.94). Although French is the official language and the language of education, 'Melanesian languages' may be accepted as part of the educational curriculum, and success in them may count towards baccalaureat results, as is the case for French regional languages. But only 4 of the 33 Melanesian languages have been so recognised, and the general impression must remain that New Caledonia's situation outside the Nouméa enclave has made little economic progress and that the Melanesian population could be quite content to become independent in 1998.

The diversity of Francophonie

The geographical spread of Francophonie inevitably poses problems to any attempt systematically to encourage closer links among independent countries. In times of Empire, economies could be managed from Paris: they were, after all, intended to produce goods of use to France or to consume goods produced by France, and only existed in relation to the needs of France. Communication which did not take place in French was ignored. Local customs, habits and traditions were simply removed, to be replaced by the imposition of French values and civilisation. But this apparent uniformity concealed an enormous range of different circumstances. Now, organised Francophonie tries to bring together not merely the economies, political customs, languages and cultures of the former French - and Belgian - Empire, including those parts still under France's control, a difficult enough task in itself, but also the very different traditions of European French-speaking countries and regions, and the equal independence of Quebec and other parts of North America and Asia, and to do so by consensus rather than by control.

Diversity is evident firstly in geography and the distances between component countries. Economies, too, are widely contrasted, with the difference of wealth and development very clear. Political systems are often different, and the lack of understanding of alternative types of democracy is clear. Populations are sometimes comparatively homogeneous but more frequently heterogeneous, containing a diversity of peoples, colours, and races. Contrasts of religion are matched by contrasts between religion and secularism, and this is particularly highlighted by the continuing struggle with Islam, whose fundamentalist views on the relation between State and religion present enormous problems for Francophonie. The conflicts between French and other languages are of three types: in the role of French in societal bilingualism, where sometimes it is a symbol of power and domination and sometimes a symbol of opposition to a ruling commercial or political elite, a symbol of freedom and openness. Conflicts between French and English, as world languages or as languages of competing influences - often between France and the United States - are widespread. Conflicts between French and Arabic, French and Flemish, or occasionally between French and other languages, are symbols of alternative social structures, values or identities. Some at least of the problems facing Francophonie, that we shall examine next, derive from the diversity and difference we have briefly investigated.

PART 2. PROBLEMS OF CONTEMPORARY FRANCOPHONIE

We shall restrict our discussion of problems facing contemporary Francophonie to five. The first two concern language: the first (Chapter 3), the range of difficulties associated with the status and use of French itself; the second (Chapter 4), the problems French faces in situations when it comes into conflict with other languages, particularly English, and into situations of competition, particularly in multilingual States. For France - and by extension, for Francophonie - the charge is still levied that the remaining possessions in the Caribbean and the Pacific are nothing more than colonies (Chapter 5). For Francophonie itself, two major problems lie in the sphere of economics (Chapter 6) and in that of the present and eventual nature of the international organisation (Chapter 7).

These problems are recognised and discussed within Francophonie, but are of importance, also, to the rest of the world. Economic contrasts, and the North-South divide, are not unique to Francophonie; colonial structures continue to affect other countries and to dominate world trade; the systematic and formal organisation of international cooperation is a significant item for many in the developed and the developing world; questions of language, culture and identity, and of the clash of cultures and their symbols are important for self-awareness across the world. But Francophonie, in all three senses of the word, often represents these problems in the most acute form.

3. PROBLEMS FOR FRENCH: LANGUAGE, CULTURE AND IDENTITY

The Number of French Speakers

Francophonie, as we have seen, is widely spread throughout the world. But its speakers are fewer in number than those of other major languages, and have been increasing at a slower rate.

Table 3.1

Speakers of world languages

Language	1928	1973	1989	Increase 1928 - 1989
	millions			%
Mandarin Chinese	400	500	834	209
English	170	270	456	268
Hindi	38	105	363	955
Spanish	65	160	308	474
Russian	80	130	285	356
Arabic	37	95	206	557
Bengali	50	100	177	354
Portuguese	36	95	158	439
Malay	-	50	64	-
Japanese	55	100	123	224
French	45 (8th)	60 (11th)	89 (12th)	231

Sources: Calvet, 1993, 73 (cols 2 and 3); UNESCO, 1989, quoted in Asher, 1994, 8, 4346 (col. 4). See also Appendix Table A1.
Note: The language names and definitions vary as between the original sources, and the figures are therefore indicative. Figures are in millions of speakers.

The number of people who use French as first language is small by comparison with other major European languages, and its main use is as second or foreign language. The figure of 104 million 'real' Francophones given above, for example, includes three categories of speaker, as defined in Etat, 1990, 27: first language speaker (i.e. 'French-speaking from birth and wherever they live'), second language speaker (i.e. 'a learnt language (4-8 years schooling) in a partially French-speaking environment') and language of adoption ('writers, artists, teachers, scientists, international functionaries who have adopted French as their language of creation or work'). UNESCO (1989, quoted in Asher, 1994) estimated the numbers of real speakers differently, arriving at the figure of 88 million for French, which, on the same basis, compares with more than five times as many English speakers, more than three times as many Spanish or Russian speakers and more than twice as many speakers of Arabic, to quote just the truly international languages among the world's twelve most spoken languages (Appendix, Table A1). While first speakers of these languages live in countries where nearly everybody speaks them, and where population growth is steady, first speakers of French tend to live in countries in which half or less of the population speaks French, and in countries - particularly in Africa - where population growth is explosive, but where the political or economic situation is such that this fact does not increase the numbers of French first language speakers.

The use of any form of French has spread very little into the general population in most countries of Francophonie. Of the full list of 71 countries and regions specifically mentioned in the 1990 *Etat de la Francophonie* report, 38 (54%) have less than five percent 'real' Francophones (Appendix Table A2). Seven countries, whose official language is French, have less than 10% 'real' Francophones (Burkina-Faso, Central African Republic, Guinea, Mali, Niger, Senegal, Zaïre). Indeed, of the 47 countries and regions attending the Summit meetings, seven (i.e. 15%) have only 0.1% of 'real' Francophones in the population: Bulgaria, Cambodia, Cape Verde, Equatorial Guinea, Guinea-Bissau, Laos, Vietnam, while fourteen (30%) have five per cent or less. 'Real' French speakers form half or more of the population in only five countries or regions: France at 98%, Quebec at 82.9%, the Belgian French Community (presumably) at 100%, Luxembourg at 80%, Monaco at 90%. Does this mean that 'real' Francophonie 'should' consist of only these five countries, perhaps together with the French-speaking Swiss cantons? Ontario, with 337,900 people who speak French at home (Année Francophone, 1992, 33) has more 'real' Francophones than any of Egypt, Burundi, Cape Verde, Central African Republic, Djibouti, Gabon, Guinea-Bissau, Equatorial Guinea, Mauritania, Rwanda, Chad, the Comoros, Mauritius, New Brunswick, Louisiana, New England, Dominica, Santa Lucia, Laos, Vietnam, Luxembourg, Monaco, Aosta, Vanuatu, Ethiopia, Sao Tome and Principe, Costa Rica, the Caribbean islands, any South American country, Iran, Syria or Turkey, Cambodia, Pondicherry, Andorra, Bulgaria or Poland. It has more than all the *TOM* and *Collectivités Territoriales* put together.

There is hence a major problem for Francophonie: in the international competition for power and influence, French is already at less than the tenth rank in terms of the number of people who use it as a first language. In no way can this position be improved, so if French is to improve its competitive position, it will have to increase the numbers of those using it as a second or foreign language. The only way this can happen is by the language becoming so attractive to potential users that they will voluntarily switch to French rather than to say English or Chinese for use as a second language; or choose to learn it as a foreign language, again choosing French over competing languages. There is of course no danger that French will not continue to be a world language. Indeed, the absolute numbers of speakers of French - first, second and foreign - are increasing, and the position compared to a century ago is 'better' (Calvet, 1987, 264). It is only relative to the similar increase in the numbers of speakers of 'competitor' languages that the problem arises. This being so, the problem for Francophonie is a psychological and social one: to give confidence to French speakers that their language can be used, and to show non-French speakers that French can be used as a vehicle for education, access to the modern world of science, technology, administration or to democracy. It is also a marketing problem: how to 'sell' French in a competitive environment. This implies a twofold strategy for Francophonie: to praise the advantages of one's own 'product' while downgrading those of the competition. Both these strategies are represented, in both official policies and in the writings of participants in the debate.

The Standard Language and Regional Variation

English has a number of regional varieties: the language of the United States, of parts of Britain, of Australia, of New Zealand, of parts of India is not quite the same as standard English. That this regional variation should exist is accepted by most English speakers without any concern that the quality of the language will thereby suffer, nor is there any generalised wish for one central standardised form to be developed or approved. English speakers from the different parts of the world will have their own assessments of the prestige, actual and social meanings of the different varieties in particular contexts, and they would probably agree that a standard English accent from the Home Counties is necessarily more prestigious than any other only in Britain, and that 'pavement' means centre of the road in the USA but not elsewhere. After English, Spanish is perhaps the most widespread of the European languages. South America (apart from Brazil, French Guyana and Surinam), most of the Caribbean islands, and Central America use Spanish for all purposes - official, domestic and commercial. There exist at least two prestigious versions: the South American and the Iberian. Despite the survival of native languages in countries in which it was a colonial imposition, Spanish is a lingua franca for the mass of the population in these areas, and indeed, in much of the southern (and, through more recent immigration, eastern) United States as well, where it is used not merely for official, public functions but also in the full range of domestic, professional and private activities. Spanish has hence developed a range of geographical, social and professional varieties. Furthermore, the languages spoken within the Iberian peninsula are sufficiently different from each other to be termed different languages. Castilian and Catalan, in particular, have different spelling conventions, different pronunciation and considerable differences of syntax. In their own regions, these languages are used in the full range of functions. Hence Castilian can in no way be described as standard Spanish, nor imposed throughout the world or even in the Iberian peninsula as the only standard form. Even Portuguese, in its Brazilian and African forms (Angola, Mozambique, Cape Verde, São Tomé and Principe), has developed a greater range of varieties than French (Hagège, 1992, 154). 'Popular' Portuguese, even in a creolised form, is widespread and used by large urban populations in Brazil and Africa.

Standard French and its users contrast with almost every one of these characteristics. Standard French has achieved such a dominant position throughout the French-speaking world that it is almost unthinkable that other forms might be used in official, public situations (Lüdi, 1992). Although functional, geographical and situational variation exists, many French-speaking communities would not expect this variation to be accepted; it is barely recognised. For French, the situation is the opposite to that of English, Spanish and Portuguese: variation, particularly regional variation, exists, but attitudes towards it are more complex and less tolerant. Indeed, one general goal of Francophonie seems to be 'the maintenance and extension of a standard spoken and written French language purified of unacceptable English language borrowings and local idiosyncrasies' (Weinstein, 1989, 53). This concept of a universal standard French, the same everywhere and unchanging in its perfection, is the basis of the belief that the French language can act as the vehicle for the transmission of a universally applicable culture. In order for it to do so, however, its standardisation must be jealously guarded: a 'balkanised' French, with different forms world-wide, would be unable to fulfil the role of a universal language. Thus Alain Guillermou (1964, 20: quoted in Weinstein, 1989, 59) declared that 'Only one kind of French can bring about the unity of French speakers: high quality French, free from a collection of idiosyncrasies, saved from English madness and respectful of the rules'. The assimilation policy of the colonial period certainly aimed at bringing standard French to the colonies for use in official administration, education, and the law. After colonisation ended, the retention of French as official language assumed, almost automatically, that the variety of French to be used would be the same as that of Paris.

Speakers of French who live in Quebec, Louisiana, Africa, the Far East, or the islands of the Caribbean or elsewhere - as well as in the regions of metropolitan France - have nonetheless, for a variety of reasons, developed forms of French which are not standard (Lüdi, 1992; Robillard and Beniamino, 1993). In Africa, for example, the *Inventaire des Particularités Lexicales du Français en Afrique Noire* (IFA, 1983 and 1988) listed specifically African vocabulary, while studies of African syntax (e.g. Lafage, 1985; Gueunier, 1992) show the influence of African languages and perception of reality on French grammar.

The 'African language' thus created may retain the outward appearance of French, but the meanings, the connotations and the intended effect of what is said diverge considerably from standard Parisian French. In some cases (the *DOM*; Haiti, Mauritius) the local mix of languages has created Creoles, whose distance from standard French is even greater. Users of these forms of language commonly experience rejection by speakers of the standard, and the attitude of metropolitan speakers is normally to valorise the standard and to condemn regional (and social) variation as inferior, which is a potential danger for the development of a friendly international Francophonie based on mutual respect (Berrendonner, 1982; Maurais, 1983). Regional norms are sometimes accepted as creating a new, acceptable, standard. Quebec, in particular has adopted a local form of French in the schools and the media and affirms its Quebec identity through the prestige it attaches to this form. There is some evidence that Belgium does likewise (Lüdi, 1992, 165). Researchers in Africa who have collected and systematised Africanisms have felt that there are so many common features that it is possible to identify an 'African French', which could be used as an African linguistic norm (Manessy in Chaudenson and Robillard, 1989, 1, 134; Hagège, 1992, 117) - although such an idea is rejected outright by Djité (1991), who favours the use of African linguae francae. Some countries - Haiti and the Seychelles, for example, where Creole is an official language - have rendered the use of a form of French official and thus tried to ensure its prestige by contrast to standard French. In France, publishers include terms from other Francophone countries in dictionaries and encyclopedias such as the *Petit Robert* and the annual editions of the *Petit Larousse*. The *Conseil International de la Langue Française* publishes French language materials for use in education in Africa and elsewhere for which standard French textbooks have been shown to be inappropriate. When new terms are agreed in the Terminology Commissions, lexicographers and industrial experts from the countries of Francophonie - admittedly usually limited to Belgium, Switzerland, and Canada or Quebec - participate in the discussions and accept the terms for their own countries.

The dilemma remains however: if one motive for Francophonie is the wish to ensure the spread of French, decisions have to be made on whether to support one variety of the language, and if so, which. If the decision is taken that this shall be only the pure standard, then Francophonie will suffer since many potential learners will find both the difficulty of the language and the attitude of speakers towards slight faults or variations distasteful. There are also linguistic consequences to such standardisation: establishing a standard necessarily fixes the language at one point in time, and the danger of sclerosis is real. If, however, the decision is taken to allow adaptations in the language to respond to local situations and real use of the language, Francophonie is open to the charge of pidginisation, 'balkanisation' and fragmentation of French - and Francophone - cultural identity. Indeed, it has been alleged that teaching any French other than the correct standard is to short-change the recipients, by refusing them the right of access to the standard, prestigious variety of French (Gueunier, 1992, 109). This argument is parallel with that of those who maintain that education, to be valuable, must necessarily be difficult, as anything that is not difficult is automatically devalued.

A crisis in language? The quality of French

Much of the debate in France turns however on the concept of the 'quality' of the standard French used by the population, and whether or not a crisis can be detected in this. The debate here joins a venerable tradition of normative writing in France: most of the evidence for the state of medieval French comes from books and lists produced to teach 'correct' grammar, and the first quotations from authors condemning 'modern' inability to use the language properly date from 1689. In the nineteenth and twentieth centuries the tradition has continued (cf. Bengtsson, 1968), although the codification of the language seems to have fixed the late seventeenth and early eighteenth centuries as the point in time to which ideal French can be referred.

Gueunier (1985) reviewed the question, and found that the achievement of contemporary schoolchildren in France in language tests did indeed show some lack of mastery of the (written) language. In grammatical points such as the agreement of adjectives the success of the sample could be as low as 10% on the written agreements in noun phrases like *les cerises rouges*, while overall annual failure rates (i.e. not achieving the required level to move up a class) could be as high as 10%. Since 1989 national tests have been conducted of the achievement, in French and mathematics, of children entering the last of two years of elementary education (notionally at age 7) and the first secondary year (notionally age 11). For French, these involve four twenty-five minute periods, testing both reading and writing, and cover comprehension, word elements (i.e. spelling and agreements), vocabulary, grammar, sentence and textual structure, and expression (Benoit et al, 1991). The 1992 results for reading (Note d'Information 94.11) showed that 20% of 7 year olds had not mastered basic competencies, 53% had mastered just these, 16% had achieved further (*approfondies*) competence ('obtained pertinent information') and 11% remarkable competence ('discriminated appropriately'). In 1991, the same tests were applied to unemployed people aged between 25 and 50, who had not succeeded in the baccalaureate and who were following training schemes. In comprehension, the result seemed to place this group between the 8 year old and the 12 year old children. In spelling, the adults were considerably worse - in dictation, 50% produced more than 20 errors against 14% of children; 20% of the adults produced incomprehensible texts. In expression the results of the adults were not comparable to those of the children, but only one third of the adults produced grammatically correct texts (Note d'Information 92.42).

Whether the crisis here is one of language use, of education or of social attitudes - or even of the accuracy of the testing instrument - the point remains that contemporary users of French do not in fact demonstrate full awareness of the rules, particularly of the written language. Yet all the public discourse concentrates on the need to protect and defend standard, classical French, to maintain the nature and characteristics of the instrument as they were when first codified. Reformation of the language itself - spelling reform, acceptance of the equal correctness of alternative syntactic forms, acceptance of changes in vocabulary even - is systematically refused.

The 'crisis' of French in Belgium, Switzerland and Quebec as well as France was discussed in Maurais (1985). Klinkenberg, in reviewing the Belgian situation (pp 95-145) and pointing out that it was a clear example of (regional) linguistic insecurity, noted that the discourse of crisis reflected social rather than linguistic concerns: 'the crisis of French is merely the result of a crisis of identity...all Belgian identity has disappeared, while the *Communauté Française* only offers an artificial framework, where the Walloons cannot recognise themselves' (135). For Swiss French, Rubattel (in Maurais, 1985, 87-91), in an extremely short contribution, questioned whether there was a crisis at all, and attributed the whole debate as one invented by the Press:

> The style and lexis of Swiss French speakers have been considered for a long time as deviant and deficient by the purists, speaking on behalf of an extremely conservative and centralising French norm. To what is after all a provincial inferiority complex is added the prejudice that Swiss French is the victim of German influence. We repeat that these are well-established prejudices, which reappear in a new form every time a crisis occurs which has other causes.

The examination of French in Quebec was more serious, and covered a number of indicators. Since the publication of the Maurais collection in 1985, the Quebec *Office de la Langue française* regularly publishes indicators of the state of the language, which include assessment of educational attainment. Particularly in Africa, but indeed elsewhere in Francophonie too, including some of the *DOM-TOM*, the crisis of French is regarded as one more indication of the decreasing effectiveness of education (Dumont, 1993). The crisis is less one of French than one of illiteracy: while up to 20% of French adults may be functionally illiterate, the figure rises to nearer 80% in Burundi and rarely drops below 50% for any of the African Francophone group (L'Année Francophone Internationale, 1994, 28). Solutions to the problem here are more oriented towards improvement of basic educational systems - although this seems during the 1990s to be unrealisable - to changing teaching methods and materials, and to establishing a workable language policy which takes cognisance of the complex language situation than towards condemnation of spelling mistakes.

Linguists agree that the language crisis is more a matter of social attitudes than of language, even that linguistic correctness and purism may be by-products of social attitudes. In multilingual societies, while a decision to ensure control of the written language needs to be clear on which language should be used, politicians often assume that the only possible policy is to educate in national or international languages, and that the 'quality' or unchanging perfection of these is part of their value. Children make better progress if at least their initial education is in the language of the home, but if this is not standard French, both politicians and social pressures can prevent success. The example of Haiti, is significant: Creole is the language of 90% of homes, and yet literacy in Creole - official language from 1983 although recognised for educational purposes from 1964 - may be rejected by parents for socio-economic and prestige reasons. The net result is that the public schools may become ghettoes and that illiteracy actually increases (L'Année Francophone Internationale, 1994, 30).

Domains of Use of French

Language of the elite

It is well known that command of the prestigious language (or language variety) is regarded by many in society as a privilege, to be jealously guarded and retained for use by the social elite. This linguistic capital enables access to prestigious employment, to leading roles in society, and to the ability so to manage affairs that the elite is able to reproduce itself (Bourdieu, 1982).

The elite is differently defined in different circumstances. But in many Francophone countries, particularly in Africa,   State education is now in a difficult situation, and private education is the only available education of quality. Access to private education, which often also means religious education, is thus an indicator of membership of the elite in some societies. But for Francophonie, reserving French to the elite in this manner is dangerous. Firstly, social or political change may change the membership of the elite, as occurred in Rwanda in 1994: since many members of the *Front Patriotique Rwandais* had trained in Uganda for their eventual seizure of power, they had come into contact with English and had converted to this language as more profitable for them in the situation in which they found themselves. Indeed, French government support for the former Hutu-dominated regime was seen by them as sufficient reason to consider Francophonie as dangerous.

Secondly, the elite may attempt to restrict access to their 'capital'. Restricting access to French runs directly counter to the aim of spreading French as widely as possible, and thus Francophonie may find itself in the awkward position of advocating education for the masses, suggesting that this should be in French, and then discovering both the impracticality of this and resistance to it from the local elite. French co-operation policies of substitution - sending French teachers, doctors and administrators instead of training local inhabitants to do these jobs - work for example in such a way that they often provide social advantage for the local elite, whose sons and daughters would be expected to provide such trained key people. Untrained local inhabitants cannot do the work, while trained and educated locals can find no work and emigrate. It is for these and other reasons that language policy in Francophonie attempts to provide language teaching in French for the greatest possible number, and that this 'democratisation' of education and of language use is part of the rhetoric of language policy.

Official language

French is used as an official language in a number of countries. The type of French is that of administrative use - formal, written and often formulaic. For Francophonie, the problems associated with the use of administrative French are of two types. Administrative French itself is not an attractive nor an easy form to acquire. Its characteristics are based on French administrative practice, which places great reliance on codified laws and administrative decisions, and assumes that posts in a large-scale public service will be open to qualified people, whose abilities will be tested - usually by written examinations - before enrolment. Enrolment by qualification requires a high degree of language ability in the general population. Such an administrative machine requires a well-developed educational and assessment system to support it, and a number of qualified people to manage the system. In the 1990s, some thirty years after the wave of countries achieving independence, the number of administrators still able to use French in Francophonie is declining. The quality of education has decreased - in some countries, dramatically - and it is unlikely that the present generation of Civil Servants, particularly in Africa, will be replaced by successors with the same skills.

Language of education

French as a language of education requires, in many countries, that it be first learnt by the schoolchild as a foreign language, then as a second language, and that it be used as such a second language from an early age. In many countries, of course, access to education at all is a rare privilege for the mass. In many countries, too, education is provided by religious foundations. The actual situation in education in Africa today is generally agreed to be disastrous - in the low level of investment, in the numbers able to participate, in the results achieved - and the future for Francophone education is therefore difficult. In many countries, too, the child's first introduction to school coincides with introduction to the language of education: the first year(s) of education are given in what is essentially a foreign language. French outside France and some other countries of the North, is fundamentally a second, learnt, language. For

Francophonie therefore, questions about education and particularly about language learning are of great importance. Thus in Senegal (mainly in Dakar - Ka, 1993) after independence in 1960 the country maintained French in the educational system despite some attempts to use Wolof. After 1981 and the resignation of Senghor as President, a bilingual educational system was proposed, as part of a new tripartite set of roles for languages: French for international communication and national administration, Wolof for national unity, and local languages for local administration. But the implementation of this policy (and indeed, its clarification) is resisted by the elite, whose control of French is part of their ability to retain their elite status.

Despite the proportion of their budget devoted to education, the presence of teachers, helpers and aid workers and the continuing presence of France in a number of ways, education in most former colonies is a 'dramatic failure' (Calvet in Robillard and Beniamino, 1993, 489). Most observers agree that the future prosperity of the former colonies must come about through education. But the dilemma is that if this education continues to be provided in French (or any other external language) it will continue to be ineffective, while if it is to be provided in national or local languages and thus be effective, that very process will spell the end of Francophonie as such and of a future for French.

Commercial language

While French is the language of commerce in many African markets (Calvet, 1992), its use is often restricted to urban markets in large population centres. Internationally, French is under pressure from the vehicular English used by American manufacturers and by many Far Eastern producers. French - and Francophone - resistance to the concept of a basic, vehicular French capable of fulfilling the mundane task of giving and responding to orders, describing machinery and exchanging finance is not the only reason why French is less and less used in this international role, but must be a factor: the major part of the rhetoric surrounding official Francophonie constantly stresses the special cultural nature of French, its difficulty and its inherent complexity. Again, a paradox is evident: French is a vehicle of culture and of values, but 'where French is making the most progress is where it is learnt by people who need it: as a language of specialism, the French of business, of science, which does not mean a second-class French, but greater adaptation and motivation' (Farandjis in Etat, 1990, 14). Paradoxically, most arguments against the spread of English condemn it as a merely a vehicular language, a language without culture; but if French is to progress, it will be as a vehicular language whose cultural content will necessarily be reduced.

French as a vehicular language

The question then arises as to whether French can operate as a vehicular language: what are the qualities of a language which make it usable as a vehicle? Are there inbuilt reasons why French is a less appropriate language than English or Japanese as a vehicle for particular domains such as science or commerce? It is generally accepted by linguists that any language has the capacity to express any human thought: there is no inbuilt characteristic of a language which prevents it being used in any domain, and no characteristic which makes one language 'better' or more appropriate than another. Languages have the same capacity for development and for 'modernisation'. If one language is more used in one domain than other languages, this is more likely to have social, economic or political causes than linguistic ones (Hagège, 1987, 170: Coulmas, 1992, 290). Nonetheless Finegan (1987, 79-82) gives the following as possible reasons for the world-wide spread of English, in addition to the 'complex social, historical and economic factors':

> Inflectional structure: only two variants for nouns, no variation for adjectives, verbs minimally inflected;
> Breadth of vocabulary: a high current growth rate of the lexicon, a large number of synonyms ('up to forty for the adjective 'inebriated' and more than a dozen for the noun 'courtesy'), extensive borrowing;
> Simple word structure: 88 of the most frequent words are monosyllables;
> SVO (Subject, Verb, Object) word order, 'enhancing processability'.

Similarly, Coulmas (1992, 286-91) gives the following characteristics of English as a 'well-adapted' (i.e., economically efficient) and indeed as the 'most advanced' language:

> rich lexicon (mixture of Latin - abstract - and Anglo-Saxon - concrete - elements), uninhibited openness to borrowing, simple phonology, morphology and syntax (making it easy to learn), extensive repertoire of technical registers (because of the size of its speech community).

The 'defenders' of French often claim clarity and precision as fundamental characteristics of the language. This claim originates in the eighteenth century, but has been frequently repeated since. Even Hagège (1987, 167) concedes that there may be some truth in the proposition that French, in some specific usages, may be clearer than English. Specific aspects of French syntax sometimes discussed as demonstrating clarity include:

> Element order (subject, verb, object);
> Reference: the precision of both gender specification and precision in the use of pronouns contrast with the vague use of 'it' in English;
> Use of prepositions: the position of *sur* in *Conférence Mondiale sur la Population* or *Conférence sur la Population Mondiale* makes the

meaning clearer than in the ambiguities of 'World Population Conference'.

But clarity may be useful in some circumstances and not in others. If efficiency (the principle of least effort) is the measure of the suitability of languages to act as vehicles, then French has to contend with a number of 'expensive' requirements, particularly the redundancy of graphic elements:

> noun phrase agreement: in *les cerises rouges*, each word bears a mark of the plural as opposed to the one of 'red cherries';
> verb phrase agreement: *ils sont partis* requires three marks of the plural as opposed to the one of 'they went';
> the accents, requiring about 25% more storage space in computers to represent the alphabet than does English.

But the main measure of the efficiency of a language as vehicle is its adaptability, in which calculation the mere size of the speech community is significant; linguistic measures are too uncertain.

Language and Francophonie

'Francophonie is an international language movement led by government and non government elites in over thirty countries where French is official or used by a significant population' (Weinstein, 1989, 53). This view of Francophonie is by no means unusual, and the belief that the only valid motive for Francophonie is that the countries concerned should have French as their common possession has only just changed. Until the 1993 Summit meeting in Mauritius the definition of Francophonie was that countries 'had the use of French in common' (*ayant l'usage du français en commun*). The formula was changed to 'sharing French' (*ayant le français en partage*), reflecting a less proprietorial and more egalitarian approach, but also indicating that French is only one of the strands of unity.

The role of the language in identity formation and in motivating Francophonie has been a matter of constant discussion. If Francophonie is to be limited to the countries and regions using French, their relationships will be based on language and their actions and policies only united in respect of language matters. Any extension of the group would be ruled out, and they would necessarily become an enclave, almost destined to be in opposition to their neighbours - for example in Africa or North America, with no possibility of anything other than conflictual relationships. On the other hand, why should such a diverse group of countries unite if their only link is that of history? The language at least offers a tangible link, as do the values and culture it conveys.

The Summits have spent considerable time debating the role of French, moving into other areas only after thoroughly airing questions of identity. Thus, one of the main areas for debate and discussion between Canadians (including those from Quebec) and French in the early Summit meetings and elsewhere turned on the question of the purpose of Francophonie (Thérien, 1993), with eventual realisation that French insistence on the centrality of language and culture would have to be modified to take account of practical realities and the pragmatic resolution of problems, while the Canadian belief in the practical resolution of immediate difficulties, particularly economic ones, was not sufficient inspiration to unify disparate countries and situations.

In the French empire, language - and education - played a role in the cultural assimilation of the conquered populations. These assimilative purposes have been clearly documented (e.g. Bokamba, 1991; Djité, 1992; Ka, 1993). Although in many colonies, education was reserved for the elite of the native population and for settlers, and religious foundations were left comparatively free to provide a basic education for others, social promotion was only possible through French, following the prescribed curriculum which could give access to prestigious diplomas and hence to employment in the public service. In some cases, the language was acknowledged as a direct weapon of assimilation: 'Since the aim of the colony's administration, in controlling the Muslim schools, was to attempt to assimilate native children, the most effective means for achieving this is to ensure that the teachers accustom pupils to listen to and understand French' (Senegal Governor, 1870, quoted in Bokamba, 1991, 180). Pupils and teachers alike therefore had to demonstrate their knowledge of French if the Koranic school was to continue to exist. Although colonial language policy was based on practice in France, and on the assimilation policy which had been followed since the Revolution, particular importance was attached to the policy in some African countries where education in Arabic through the Muslim schools was well developed. Colonial language policy did not apply solely to education. The use of French in all administrative and official functions was an important element, following the principle of assimilation, and entailed the prohibition of the use of any native languages in such functions. As a result, the sort of scholarship and awareness of the native languages which informed much British work on languages and linguistics, and which indeed affected the development of British linguistics in Malinowski, Firth and their successors such as Halliday, did not take place until more recently in France.

How far is a knowledge of French still a unifying factor in Francophonie? For the countries and regions in which French L1 speakers are the majority the language naturally remains a symbol of identity, and Francophonie remains defined in terms of those who speak French: the norm is still that of the Parisian standard. Outside these countries, however, the Parisian norm cannot act as a symbol of identity in the same way. For some, the acquisition of standard French is a motivating force, and in this it may well be that a social divide is significant, with the elite seeking a means of social advancement. For other countries, the defence and promotion of French is a common cause, but the debate over whether, and how far, to accept modernisation and polycentrism in French recurs as a leitmotif. For countries attracted more recently to Francophonie, however - Bulgaria, Romania - motives are more complex than the defence of the quality of French or the spread of the language, and we must seek further to identify the values which motivate their desire to join organised Francophonie. Are the culture and values which lie beyond language sufficiently attractive to encourage them to join?

Beyond Language: Francophonie and Cultural Identity

'Although there are political, military and diplomatic alliances, there are few examples of international communities founded on linguistic and cultural conviviality' (Farandjis in Etat, 1990, 11). The role of the cultural identity conveyed by language is, for many, central to Francophonie and distinguishes it fundamentally from the British Commonwealth, the European Community, the Council of Europe, the Organisation for African Unity, the League of Arab States and many other international groupings.

It is impossible to define briefly the components of French-based culture. The word has two main meanings, interpreted in French as, firstly, *civilisation* - the ways in which any society establishes and represents its social structure and its social significance, and which could be labelled 'ways of social meaning'. Secondly, *culture* is normally understood as the manifestations of the artistic and intellectual, and could be described as 'ways of individual expression'. Both meanings of culture are loosely applied to the universe which is familiar to those born and educated in France, and which is represented by the values, beliefs and attitudes of those who speak on behalf of France. For some, the defence of Francophonie is the same thing as the defence of (both types of) French culture.

This defence leads to a paradox: defending French culture and civilisation requires that that culture and civilisation be unique, and preferably unchanging. To an extent, the standardisation of culture is parallel to the standardisation of language: in order to be recognised and to be accepted everywhere, it must be the same everywhere. But French *civilisation* - the structure of social cohesion, the institutions, the traditions and practices of political, social and economic life - does not altogether translate to other societies. African political life, for example, has found it practically impossible to ignore the ethnic component, and politics based on opposing views of State organisation are not part of African civilisation. Even Quebec works within a different political context, and Quebec *civilisation* has notable differences from the French. French *culture*, too, is difficult to export. It is essentially written or performed, rooted in the Greco-

Roman tradition, dependent on a European view of the world and on an educational system which gives priority to language and the graphic arts - hence the condemnation of writers such as Noguez for the mathematics- and economics-oriented educational reforms of France in recent years (Noguez, 1991, 65). Creole, African and Arab writers, if they are to create in and through French, have therefore to 'write, write in French, and write differently, by territorialising and deterritorialising French' (Jouanny in Vigh, 1989, 297). They have to change and transform from the inside.

Both types of culture are hence shaken by exposure to other, alternative ways of meaning. Traditional monocentric culture must give way to a polycentric approach, and the culture of France will necessarily in these circumstances no longer be the only model (Tétu, in Vigh, 1989, 306). But there is no doubt that traditional French-based culture is and remains a fundamental motivating force within Francophonie, particularly for France, and it is the experience of organised Francophonie which has brought about a certain degree of change. This change is represented both by a shift of interest, led by Canada, towards practical matters of aid and politics, but also in a sometimes grudging acceptance that culture itself may have to change:

> The Francophone Community is a singular Community because the use of French was its starting point and remains one of its preoccupations, while its present aim is, more widely, the illustration of linguistic conviviality between all the languages which coexist with French, the dialogue of cultures and multilateral co-operation, in the cultural domain as much as in the scientific, technological and economic.
>
> Francopolyphonie, one and multiple, universal and plural, can be a privileged laboratory, in this respect, for the humanism of the new age. This humanism will give a soul to the civilisation of the universal, the true and new spring of humanity (Farandjis in Conac et al., 1990, 43).

Hagège (1987; 1992, 108) traces the origin of the belief in the universal vocation of French culture - including its language - to the two periods during which French and French values were widespread: medieval times and the eighteenth century. However, the rise of nationalisms in the age of Bonaparte, the progress of English through the commercial dominance of Britain and then the United States effectively destroyed any justification for such claims, and the revival of French pride under - and after - de Gaulle has produced a situation in which 'nostalgia for the past and the future' has created the belief - 'a sort of routine expectation ' - that 'the two periods of glory are ... manifestations of a mission inherent to French, rather than flashes linked to defined sets of circumstances. If another language seems to be replacing it, this is felt as a dethronement...'.

French culture, too, has a distinctly elitist origin, which is perhaps why popular culture in French-speaking countries draws much of its inspiration from other countries. Liehm (Le Monde, 8.3.1995) points out for example that the international appeal of American films lies both in the melting pot of US origins, drawing on a variety of traditions, and also on the deliberate attempt to communicate with all parts of society. The cowboy film has universal themes - adventure, action, love, the battle of the rich and the poor - and the purpose of entertainment is precisely to entertain.

Both the meetings held by the *Agence de Coopération Culturelle et Technique* (*ACCT*) and the Summit meetings of organised Francophonie stressed the cultural and linguistic aspects of Francophonie at first, and have moved away from these as sole preoccupations. Whether this move demonstrates the impatience of the developing countries to ensure that their practical problems are discussed, the pragmatic nature of the Canadian contributions in the belief that on these, at least, agreement is more likely (Thérien, 1993), or a general move to modernity - away from the theoretical to the practical - as the organisation of Francophonie develops (Guillou and Littardi, 1988), is impossible to say. But in general organised Francophonie seems to accept and approve the move.

Beyond Language: the Values of Francophonie

The Declaration released at the end of the 1993 Summit in Mauritius summarised what Francophonie represented for those gathered together:
> Francophonie is a space for dialogue, co-operation and partnership in the most profound respect for its diversity. Its unity is based on a community of values and languages, dedicated to promoting peace, justice, security, solidarity and democracy together with respect for the rights of Man and fundamental liberties, which are universal and inalienable (Lettre de la Francophonie, 66)

In the concluding section of the *Etat de la Francophonie* report for 1993, Stélio Farandjis, the Secretary-General of the *Haut Conseil de la Francophonie* drew up an analysis of the situation in regard to the 'spirit or ideal' of Francophonie. In this, it was his view that Francophonie had to make its way between the 'coca-cola' or the 'ayatollah' - the 'universality of the desert or the jungle of ghettos'. For Farandjis, the image of Francophonie joined scientific and economic modernity, solidarity (co-operation for development) and pluralism (dialogue of cultures, creativities and exchanges). These three are symbols of the humanism of modern times, and represent a universal civilisation. The parallel report in L'Année Francophone (1992) had similarly noted that the Declaration of the 1991 Summit at the Palais de Chaillot had linked democracy and development, insisting on the necessity of the rule of law and (in the words of the Canadian Prime Minister, Brian Mulroney) 'without true democracy there can be no durable development, and without continuing development, no solid democracy'. The discussion had been oriented towards help, by northern States for southern States, particularly in Africa, as was clear in the press reports of the Summit. For Albert Salon, French Minister of Cooperation at the time, Francophonie

> as the use of French - as is the case with English, Spanish or German - is a key to development and modernity...But Francophonie is also the construction of a geocultural whole...sharing French and wishing to develop in common not only their languages and cultures but also their economies and links between their institutions. In this sense, Francophonie is a novel framework for the development of privileged international relations between very different countries...with varied religions: Christian, Muslim, Buddhist, Hindu...with linguistic groups...with other groups such as the Commonwealth, the Spanish, Portuguese, the Arab League....

Salon noted also that multilateral Francophonie had 'rediscovered its true vocation, which is basically "cultural" in the broad sense, as the condition and motor of development...working for the bases of development (rather than for individual projects)'. Shirin Aumeeruddy-Cziffra, Mauritian Ambassador to France and President of the *Conseil Permanent de la Francophonie* at the time, and speaking on behalf of the Francophone Community to the World Conference on Human Rights in Vienna in June 1993, noted that the objectives which had united Francophones were the 'principle of universal rights, their interdependence - of economic, social, cultural, civil and political rights - and that of the independent sovereignty of States, even if this implies duties as well as rights; and finally the right to development' (Lettre de la Francophonie, 62, 1.7.1994). 31 representatives of Francophone countries expressed similar feelings, even if some of these came from countries where human rights were in the process of being systematically destroyed (Rwanda's previous government was represented at the meeting).

In general then, it seems that contemporary organised Francophonie has agreed that it is a voluntary community linked by a common wish to co-operate, and that its values involve dialogue, co-operation and partnership, particularly directed towards the development of less developed nations; (a somewhat recently discovered) respect for linguistic diversity, but well-established respect for cultural and religious diversity; and widespread acceptance of the correctness and universal applicability of the traditional declaration of the Rights of Man and of the fundamental liberties.

There remains a certain lyricism and potential for unreality surrounding the expression of Francophonie, and particularly its cultural values. French imperialism was never as practical, realistic or simple as that of the other colonial powers. A strong influence on those who supported colonial expansion in the nineteenth century was the belief in the indefinably superior nature of

French civilisation and culture, and particularly the belief that France had a special role to play in bringing her culture to the world. The 'role of empire...was laden with symbolism. (France had) an intangible view of power, based more on prestige and influence (*rayonnement*) than on military or economic capabilities' (Thérien, 1993, 505). Many political leaders, even after decolonisation, retained a poetic view of Francophonie. Senghor, for example, was convinced that '*Négritude*', awareness of the African values, could and should make a major contribution to Francophonie, seen as the culmination of the civilisation of the universal. African Negro values contributed warmth, emotion, intuition and participation to the European values of discursive reason (Kazadi, 1991, 70); but for Senghor the culmination of this contribution was to the ideal of assimilation to a universal culture and to a nearly mystic view of Francophonie as the sole vehicle of such a culture. According to his critics, 'the link (he makes) between Francophonie and French culture is a necessary link...hence, the humanism of Francophonie is nothing more than French civilisation enriched by exotic gifts from peoples whose 'negritude', 'arabness', 'indochineseness' and other '-ness' are nothing more than vague reminders of long-lost identities'. This interpretation is in fact underlined by Senghor himself: 'Francophonie is, over and above the language, French civilisation, or more precisely the spirit of this civilisation: in other words, French culture' (Kazadi, 1991, 75). Senghor's views were by no means generally accepted among African intellectuals, as Kazadi's discussion of their reception shows. Indeed, certainly in more recent times, Francophonie has been more closely assimilated to imperialism than to any form of universalist culture. For some, Francophonie is nothing more than the last battle being waged by the French using African 'troops' to protect their own language; for others, French is a device serving to cut African nations in two: the elite, speaking French, and on the other side, the masses, 'walled into their local languages and therefore having no way to gain access to national life, and blocked off from modernity and history' (Kazadi, 1991, 79).

General de Gaulle had a particular view of what role France should play in the world: 'The key to Gaullist symbolism is the perception of France as having a particular - and unique - identity which is internalised by the French people and itself becomes a significant social bond. This is de Gaulle's "certain idea of France" (which) ...de Gaulle built out of ...historical anecdotes and into a structured myth...This process can combine and blend together that which was previously divided and divisive...the pursuit of *grandeur*' (Czerny, 1980, 85-8). This *grandeur* required that France 'be able to exercise influence disproportionate to her material means' through the deployment of 'resource power' - a mixture of military might, economic capability and, most important of all, ideological power (Czerny, 1980, 93). The charge that Gaullist delusions of *grandeur* still motivate French foreign policy has been made in many recent assessments of Mitterrand's period in government (e.g. Aldrich and Connell,

1989) and more recently about the Balladur government (Bremner in The Times, 6.8.1994):

> 'France has a calling to be a great world power' said Edouard Balladur...the modern version of the creed proclaimed by Charles de Gaulle, according to which 'there is a pact between the grandeur of France and the freedom of the world'...The theory that France has a duty to act as the conscience of the world was developed by President Mitterrand's Socialist Administration and has been enthusiastically pursued by Mr Balladur's Gaullist team...lofty aims...humanitarian ideals.

Despite the declarations at the Summits, and despite the rhetoric of co-operation and diversity, there must remain a lingering suspicion, in view of the facts of France's own involvement world-wide, that the cultural and spiritual values uniting Francophonie are those of the French tradition rather than freely chosen by consenting partners.

4. THE PROBLEM OF ENGLISH AND OTHER LANGUAGES

French in Contact with Other Languages: Conflict

In some situations, French is in active conflict with another language. The best-known examples of this are Belgium, where the conflict is with Flemish, and Quebec, where the conflict is with American English. Both these regions have been discussed above (Chapter 2). In France itself however, French is often considered to be subjected to intense attack from English, and the debate over the defensive 'Toubon' law of 1994, aimed at keeping English influence to a minimum and at imposing, on public servants, an official terminology replacing American technical terms by French ones, has strengthened the intensity of this feeling among both supporters and critics of the law. For any serious analyst the actual danger to the French language is minimal. Hagège (1987, 24-74) in a detailed survey of the whole question, refutes absolutely any idea that French is in danger: 'In spite of the often sombre prophecies which we hear, there is nothing to indicate that French is today submerged by a tidal wave of Anglicisms'. He exemplifies this conclusion through a study of pronunciation, morphology and syntax. English and American pronunciation have practically no effect on the way French people pronounce borrowed words. French speakers can understand *tee-shirt* or *shooter* although a native English speaker might well have difficulty in recognising them when spoken. The suffix *-ing* is the only element which might have had an effect on the French pronunciation system, creating a new phoneme, but even this is not widespread and is only used in borrowed words. In morphology and syntax the actual changes to French are minimal: most borrowings are simply absorbed into French within a short time. Suffixes such as *-man* are used to create new French terms (*tennisman*), while changes in the normal adjectival position (after the noun) - *l'actuel gouvernement* instead of *le gouvernement actuel* - in journalese are not serious inroads on French.

Calvet (1993, 145) comes to a similar conclusion, refuting any suggestion that French could die out or even that it is under serious attack. He points out that there are at least three ways a language can die: by transformation, like Latin; by substitution, when a dominating language absorbs a dominated one, as Gaulish was absorbed into French; and by the extinction of its speakers. There is no immediate danger for French in any of these. Indications of the process of disappearance are well-known - a reduced phonology with increasingly wide variations from the standard; syntax imitating that of a dominating language; falls in the transmission ratio between children and parents using the language (i.e. children's language deviates from that of their parents).

> From all these points of view, the official languages of Europe are not threatened: French, Spanish and Portuguese, on the contrary, have an increasing rate of vehicular importance...borrowings have never been a factor in the disappearance of languages - the best example is English, the archetype of an expanding language, whose vocabulary is half of Romance origin.

Despite these reassurances, there is a widespread belief that there remains a real and abiding threat to the very nature of French. In the post-war period this reached a height in the late 1960s, when René Etiemble, in a series of books starting with *Parlez-vous franglais* in 1966, touched a chord among those who had noticed growing numbers of borrowings from American and who, at the time of de Gaulle's return to power and affirmation of French independence, wished to underline the dangers of imitation and subservience to American culture and language. Trescases (1982) in assessing the extent of English penetration of French 'twenty years after', repeated the sombre warning.

Pergnier (1989, 200), also an academic linguist, acknowledges the importance of English as a vehicular language, and notes that the French-speaking world can do nothing about modifying this fact. Indeed, English will if anything become even more significant, and 'even if this role for English depends on the economic, political and military power of a nation which profits by it, the contemporary world is not opposed. More than ever, the world, because it is becoming narrower and more homogeneous through the acceleration of the circulation of information, hopes for a transnational vehicular language'. But to say this is not to say that French itself is not being affected by English. Pergnier (126) believes that French is undergoing major change: 'In a few centuries franglais might give birth to a new language, as different from contemporary French as the English of the Renaissance was different from contemporary English'.

The perception of the English language as a threat to French is matched by a feeling, said to be widely shared, that the values and culture conveyed by English represent a threat to French identity. It is rare (although not unknown), at least among the politicians and intellectuals adopting this attitude, to find the literary and artistic culture of the English-speaking peoples condemned. Condemnation is usually reserved for American TV and its soap operas, for the food, drink and other aspects of everyday life imported to Francophonie and particularly to France, for the values and attitudes expressed through language, and for 'Anglo-Saxon' social and cultural norms of behaviour. 'Globalisation', or the belief common among many marketing and communication specialists that cultural specificities need no longer be addressed, lies behind what is often condemned as American or Anglo-Saxon. Much of the globalisation approach derives from an article written in 1983 in Harvard Business School, suggesting that 'once and for all the needs and wants of customers had been homogenised, making it possible to sell the same products to similar market segments all over the world' (Niss, 1994, 162). Condemnation of such a view, and the drawbacks of associating globalisation with Americanisation are very clearly expressed in some of the statements by the Secretary-General of the *Haut Conseil de la Francophonie*, Stélio Farandjis:

> What is frightening, is the fact that certain cultural goods, songs, films of English origin, are spreading and imposing themselves on Francophonie or on other linguistic universes. It is not the English language which is the problem. One should find an expression to distinguish between 'English-speaking' and 'the Coca-Cola civilisation'. No young people make progress in English because they have spent their lives listening to disks in which they often understand nothing, nor have they enriched their culture because of American TV series. We should make a distinction between this demeaning civilisation, without culture, and English-speaking culture, that of authors and poets. Our opponent is not English, it is the deculturising process (Etat, 1991, 14).

Others confuse the two, but accept that things are not the Americans' fault. Noguez (1991), for example, fears that French civilisation is under serious attack in France:

> What is at stake is the essential core. It's a question of the identity - the life - of a bedraggled, panting, social body which has practically gone down to that moment when the reflexes don't work, when breathing is interrupted. We're on to artificial respiration. I insist that it is less a matter of the imperialism of others than our own tetanus. The others - the Americans, the multinationals - are after all acting logically, I was going to say they are quite right to do so: by trying to concentrate in their own hands all the levers of all national economies, to expand their markets, to settle, to the advantage of their own, all these annoying questions about language which up till now have been brakes on their expansion and profitability; they are, I say, doing their job as Americans and capitalist multinationals. We are the ones who are not doing ours: all we seem to want is to become the wops of the States. We are not doing our job as a friendly, but distinctive, people (Noguez, 1991, 227).

Outside France, linguistic insecurity in relation to English, and a consequent desire to raise the prestige of French in everyday life has been one of the motives for the series of language laws in Quebec - although economic pragmatism and a desire to protect social and cultural characteristics are equally strong motivators, and indeed language protection is in many cases a symbol for other motives. The language laws were given particular emphasis after the election of the *Parti Québecois* to political power in the 1970s, although moves towards greater independence for Quebec from American economic domination had started well before in the 'Tranquil Revolution' of the 1960s (cf. Bourhis, 1984; Mougeon, 1994). Mougeon notes that the Gendron Commission of 1972 on the situation of French in Quebec, having quantified the feeling of linguistic inferiority most French-speaking Quebeckers had, identified four threats to the future of French: most immigrants from backgrounds using neither English nor French sent their children to English-speaking schools, and adopted English for use in the home; most organisations controlled by English/American interests used English and made no provision for French speakers; most industrial and commercial sectors were dominated by English speakers and French speakers only rarely occupied management posts. Deliberate Governmental language policy to reverse this and raise the prestige of French followed: Law 101 (Charter of the French Language) of 1977 and subsequent legal measures, the creation of enforcement agencies, and a public campaign to raise awareness of the situation and to strengthen the Quebec identity. These policies coincided with a heightening of the Quebec sense of nationalism, with constant political debate about the future of Quebec within or outside the Canadian federation, and with the eventual rejection, by Quebec and the other provinces, of the Charlottetown Agreements of 1992. Most commentators now feel that the autonomy of Quebec is only a matter of time. The self-image of Quebec French speakers has notably improved over the years between 1960 and the 1990s (Mougeon, 1994, 42). It is particularly significant that the educated Quebec norm of speech is now regarded by the Education Ministry as that to be adopted and taught, rather than the Parisian norm: not merely has Quebec apparently successfully resisted the linguistic insecurity imposed by its relationship with American English, but also that imposed by the status and prestige of Parisian French.

In Africa, the conflict between French and English is a battle between exogenous languages for a role in the communication pattern of independent States, most of which have been left a difficult situation after colonialism. Gueunier (1992, 109) points out that in Africa, the Francophone area contains 22 States and 140.5 million people, while the Anglophone area contains 20 States and 309 million people; the Arabic-speaking area 4 States and 52.2 million people, and the Portuguese-speaking area 5 States and 26.2 million people. The language policies followed during colonisation were different: regional languages - some of which have become national languages - were encouraged by English colonisers under the policy of indirect rule, and local versions of English developed rapidly. Among the Anglophone States is Nigeria, whose population (100 million) and significance make it the most important single

African State after South Africa - also Anglophone. The possible attraction of English to Africans should not therefore be underestimated, particularly when it is noted that the African languages are spoken in both 'Anglophone' and 'Francophone' areas: Housa in Nigeria and Ghana but also in Benin and Togo; Swahili in East Africa but also in Zaïre. The Rwandan conflict has certainly been coloured by French perception of the Patriotic Front as Anglophone, supported by and supporting Uganda after their exile in the camps there; and much French policy towards its bloc of countries in West Africa is said to be motivated by the desire to protect it from the influence of Anglophone States.

Other parts of Francophonie may have adopted some of these attitudes, as we have noted in relation to Cameroon, where the Francophone majority is said to be dominating the Anglophone minority in employment, social advancement and access to education. Similarly, conflict may take place with other languages: language conflict in Belgium for example takes place between the French-speaking Wallons and the Dutch-speaking Flemish, as we have noted above (Chapter 2). In this case, the conflict is as severe as that of Quebec, and the reaction has been as violent, leading to political and financial separation of Belgium in 1994 in a way that is clearly hoped for by those supporting the independence of Quebec.

French in Contact with Other Languages: Competition

Stability in language use within a society can be said to be achieved when two or more languages have achieved a state of mutual tolerance, and neither is actively changing its role or proportionate importance. Stability of this sort is only obtainable when the languages used within a community have clearly defined roles and functions, and when the general political and social conditions within the community indicate that radical change is unlikely.

Bi- or multi-lingual States fall into one of two main types. The first, societal bilingualism, includes those in which different languages are used by different communities, and individuals within those communities can be and remain more or less monolingual, but nonetheless function within the same State. The second, individual bilingualism, applies to societies in which, in order to be citizens, individuals have to use more than one language in the different functions and domains in which they need to communicate. In the simplest such diglossic societies, citizens have to use two languages: a High status language (H) is used in public domains, while a Low status language (L) is used essentially for the private, domestic roles which do not require formal or official uses (Ferguson, 1959). The 'status' of a language therefore indicates the number and standing of the domains of usage. As a consequence of the domains of its usage, the attitude of members of society towards the H language will accord it greater prestige than they accord the L language (Mekacha, 1994). Because of the complex nature of regional and social variation in French, it is thought by some commentators that France itself is now approaching this type of diglossia (Lodge, 1993, 260).

Although the language situation in many colonies could be classed as diglossic, in recent years in the remaining *DOM-TOM*, and indeed in many of the independent countries of Francophonie, local and indigenous languages have officially been allowed increasing recognition in the public sphere, and have thus improved their status. As a consequence, they have greater prestige. Changes in status and prestige are associated with changes in political dominance and in ideology: 'while the language of higher prestige will be that of the dominant ideology, a language of higher status will be that of the politically dominant class' (Mekacha, 1994, 114). In French Polynesia, for example, as the political power of Tahiti increases with internal autonomy, and television is spread to the other islands, Tahitian is displacing both French in some public domains and many of the Polynesian languages used for normal communication in the other islands, and thus bringing into existence a different kind of domination and potential diglossia.

Various 'typologies of Francophonie' have been published (discussed by Chaudenson 1991, 9-23). Chaudenson (see also Chaudenson 1993), in a research programme started in 1985, identified a sophisticated procedure, which nonetheless produced a simple pictorial representation - an 'analytical grid' - for classifying language interactions in Francophonie, with particular application to Africa. The axes of the grid are the 'status' (vertical axis) and the 'corpus' (horizontal) of French, with high values of 'status' being accorded if the society uses French in the more official domains, and higher values of 'corpus' being accorded if members of the society (a) use French a great deal and in a higher proportion than other languages and (b) are more competent in their use of French. This definition of 'corpus' is quite different from that normally used in language planning, and is closer to that of the prestige dimension outlined above, but the purpose of the grid is practical.

There is great diversity in these situations. The majority of countries in Francophonie show high 'status', but low 'corpus' levels for French: that is, French is the official language used in high status domains, but known by a small number of citizens. The outline graph in Figure 4.1 illustrates this with five communities. The majority of States in Francophonie fall in the top left corner of the graph, although only two examples are shown here; the other communities demonstrate that in the Belgian French Community, French is the high status language and also the practical language of the entire population, while in Brussels, although the language is used by about 90% of the population its official status is not so high.

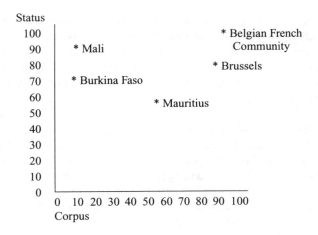

Figure 4.1 Typology of Francophonie
Source: Chaudenson, 1993, 362
Note
'Status' is a composite score obtained from allocating a numerical value to the use of the language in 5 domains: official language, institutional language (law, administration, justice, local administration, religion), education, media, economics.
'Corpus' is a composite score obtained from allocating a numerical value to the method of acquisition, vehicular and vernacular uses, competence, language production and consumption

Studies of actual language use in Africa show that multilingualism is the norm, and the absolute necessity to understand and use, for different purposes and usually with different interlocutors, up to nine languages. Calvet (1992), for example, groups studies of market places in seven African countries, where language use can be very variable. The conclusions of the Mali study (p. 215) were (languages mentioned are given their French spelling):

(1) ...Bambara certainly functions everywhere as a vehicular language, but it is not the only one (Songhay plays this role in Gao, Denné, etc.) and it does not replace the vernacular languages...

(2) ...In Bamako, two types of 'market callers' were found: mother tongue Bambara speakers who were usually monolingual, and those who have another language as mother tongue and were bilingual at least, using Bambara. The situation is the opposite in Gao: the Songhay speakers were monolingual...

(3) African multilingualism has often been presented as the addition of monolingualisms, the only multilingual site being towns....and the language practices that we have seen are therefore mechanisms for managing (interaction between) monolingualism. This is most often done through a vehicular language...Songhay dominates as vehicular language in Djenné (57% of interactions)...

(4) Societal bilingualism (many languages in contact) brings about individual bilingualism (individuals speaking many languages) when it does not impose a vehicular language. In Gao, as in Bamako, monolinguals are the most numerous, followed by bilinguals, while in Mopti trilinguals are the most numerous, followed by bilinguals then quadrilinguals...

The conclusions Chaudenson draws from his typology are that no one policy can apply to all situations; that the pressing need is for 'real, effective and adapted diffusion of French', and that the grouping of States by their proximity on the grid shows a possible solution in exchanges and co-operation between them (i.e. rather than by unidirectional policy from countries in radically different situations). These policies, of course, leading to the extension of French, assume that the spread of French is in the best interests of the States involved.

Language Policy in Francophonie

Intervention and defence

Francophonie generally has followed the French tradition of an interventionist policy in matters of language. There is a long history of governmental interest and decision-taking in language matters in France, going back to the fifteenth century (Grillo, 1989; Judge, 1993; Lodge, 1993). For Stélio Farandjis, writing in 1991, the decision to continue with this interventionist approach is obvious:

One must always defend a language, contrary to the opinion that laissez-faire and spontaneity are sufficient to guarantee its life. In the French and Francophone tradition, internationalisation, regulation and schools have always played an important role in maintaining linguistic unity between the generations. To avoid dispersion and divergence, intervention is essential, and one cannot leave things to take place naturally (Etat, 1991, 13).

Many linguists and others are worried about such interventionism, as became clear in the newspaper and television debates between January and July 1994 on the French 'Toubon law'. This law, strengthening the provisions of the 1975 Bas-Lauriol law, and prepared - but not presented - by the previous Socialist Minister, Catherine Tasca, included the following provisions:

- prohibition of recourse to terms and expressions in a foreign language when there exists an expression or term in French having the same meaning: fines of up to 10,000 francs or 20,000 if the offence is repeated;
- this first requirement applies to documents relating to goods and services, and publicity for these; documents (such as posters) visible to the public (e.g. on roads or in public transport); to contracts affecting

local or national administrations; to employment contracts; to documents governing general working conditions (e.g. trade union agreements) or enterprise level agreements; to the whole of radio and television broadcasts except for works broadcast in the original language, and to musical works whose text is in a foreign language;
- the language of education, examinations and competitions, theses and dissertations (other than in the teaching of regional or foreign languages) is French;
- in publicity,
- in colloquia, congresses and meetings organised in France by French nationals, every participant has the right to use French, and any communications in a foreign language must be accompanied by at least a resume in French; a translation service must be provided in certain cases;
- subsidies for teaching and research are only available when guarantees are given that publication will be in French (Law 291, Senate, tabled 1.03.1994).

The Constitutional Council, in July 1994, decided, quoting the 1789 Declaration of the Rights of Man, that the State could not determine what was and what was not French, by imposing on private individuals the use of terms taken from the *Dictionnaire des Termes Officiels*. The Council (decision 94-345 of 29th July 1994) also made other minor changes, and it remains to be seen whether the law will be put into effect, and if so, how. Calvet (1987, 261) had already warned that it was possible to find similarities between French interventions and the language laws of Fascist States:

> Four constants reappear in Fascist language laws: xenophobic purism for the national language; anti-dialect centralism; nationalist centrism directed against national minorities; colonialism or linguistic expansionism abroad. These four tendencies can be found in many language policies, particularly those of France at different periods in her history...(French policy) is surely not Fascist, but evidently jingoistic and inefficient because it is just not based on any serious analysis of the situation. It's a sociolinguistic problem, not a linguistic one, and you won't change the power of the Anglo-Saxon countries by fighting against borrowings from English.

Libération (24.2.1994) noted the opposition of the *Académie des Sciences*, the publicity industry, computer experts and two Government Ministers - Industry and Enterprises - to the Toubon law. L'Express, in an editorial on 21.4.1994, while generally approving intervention and applauding M. Toubon for his moderation, was very cool towards some of the products of language planning such as the *Dictionnaire des Termes Officiels*. Le Figaro (3.3.1994) thought the idea of publishing a law banning English 'vain and futile', particularly when politicians were supporting the 'multicultural society' - but nonetheless proposed 'restoring the teaching of grammar and spelling', and 'increased control of the audiovisual'.

The defence of standard French is nonetheless systematised in France (Ager, 1990, 218-49; Lodge, 1993, 230-60). The French Academy, the *Conseil Supérieur de la Langue Française*, the *Délégation Générale à la Langue Française* are all official bodies established with the purpose of planning and controlling the language; specific legislation was enacted in 1975 and has been reinforced in 1994 to enforce the use of 'correct' French; Terminology Commissions work in each Ministry to identify and enforce correct terms for their specialism; and innumerable Ministerial circulars define the duties of public employees towards the language. One such was the Circular to Ministers (4057) from the Prime Minister of 20 April 1994, advising that 'the interest and zeal shown towards respect for French' was to be a factor in the annual appraisals of Civil Servants (Le Monde 2.7.1994).

Similarly, each of the main Francophone countries has a Council for French (*Conseil de la Langue Française*), whose task is to provide 'expert' advice from authors and significant leaders of opinion on what should be accepted and what rejected, and on language policy matters generally. Some countries have instituted a 'language police' to monitor the implementation of their language laws, although generally speaking the punitive approach has been avoided. Le Monde (2.7.1994) noting the final passage of the Toubon law, considered that it was the pressure of other Francophone countries that had forced the French to act: 'African and Arab Ministers had asked whether they should continue teaching French to their children when public enterprises, banks, hotels and Parisian suppliers, not to mention the *Centre National de la Recherche Scientifique*, reply in basic American English to their documents in French'.

Language planning and policy measures are generally divided into those affecting the status or prestige of the language (or of a variety of it) and those concerned with the language substance itself (its corpus: spelling, terminology and vocabulary, but occasionally also syntax). The 1994 'Toubon law' was a clear example of status planning, while corpus planning continues in the work of the Terminology Commissions present in each Ministry since the mid 1970s, and in the *Délégation Générale à la Langue Française*. Such corpus policy is often directed towards ensuring that French can be modernised where necessary to ensure terms and expressions are available to replace borrowings; on rarer occasions, corpus policy deals with social pressures such as that for example to ensure that French can provide non-sexist terms to describe occupations or other aspects of life.

Language policy in Quebec is clearly directed against American English. The basic provision is that of the 1977 Charter of the French Language, which insists on the use of French in a number of high prestige domains in Quebec: in public service, in commerce (all enterprises have to obtain a 'Francisation Certificate' to show that they use French internally), in education. Despite a number of setbacks, the results of the policy have kept American at bay; Quebeckers now have more pride in their language and it is not now possible for monolingual English speakers to dominate Quebec's commercial or public life.

Francopolyphonie

French in Francophonie is, as we have seen, not the sole language used by the population, even in France. For most members of Francophonie, this means that policies towards language(s) must reflect the diversity of languages and cultures within Francophonie and must develop ways in which countries including France can feel comfortable with the resultant multilingualism. The unlovely word 'Francopolyphonie' has been used to describe the concept of a multilingual Francophonie. 'Mauritius, for example, is at ease in Francophonie, but in a pluralist Francophonie. A language is as important as those who speak it: the importance is rarely that of their number' (Shirin Aumeeruddy-Cziffra, Mauritian Ambassador to France and President of the *Conseil Permanent de la Francophonie* in Lettre de la Francophonie, 64, 1.10.1993). Most participants in the same conference shared the sentiments of a necessary diversity of languages within Francophonie, although it had not been until the 1989 Dakar Summit that President Mitterrand had declared support for the idea of linguistic and cultural diversity within Francophonie (Calvet in Robillard and Beniamino, 1993, 490). Indeed, for some commentators Francophonie, is even now, inherently incapable of any language policy which does not mean the continuing imposition of French: 'There is no difference between the language policy in France after the Revolution and that of the colonial era, as there is no difference between the language policy of the colonial days and Francophonie: the latter is a continuation of the former' (Djité, 1992, 175).

Francophone organisations, at first, adopted a policy towards supporting French and generally tried to impose its use. In France, the organisation set up in 1966 was at first named the *Haut Comité pour la Défense et l'Expansion de la Langue Française*, and language policy adopted the simple approach of insisting that French be used. This neo-colonial approach was reversed when the organisation was renamed as simply the *Haut Comité pour la Langue Française* under President Pompidou. The search for identity also characterised the early years of the *ACCT* (founded in 1970):

> The Agency seems to have gone from affirming its identity and identification as Francophone (specifically by opposition to English), and thus from a Francophone affirmation as French-speaking, (which

it) sought through the nature of its programmes, to one of a certain realism towards the real sociolinguistic situation of Francophonie, and a use of French to achieve (economic) development (Arnold, 1989, 119).

It took some time for the realities of the world to be brought to the attention of the Francophonie movement, and indeed, some relics of the desire to see French imposed everywhere remain, as was seen in the 1992 debate over the phrase 'French is the language of the Republic' which had to be replaced by 'The language of the Republic is French'. The term *rayonnement* (sometimes translated, particularly in the South Pacific - with a wry smile, in view of the nuclear testing centre in Mururoa - as 'radiation') is still commonly used to describe the actions of the *Alliance Française* or indeed of Francophone governments in supporting the use of French. In Africa, however, *ACCT* set up a *Conseil International de Recherche et d'Etude en Linguistique Fondamentale et Appliquée (CIRELFA)* in 1980, with the original intention of reinforcing the teaching of French: 'the Council did not take long to realise the absolute necessity of taking note of the national languages within a global Francophone strategy' (Arnold, 1989, 120).

Policy in the mid 1990s is to support the concept of linguistic diversity: to recognise, and indeed to celebrate the legitimate role of other languages within Francophonie, as is shown by the institution of the ten-year programme on language and culture as one of the basic programmes following the Dakar Summit. In follow-up programmes outlined at the 1993 Mauritius Summit, the 'Francopolyphonie' programme set the following aims, as much concerned with the development and use of national languages as with that of French:
> - to ensure the development of French by the creation of linguistic resources and to follow the evolution of appropriate technologies;
> - to consolidate the ability of the languages of the South to carry out all linguistic functions in complementarity with French;
> - to keep up to date an information bank and to ensure the dissemination of French for Special Purposes;
> ... Francophone co-operation will support, in the South, the establishment of national language policies aiming to approve the use of some vehicular languages, particularly in the public sector (Lettre de la Francophonie, 65).

The 'Francopolyphonie' policy sharply poses the problem of deciding what is meant by Francophonie, and indeed, whether the use of French is any longer the real basis for co-operation between countries. Arnold (1989, 129) baldly stated that
> Francophonie does not need French as a basis...Francophonie only exists, continues and has a reason for existing insofar as it allows for political, economic, cultural and linguistic co-operation. Such co-

operation which, in a certain number of countries is based on the existence of communities using French, has no purpose in Africa other than development - multifunctional, multispatial and multilingual.

The link between the countries of formal Francophonie is now that they share - rather than use - French (*ayant le français en partage*), but as we have seen, unequally: some of the countries in organised Francophonie have fewer Francophones than many outside it, while if one includes second and foreign language use in order to increase the apparent weight of French speaking within a country, many countries - including Britain - would show as high a proportion of such usage as Vietnam and much higher than most of the African countries of Francophonie. For Francophonie, the problem of conflict and competition between French and other languages may be resolved by acceptance that the French language is not as valuable or necessary a symbol as had been thought.

5. THE LAST COLONIES? THE *DOM-TOM*

The *DOM* and the *TOM*

For many commentators France is still a colonial power (Bokamba, 1991; Connell and Aldrich, 1991; Djité, 1992; Chand, 1993). Early in the twentieth century it possessed the world's second largest colonial empire; now, it retains a group of *Départements (DOM)* and *Territoires d'outre-mer (TOM)* which continue to show the main characteristics of colonialism: political, economic and cultural dependence on the mother-country; few or non-existent relationships with other countries of their geographical region; mixed populations with a significant role for an elite whose origins are often not local; systematic discrimination against the local population in employment, status and political life. There is little local political control, and even less local financial autonomy; in education, local populations have little control over the syllabus; in language, the territory has total reliance on a language external to the history of these countries and regions. How true is this picture?

The remaining *DOM* and *TOM* number some one and a half million citizens, considered as fully (in the *DOM*) or partially (in the *TOM*) French. The four *DOM*, located in the West Indies (Guadeloupe, French Guyana and Martinique) and the Indian Ocean (Ile de la Réunion), are administered as both *Départements* and *Régions*, although the decentralisation laws proposed in 1982 intended there to be only one local assembly. They have an elected *Conseil Général* for the Departmental role and another elected *Conseil Régional* for the Regional one, and the latter has a greater role than metropolitan regions: it has competence over the import taxes (*octroi de mer*), international agreements affecting its region, infrastructure development and relations with the European Union. Integration with France is ensured, as in other *Départements*, by a Prefect who represents the State and shares the executive role with the *Conseil Régional*, the population of the *Département* returns *députés* and *sénateurs* to the Paris government and participates in local and national elections.

The four Pacific *TOM* - French Austral and Antarctic Lands (*TAAF*), French Polynesia, New Caledonia, Wallis and Futuna - have greater differences from France and each has a different regime: theoretically, they are merely administered by France. The representative of the State has different titles - an *Haut Commissaire* in French Polynesia for example - and his internal executive functions are limited (but include policing); there is an elected government responsible to a territorial assembly, called the Congress in New Caledonia, with powers over a range of internal matters including many economic and fiscal questions, infrastructure and employment law; its opinion must be sought on relevant international matters and it may manage certain financial activities such as the Economic Zone or overseas investment. The *Conseil Economique et Social* is a consultative organ similar to that in the metropolitan regions and the *DOM*, but other groups may perform specific tasks - for example, the *Conseil Coutumier* in New Caledonia protects *la coutume* (Melanesian customary law and practices). The territory returns fewer *députés* and *sénateurs* to Paris than would an equivalent *DOM*. The statute of the *TOM* has generally followed the decentralisation measures of 1982 which been modified in each case, particularly after the problems of 1988 in New Caledonia and the subsequent Matignon agreements, and the 1992 Maastricht amendments to the Constitution.

French law does not fully apply in either the *DOM* or the *TOM*. Laws voted by the Paris Parliament apply in the *DOM* unless there are specific modifications for them, in which case the opinion of each departmental assembly is sought - and in practice the advice of the regional council is also sought. In the *TOM*, only 'sovereignty laws' apply directly: those affecting constitutional matters, the functioning of the State, the status of the population and the major jurisdictions. Laws deriving from international agreements - provided they are not merely regulatory - must be 'organic laws' if they affect a *TOM*, and hence require the approval of the (Paris) Constitutional Council as well as an absolute majority of the (Paris) National Assembly. The customary laws take precedence in some cases, and the Minister for the *DOM-TOM* retains certain administrative responsibilities over all the overseas possessions. In monetary matters, the currency is either the French franc itself or a local franc, backed by the French Treasury and convertible at a fixed rate, and credit is controlled by the State.

The two *Collectivités Territoriales*, St Pierre et Miquelon and Mayotte, also have their own specificities. They have a *Préfet*, a *Conseil Général*, and elect *Députés* and *Sénateurs* to the French Parliament.

In the preparation for the eleventh national plan, a Working Group consisting of civil servants, representatives of commercial interests, trade unionists and representatives of the councils produced a report published in January 1993 (Belorgey, 1993), updated and presented to a wider public eighteen months later in Belorgey and Bertrand, 1994. This reviewed the general position of France's overseas possessions, avoiding the debate about colonialism and instead concentrating on possible solutions and arrangements for the future. But the analysis of the present position of France's possessions highlighted their legal status, their handicaps and the arrangements for their future support.

Economic Dependence

The structural problems outlined by Belorgey, whose study provides most of the factual material for this section, were three: demographic, economic, and social. Population increases were still four times the metropolitan rate - even though they were falling - and the population was young (37% under 20 compared with 27%). This population was either crammed into small areas or spread over enormous distances of often unusable space: the sea, mountains or forest. The economic base was insufficient, being founded either on the export of raw materials (minerals, tropical products) or the local manufacture of goods required by the comparatively small populations. Indeed, apart from exceptional cases - nuclear testing in the Pacific, space research in Guyana - and traditional natural resources, any possibilities of economic activity were precisely those where low-wage economies (Taiwan, Malaya, the Philippines) have already obtained command of available markets. Because of their geographical isolation, climate, and natural risks, the *DOM-TOM* form a series of micro-markets where industry survives behind a protective regime of special taxes on imports, special VAT regimes and income tax arrangements. Economically, the *DOM* and the *TOM* are hence dependent on France, with a balance of trade massively to France's benefit. It is direct subsidies that support the local economies, covering the gap between imports and exports (four fifths of the import bill in French Polynesia and 99% of it in Wallis and Futuna), helped by indirect payments in the form of the salaries of an extended bureaucracy and subsidies for social payments. Bureaucrats receive salary supplements of at least 40% and up to 105% of the French salary (even if locally recruited, and even if working for the local government), and pay no local income tax. As a result, the public sector is bloated and there is often little incentive to join the commercial economy. The standard of living, lower than in France, is far higher in these islands than in their neighbours: Haiti is one of the poorest countries in the world while Martinique and Guadeloupe have the highest standard of living in the Caribbean; New Caledonia is wealthy by comparison with Vanuatu; Mayotte by comparison with the Comoros. The setting up of such 'transfer' economies does not benefit all the local inhabitants, either: most of the imports are of French consumer goods or 'European' food and luxury items, while much of the wealth is returned to France in purchasing French goods: most personal capital and savings originating in the *DOM-TOM* is invested in France. 'Public money flows out, and private money flows back' (Mathieu, 1988, 19).

France subsidises each *DOM* inhabitant to the extent of 7,750 francs per annum, and each *TOM* inhabitant at 12,000 (ignoring military expenditure and net of fiscal receipts). Taking into account the special VAT regime and the absence or reduction of income tax, the subsidy for the *DOM* rises to 13,550 francs annually (Belorgey, 1993, 21). In effect, the inhabitants are living in Third World economies on a developed world income - and with the consumer tastes of the developed world, too. Capital development projects are not intended for local benefit, either: the French space station in French Guyana, the nuclear testing site in Mururoa, are the single most important investments in these areas, maintaining local employment and generating ancillary services, but they could be switched to other areas at France's will. Some of the economic benefits of her 'colonial empire' accrue to France: nickel, in New Caledonia is the largest single product of economic value, and the 200-mile fishing and exploration zone (Exclusive Economic Zone - EEZ) around each part of each *DOM* or *TOM* provides an invaluable potential wealth. The economic benefits of licensing Korean fishermen to exploit Pacific waters accrue to France, not to French Polynesia.

Generally speaking, the local resources available to the *DOM-TOM* are limited. The four *DOM* produce sugar-cane, sugar, rum and tourism: Martinique and Guadeloupe, bananas; French Guyana, wood and seafood. Among the *TOM*, Tahiti's pearl industry and New Caledonia's nickel extraction are major resources. But in all areas, the proportion of the commercial sector in the local GDP is less than that of France, and the possibilities for expansion are small. The Bank of France controls all monetary matters: in the *DOM*, the currency is the metropolitan franc, while the *TOM* use the Pacific franc (*Franc de la Communauté Française du Pacifique*, issued by the *Institut d'Emission d'Outre-Mer* which acts as the banker for the region), convertible with the franc at a fixed parity of 0.55 French francs. Without this, it is almost inevitable that internal inflation, the contrast with the regional situations and the poor internal economic situation of the *DOM-TOM* would lead to 'absolute monetary depreciation' (Belorgey, 1993, 22).

Although the *DOM-TOM* are directly subsidised by France, they cost only 0.2 to 0.3% of the budget, and the means are clearly available to support France's global ambitions. The economic burden is shared with the European taxpayer and France is particularly good at defending the interests of her overseas possessions: in the 1993 negotiations with the Union, France secured an increase from 880 million ecus for the period 1988-1993 to 2 billion ecus for the period 1994-2000 in regional development funds. Admittedly these funds covered Corsica, and from 1994, the Hainault region of France itself as well, but the doubling of the available funds is a remarkable achievement (Deloire, 1994). It is doubly remarkable in that the *DOM-TOM* retain the ability to tax imported European products while freely exporting to Europe. In the future, these import taxes will have to apply to imports from any European member country, and the existing and marked preference for French goods may be difficult to sustain. Similarly, the application of European laws may require that certain employments now reserved to local dwellers exclude French nationals as well as other Europeans and that the immigration laws permitting free movement between member countries enable other Europeans to settle as freely as the

French. Both the European sugar and the banana markets were reorganised in 1993 to retain significant advantages for these products from Martinique and Guadeloupe - although there remain problems with the Latin American producers, traditionally exporters to Europe, and with the price rises the policy has brought to Germany as well as other consumers (Le Monde Diplomatique, July 1994). A degree of resistance to further support for the ACP countries generally was notable in 1995, when France was obliged to scale down demands.

But as significant as these economic facts is the sociology of economic production and management in the *DOM-TOM*. Their history as colonies means that economic life had traditionally been controlled by 'clans' - 'the same groups controlling the land, mines, distribution channels, immediately profitable areas of diversification (food businesses, construction, transport, tourism)' and both the export of tropical goods and the import of consumer goods and equipment. Additionally, there is a large minority of well-paid bureaucrats, little or no local taxation of incomes, and a generally poor level of social payments. The social inequalities this produces means that unemployment is rife (25 to 40%), the population is under qualified, gambling is growing fast (the *Française des Jeux* gets 6% of its turnover - twice the metropolitan rate - from overseas), the informal economy is active, and there is a large and growing 'apparent role, in some geographical areas, of resources which might be obtained from drugs and laundering drug money' (quotations from Belorgey and Bertrand, 1994, 30 and 31).

From the point of view of an external observer, it is difficult to see simple answers to this range of structural socio-economic problems, and little has been done in policy terms to meet them. When 65% of local wealth is provided by transfers from the mother country, unemployment rates are high, resources for economic activity lacking, and local management subject to local pressures little understood in Paris, the future for these tropical micro-markets with European income levels is dependent on their attachment to France and now to Europe. Regional co-operation might possibly help - for example in joint ventures or technology transfer between different countries of the region. But for these to be effective, either the management of projects and their resourcing would have to be less dependent uniquely on France, or, if France was involved, French management would have to deliberately use the *DOM-TOM* as channels of access to wider local regions.

It is not altogether clear whether, and how far, French policy envisages any slackening of the economic dependence of the *DOM-TOM* on France. Belorgey's overseas group in 1993 considered that it was impossible for any of the countries to stand on their own, and noted that no-one had suggested such complete autonomy. Any solutions depended on further integration with one of four possible partners: the franc and the franc zone, together with its eventual monetary unification with the European Union; the French nation; the European Union; and/or groups of countries located in the region. But each potential partner presents problems. Of the suggestions outlined in Belorgey, 1993, 124-145 for the eleventh Plan, and those that were picked out a year later in Belorgey and Bertrand, 1994, 108-110, some tended to align *DOM-TOM* economies on those of the metropolis and some strengthened what were seen as necessary differences. Proposals implied greater metropolitan support - in infrastructure and more targeted search for markets, in specific tax relief for capital investment, in unemployment support and in job creation; but also in suggesting an income tax like the French one. The proposals also suggested changes from this idea of integration with France: decreased support for a high birth-rate through the French family allowances system, since overpopulation was the problem in the *DOM-TOM*, the direct opposite of the under population of metropolitan France; compulsory deposit in local banks of part of the excessive bureaucratic salaries; financial discipline to be instilled and be controlled by France; a greater input than is normal in the metropolis to the admittedly much larger requirement for infrastructure projects.

What was clear in the economic proposals was that change was needed from the traditional bilateral economic relationships with France. Europe could help, and this might require bilateral negotiations between each *DOM* or *TOM* and the European partners, thus potentially losing French undiscriminating support; regional collaboration might help even more, and this would require the *DOM-TOM* to develop service arrangements with their neighbours, rather than continuing to rely on Paris as intermediary. Perhaps one of the most interesting observations was that collaboration was necessary to avoid competition between one *DOM* and another or, indeed, between one arm of French government and another: bananas imported from the Cameroon in order to help that economy merely competed with those from the Caribbean. Apart from this rather negative suggestion, the existence of organised Francophonie was not even mentioned in the Report, and most proposals indicated the awareness that the economic future lay, if anything, in greater political dependence on France.

Political Dependence

The *DOM-TOM* do not participate directly in international organised Francophonie, either at the level of the Summits or in regional co-operation. As dependent territories, they apparently have no external relations of their own, despite the formal arrangements for consultation. The overseas territories are in effect closed off from their own regions, closed off from access to the Francophone world, and unable to put forward their own view to international agencies and organisations except through the 'colonial' power. If they wanted independence, the Territories would have to vote for it, and the vote would have to be conducted by the French Republic - as indeed happened in the case of Djibouti in 1977 and the Comoros in 1975. Politically, it is France that gains a global role from her presence in the Pacific, in the Caribbean, and in the Atlantic. She is not limited to Europe, and it is her views - not those of her possessions - that must be taken into consideration by the Pacific Forum, by the Atlantic powers, and by the United Nations. The 'loss' of Vanuatu in 1980, when it became independent at British (and mainly Anglophone local) insistence provoked a French reaction to any further independence, and the *DOM-TOM* are seen as important components in France's desire to retain a balance of power and to remain a global power in addition to her European role.

It was the interests of France alone which were considered when nuclear testing in Mururoa was started in 1960, when it was temporarily halted in 1992, and when it was restarted in 1995. The financial consequences of the halt in 1992 on Tahiti were not part of the consideration of the matter, which followed geopolitical strategic considerations such as the halting of Russian and American testing, and in 1995, restarting of the tests was conditioned by the imminent Comprehensive Test Ban Treaty which would outlaw all testing by June 1996, and a number of other factors: the 'experts' report by Admiral Lanxade, President Chirac's known views - he had frequently declared the necessity to ensure independent military, and particularly nuclear, capability - the impact of new testing on the nuclear submarine programme at the Cherbourg yards, the missiles branch of Aérospatiale and the nuclear programme at the *Commission à l'Energie Atomique, Direction des Applications Militaires* (Libération, 6.6.95). Consideration of Polynesian views, likely to be in favour because of the economic consequences, and of those of the South Pacific Forum, certainly opposed, was simply disregarded.

The overseas possessions seem by now to be closely integrated into the political life of the mother country. Since the *DOM*, and to a lesser extent the *TOM*, participate in French as well as local elections, they represent a political force of 22 members which must be reckoned with in the National Assembly, but they do not form a coherent bloc. Usually, they act in support of stability and legitimacy, voting for the Right up to the early 1980s, for the Government in power since, although both independence parties and the *Front National* are present in the political scene, and the vote for stability may reflect the political awareness of settlers and expatriates rather more than that of the local population. The 1993 French legislative election results produced 15 *députés* of the Right and 4 of the Left, while the 1995 Presidential elections are more indicative of basic political allegiances, with the *DOM* voting for Jospin and the *TOM* for Chirac (Appendix A6). Indeed, these 1995 elections demonstrated at least two characteristics: increased voter turnout - particularly in the Caribbean - usually helped Jospin rather than Chirac, while the settler-dominated societies such as Nouméa in New Caledonia voted solidly for the Right.

Abstention from elections, support for the party in power (*légitimisme*), virtual monopoly of the local Press, the political role of groups and organisations such as the Chambers of Commerce or the Trade Unions, and the lack of representation for those situated far from the seat of local power are all characteristics of *DOM-TOM* politics (Aldrich and Connell, 1992, 186-92). Considering for example the 1995 Presidential elections, the main characteristics and differences between the individual *DOM* and *TOM* become clear. Guadeloupe, voting for Jospin (55% to 45%), rejected Lucette Michaux-Chevry's militant support for Chirac and increased voter turnout in the second round (44.82% as against the first-round 35.47%) ensured that left-wing sympathies were better represented: in the first round, Chirac and Balladur together had collected 52% of the vote. Martinique also supported Jospin by 59% to 41%, as indeed it had in the first round. Guyane was closer to the majority of French metropolitan Departments, but Réunion voted solidly for Jospin, the vote being helped again by increased participation in the elections; Réunion gave a significant 10% to the Communist candidate Hue. Interestingly, Jacques Chirac, during his campaign - both he and Balladur had visited Réunion - had promised 'social equality' for the *DOM*, extending to them the level of social payments normal in metropolitan France: since three of the four voted Jospin in the second round, this did not seem to have had much effect, and the social inequalities of the *DOM* meant that generally they preferred the Left. In the *TOM*, *TAAF*, whose minute population is composed of scientists and explorers on tours of duty, did not figure in the early statistics. New Caledonia's right-wing voters returned a massive 74% for Chirac in the second round, repeating the right-wing dominance of the first round, where he and Balladur together had obtained nearly 70%. Unsurprisingly, the Chirac vote was based in Nouméa, where 85% of his voters originated: the North and the islands voted for Jospin. In Polynesia, Chirac scored 61% in a small turnout, while he also won by a smaller margin in Wallis and Futuna. Voters in both these *TOM* can hear the result of the metropolitan vote (although it is not broadcast by French radio) before polls close, and there is little point in Jospin supporters continuing at that stage. But the *TOM* generally voted for Chirac. The two *Collectivités* also voted for Chirac and the Right as they traditionally do, although there were under 3,000 voters in St Pierre and Miquelon in total and Mayotte, with a high level of abstentions in the second round, followed its traditional legitimist political approach. Within each *DOM-TOM*, local parties elected to the *Conseil* or the *Gouvernement Territorial* similarly follow the party structure of France to a large extent.

Since the 1984 decentralisation measures which applied to the whole of France, and, with some adaptations, to the *DOM-TOM*, commentators have noted the growth of a number of problems with local political control. These have been particularly acute in the *DOM-TOM*, where the main employer is the public service and there is a high rate of unemployment. Belorgey's commission regretted the lack of power and ability (through the absence of adequate statistics) for the State to intervene (1993, 42):

> The most obvious difficulty is the frequency of loose management which the State has not been able to control: not only in Polynesia (where local autonomy practically excludes control) but also (despite the means available to the Administration for oversight) in all the American regions (French Guyana, Guadeloupe, Martinique), sometimes at regional level, sometimes in dependent organisations...

The Belorgey comment referred to an incident in late 1992, when the High Commissioner in Polynesia 'seized control of the territory budget' (Pacific Islands Monthly, September 1992, 12), after Tahiti's government - which until then had relied on the customs duties on imports for the nuclear test centre for most of its resources - refused to face the deficit of a billion francs CFP by taking the sort of deflationary and credit measures France thought appropriate.

Keating and Hainsworth (1986), Aldrich and Connell (1992) and Palard (1993) all note the greater role since decentralisation accruing to the President of the *Conseil Général* or his equivalent in the *TOM* in real power, for example over budgets; the intensification of the system of local notables through continuation of the system of the *cumul des mandats*, by which a politician can hold both a local and a national role - Lafleur in New Caledonia and Gaston Flosse in Polynesia are two examples; and the growth of clientism. These characteristics are not unique to the *DOM-TOM*, but are more marked there.

The role of local notables and the association of the local elite with government is reflected partly by the continuation in office of certain individuals, who gain credibility by their ability to intercede with the 'colonial' power. In 1994 Gaston Flosse, also first President of the Territory under its revised constitution, was again President. His right-wing party, Tahoeraa Huiraatira was out of office from 1987 to 1991 when Alexandre Léontieff was President. Léontieff had nonetheless been a close compatriot of Flosse and Minister in his first government, and although there had been 35 Ministers in the ten years and ten governments to 1994, politics at this level had been mainly a matter of 'palace revolutions'. Chesneaux and McLellan (1992, 130) are extremely critical of the role of such local politicians:

> Gaston Flosse, mayor of Pirae, head of the main Assembly party, head of the territorial executive government from 1982-7, Minister of Pacific Affairs in the Chirac Government in France in 1986-8, is the archetype of the Polynesian 'boss': never criticising the principle of French sovereignty or the nuclear base, he plays adeptly on his status as a *'demi'* (of both French and Tahitian origin) to pose as a defender of the territory's interests...he does not scorn real estate speculation and has been incriminated for his hidden participation in petrol importing firms.

Opposition in the DOM-TOM

The largest of the movements towards independence in recent years has been the rebellion of the *FLNKS* in New Caledonia and the movements in Guadeloupe, outlined in Chapter 2. But there are two major difficulties for internal independence movements: a democratic vote did indeed take place in 1958, when the regions had their chance to declare independence - and there is always the possibility for further democratic votes on the model of Djibouti or the Comoros; and the socio-economic situation since has ensured that it would be foolhardy for the existing *DOM* and *TOM* to contemplate independence without securing their economic future.

There is a tradition of opposition in Polynesia, for example: not merely is the French presence the result of conquest, Tahitian political life is also affected by groups such as the Protestant Church, using maohi as its preferred language and now mainly organised by Tahitian, rather than overseas, priests. The evangelical Church has condemned Mururoa, the French educational system (as a 'race for diplomas'), schemes for exploitation of phosphates on Mataiva or for the construction of a casino. It supports the promotion of the language and of the local culture, as does the formal political opposition. The independence movement during the 1950s was led by Pouvana'a through a *Rassemblement démocratique des populations tahitiennes (RDPT)*, and supported at that stage by two thirds of the Tahitian population. But in 1958, when de Gaulle gave the former Empire its chance to vote for its future status, French Polynesia voted to remain as a Territory, and the Pouvana'a movement was crushed when the French established the nuclear centre in the early 1960s. Since then, the main independence party is the *FLP (Front de Libération de la Polynésie)*, led by Oscar Temaru. By contrast with most Tahitian political parties, for the *FLP* links with other Pacific countries take priority over those with Paris and the party sees itself as centred on the Pacific rather than as a movement interceding with France for better treatment.

In 1991, a strike against increased petrol prices led to violence, to the burning of the French flag and to demonstrations. In 1993, in the legislative elections, the two *députés* elected from Polynesia were Juventin (mayor of Papeete) and Flosse, head of the Territorial Government. An acid review of the result (Pacific Monthly, May 1993, 17) noted that Flosse 'who is more metropolitan than Tahitian, as he is the son of a French businessman and for 20 years has been the leader of the local section of the French Gaullist party', obtained only a slight majority in one area, 'mainly because half the voters are expatriate French soldiers, sailors, nuclear technicians, government officials and businessmen' and elsewhere 'Flosse had often visited remote islands on government vessels and airplanes and had offered the inhabitants gifts and advantages'. The final vote was 15,776 for Flosse and 15,692 for the other five candidates 'all in favour of independence'. Temaru, in the second round in the second constituency, lost by 19,059 votes to 23,966. But the Pacific Monthly observes that if the total votes cast for Flosse (and therefore France) was 15,776, the total against, in the first round of the two constituencies, was 35,457, and there were 37,644 abstentions. Even in formal votes, therefore, there is a feeling that independence parties have retained credibility and that the question of independence is still on the agenda. One region of Tahiti itself - Fa'a - votes solidly for independence candidates, and resolutely refuses to participate in ceremonies such as the national fete on 29th June, and certainly does not send representatives to the French national day on 14th July.

Paul Vergès, leader of the Communist Party in Réunion, was also an early supporter of independence (Vergès, 1993). His demands for equality for individuals and rejection of France moved towards a fight against centralisation and against overt repression. Like many Left-Wing politicians, the election of Mitterrand in 1981 took much of the sting out of his demands, and he shifted towards grudging, and critical, acceptance of Socialist approaches, finally agreeing that the solutions put forward in the early 1980s were impossible and had to face economic realities. His present position seems to be that the situation of Réunion as a *DOM* is the best that can be considered; that France is the best partner possible in the face of the European Union; and that autonomy with all the financial advantages of France as a partner is preferable to independence without them.

Independence movements have thus usually been bought off with the financial support of the transfer economy. Some refuse to participate in elections - the *FLNKS*, the *Union Populaire pour la Libération de la Guadeloupe* - and this lack of local protest despite occasional violence enables France to take no notice of anti-colonial groups in France or elsewhere, of opposition to the French presence by other countries in the region - for example in the South Pacific - or, indeed, of international organisations such as the United Nations. Opposition to France's colonial role has anyway usually come from small countries of little international significance such as the Solomon Islands or Vanuatu. The only significant opposition has come from the South Pacific Forum, as occurred for example with the deputation in June 1995 led by the Prime Minister of Australia, protesting at the resumption of nuclear testing in Polynesia. In France, opposition to the continued existence of the 'colonies' is weak and, in France, there is no significant anti-nuclear lobby to protest about the testing programme in the Pacific.

Each of the *DOM-TOM* also acts as a cultural showpiece for French civilisation. This may take the form of TV broadcasts through TV5, tourism for French nationals and others, or the deliberate fostering of cultural and educational links: New Caledonia exercises considerable attraction for Australian schoolchildren and University students learning French. There are other links too: the population of the *DOM* and the *TOM* is linked to the French population by migration - some 500,000 *DOM-TOM* citizens have moved to France although in recent years there has been a significant return movement. French tourists retain their preference for visiting French *DOM* and *TOM*. Those overseas who succeed in secondary education go to France for higher education. Many French citizens, not just those who were originally born there, establish themselves overseas. The *DOM-TOM*'s direct participation in French internal politics, where political parties - on the surface - reflect those of the metropolis, the constant flow of public servants to them, and the increase in tourism, should have provoked considerable interest among the general French population; despite this, the *DOM* and the *TOM* appear to provoke little concern among the French population, which remains mostly ignorant of their existence and 'tempted by the prospect of abandoning them'. Much of the tone of the Belorgey report and the subsequent book indeed smacks of the white man's burden: the *DOM-TOM* are no longer the 'confetti of Empire', they are the 'frontiers of the Republic'; 'the French nation is not defined by the frontiers of ethnic groups, nor by the barrier of a profit and loss account. It is the fruit of the responsibility which history has conferred on it' (quotations from Belorgey and Bertrand, 1994, 23).

Politically, therefore, it is hardly surprising that France retains in effect total control over all external matters and has ceded very little in terms of internal autonomy, nor that internally, independence movements have made little headway. Any external interference, for example by the Solomon Islands or Vanuatu, hoping to encourage UN decolonisation missions to visit New Caledonia to check on progress, is rejected out of hand (Chand, 1993). Indeed, the additional funds provided for the *DOM-TOM*, together with the high proportion of employment available only through the public service, can be seen as ways of making the local population so dependent on France that they will refuse autonomy anyway. Certainly, in view of the economic situation, independence from France could lead only to bankruptcy and poverty.

Attitudes in France: for or against colonialism?

Colonialism in its strongest manifestations during the late nineteenth century was based on motivations, many of which are no longer tenable in the twentieth century. But there was a strong belief, too, in the existence and value of a unique French identity which could be transferred to other countries and other peoples, and the consequential belief in the universality of the French scale of values. This attitude remains visible today, perhaps in its strongest manifestations in regard to the continuing Pacific *TOM*. Chesneaux and McLellan (1992, 113) describe this belief in French-centred views as '*Franconésie*', and gives an example:

> You cannot understand why we say that New Caledonia is a part of
> France. It is so because in our spirit, in our history, as well as in our
> Constitution, we have worked towards the assimilation of these
> peoples...You cannot abandon a part of France, a part of our family
> (French ambassador to Australia, speaking in 1987).

Pushed to the extreme, this attitude is self-justifying:

> We are at home, what we do concerns us and us alone, we do not have
> to discuss it with you, in any case we are right because we speak the
> language of Descartes, that is, of reason.

The prime example of the Francocentric view is that of the Rainbow Warrior
affair. France and the Pacific countries simply did not understand each other's
attitudes in the subsequent period: the Pacific countries were outraged by the
violation of law and morals while France feted the two patriotic agents who had
saved France's possessions from an Anglo-Saxon attack. France simply bullied
New Zealand for having arrested and imprisoned her agents, on the argument
that by allowing the Rainbow Warrior to dock in Auckland she had in effect
been supporting anti-French actions. The threat to block meat exports to the EC
and to black all trade from New Zealand was sufficient to force the country to
hand over the two agents who were released after a minimum time of
imprisonment in the Pacific. France was simply not prepared to listen to the
views of minor countries situated a long way from France and who did not
possess the same sense of realpolitik which was built into French external
affairs. 'Identified with France's higher interests, French positions in the South
Pacific are expected to withstand censure and unpopularity' (Chesneaux and
McLellan, 1992, 114).

Yet the French view does not amount to colonialism, and it would be quite
unthinkable today to reproduce the same motives and practices as those which
supported the expansion of a hundred years ago (Benot, 1994). The Belorgey
report of 1993 shows clearly the widespread feeling that contemporary France
must take responsibility for the present and future support of her continuing
dependencies, rather than continue exploitation or cut them off without
recognising the economic disaster which would follow. Indeed, French
representatives accuse their critics of a mixture of ignorance and perfidy:

> (Overseas possessions today are) a series of situations, certainly
> characterised by different populations, but where the clash of interests
> was not regarded as fatal, either because these could be brought
> together in time or because those of the indigenous population had
> been largely stifled (as in New Caledonia). In these cases, the Republic
> thought it could both decolonise and consolidate while further
> involving itself. This change within continuity has sometimes been
> regarded ironically, if not perfidiously, by a certain number of foreign

powers, particularly Anglo-Saxon ones, whose culture does not permit them to understand French constitutional concepts based on universal rights and hence to admit that collectivities, unusual on the ethnic level, might be part of the Republic without being colonies. In addition, this suspicion of colonialism has sometimes been useful in providing a good conscience for partners when France has had to defend her overseas interests when these conflicted with theirs (Belorgey and Bertrand, 1994, 14).

Cultural Dependence

In significant ways, and despite the long history of control, the culture of the overseas possessions does differ from that of France. In this regard, the situation of the Caribbean *DOM* is quite different from that of the Pacific *TOM*. In the Caribbean, the original populations were slaughtered or exiled in the seventeenth century, and the 'local' culture is that of the ethnic mix: mainly the descendants of imported African slaves, now speaking Creole, descendants of intermarriage between the Africans and the white settlers, immigrants from the Indian sub-continent or Asia, and expatriate functionaries. Contemporary tourism stresses the exotic attractions, not merely of tropical islands, but also of an easier-going way of life, different food and music. More seriously, there are social differences with European culture, particularly in family structures and the education of children, which most probably derive from the attitudes of colonial settlers towards the family life of their slaves and servants:

> On the one hand (family structures) are broader than in metropolitan France; on the other hand, they are marked by a strong nucleus. The percentage of bachelors over 25 reaches 26% in the *DOM* against 20.4% in the metropolis, and 24% for women against 19.7%. The birth rate is lower everywhere than in the metropolis (5%) except in Réunion (5.1%). The average number of people per household is 2.57 in the metropolis while it varies from 3.3 in Martinique to 3.8 in Réunion. There is a higher proportion of one-parent families. This phenomenon can be observed also in families from the *DOM* living in the metropolis (Belorgey and Bertrand, 1994, 27).

General education, despite the enormous investment since 1946, still leaves a higher proportion of illiterates than in metropolitan France (23% in Réunion: Chaudenson, 1989a, 186) and there is classic diglossia with French, so that standard French is at least a second language, and for many children is best taught as a foreign language. The proportion of the population knowing and using standard French is nonetheless said to be high, and they are counted in the statistics of Francophonie at 100%, although Chaudenson (1989a, 156) considers the following proportions of monolingual Creolophones more realistic: Guadeloupe: 40%; Martinique: 20%; Guyane: 70%; Réunion: 60%.

In recent years Creole and *créolité*, distinguished both from the *négritude* of Africa and from French culture, has become more a source of pride, and for the independence movements, both a symbol and a political declaration. Aimé Césaire, reflecting and developing Senghor's concepts of the importance of African culture and applying it to the Caribbean (1947: *Cahier d'un retour au pays natal*); Fritz Fanon, writing in the 1950s and 1960s (1952: *Peaux noires, masques blancs*), and more recently Edouard Glissant (1981: *Le discours antillais*) sought for a new identity - not restricted to that of the French Caribbean but uniting former Dutch and British colonies. Authors such as Chamoiseau and Confiant use and develop these concepts, although it is their work in French that is more widely known. These attempts to first identify, and then support, separateness and a special character for the Caribbean - and to a certain extent, for Creole speakers in the Mascareignes (Mauritius, Réunion and the Seychelles), although on a different basis - rely to a certain extent on the concept of Creole as a distinct language, with its own characteristics and capable of acting as a symbol for cultural pride.

Linguistically, the *DOM* use standard French as their official and public language, internally as well as externally, and education uses French as its medium, following the syllabus and examinations of education as in France. Access to higher education - which mainly takes place in France - is through the standard Baccalaureate. The situation is hence apparently one of the classic diglossia typical of colonialism: an external language used by the elite and in official functions, while the local population is excluded from the social and economic advantages associated with the use of this external language. Instead, the local population uses Creole for domestic and family functions, for local shopping and the informal economy, and as we have noted, may be excluded from State activities unless it manages the official language adequately.

The *TOM*, by contrast, have retained their original languages and, despite the best efforts of the missionaries, the original culture of the native populations: the 33 Melanesian languages in New Caledonia, the range of Polynesian languages in Polynesia and Wallis and Futuna; highly structured systems of social relations; the influence of Protestantism in Polynesia; the connection with specific areas of land in New Caledonia. But the *Territoires*, too, suffer from the lack of prestige of local languages and cultures: it was not until the 1970s that any serious attempt was made to understand the Melanesian way of life, and the 1975 exhibition organised by Jean-Marie Tjibaou on Melanesian culture was the spark leading both to the independence movements of the 1980s, and to greater French awareness of the need to understand and not ignore ingrained traditions and cultures. Only from 1994 however could Melanesian languages be accepted for credit within even the New Caledonia educational system - although in order to be accepted there they have to be accepted throughout the Republic now - and despite the acceptance of Tahitian on local TV in Tahiti (under the regime of local languages, parallel with the provision of regional languages in France) the proportion of time allocated to programmes in the language is far less than that accorded to French, and is limited to nightly news and the occasional programme.

Yet, in both *DOM* and *TOM*, intermarriage has produced significant groups of *métis* (*DOM*) and *demis* (Tahiti) who often support yet closer integration with France rather than autonomy. The prestige of France has always been high, and it is not until recent years that either the ethnic mix or its culture has either been recognised or been a source of anything other than shame. If *créolité* and the identity of indigenous peoples has been rising in importance, this is not to say that the power and prestige of metropolitan French culture has not been overpowering.

But...

Nonetheless, there are coherent arguments on the other side, too, in France's defence. The four *vieilles colonies*, now the *DOM* of Martinique, Guadeloupe, Guyane and Réunion have been in French possession about as long as Alsace, longer than the Savoy region of France itself, and considerably longer than the American mainland has been independent. The *TOM*, too, have known at least 150 years of French influence, and there is no doubt that France has brought advantages and progress to her possessions, nor that she has invested in them to their benefit. The integration of the *DOM* into the French State is exactly the same process as that which has been followed in the case of Hawaii, now a State of the USA, and France has nothing to reproach herself with by attempting to ensure that the citizens of the overseas *Départements* receive the same type of benefits as do those of European France, including access to European funds of all types. Indeed, France can take pride in having been 'far in advance of its imperial partners in granting civil and political rights to its subjects' (Aldrich, 1993, 346). Citizens have rights of abode in France, and universal suffrage in electing the President, members both of the *Chambre des Députés* and the Senate, and the local Councils or, in the *TOM*, Governments. Admittedly Melanesians in New Caledonia only received this right in 1957, but then aborigines in Australia only became full citizens in 1986, some thirty years later.

Admittedly, too, the French approach to citizenship and nationality, even after the 'Pasqua' laws of 1993, assumes that individuals, not groups, have rights and duties. The traditional - and Constitutional - refusal of the French to accept the idea of multiculturalism, or indeed the specificity of any group, community or race, within political life is both a strength and a weakness, but it does mean that, at least in theory, individuals have the same rights throughout metropolitan and overseas France to education, to social progress, to membership of the elite.

A consequence has been that the development of a 'local' elite, educated and trained in French ways, has a personal stake in the future of the connection with France: they can participate in the administration of the region and thus avoid the 'colonial' despatch of administrators with no local connections, and indeed they themselves can become teachers, bureaucrats or researchers in France if they wish.

Internal autonomy in the *DOM* is on the same basis as that of the French regions, and citizens are no more disadvantaged in control of their own local affairs than are those of Brittany or Provence. In the *TOM*, again, internal autonomy enables local governments to determine their own affairs to a large degree, with some very limited restrictions: indeed, the central State has been generally scrupulous in not intervening, to the extent that Belorgey (1993, 51) thought it ought to have intervened further to ensure basic moral and efficiency criteria were being met in the local management of affairs.

Many of the other ex-colonies have retained some degree of oversight from their previous colonial masters: American Samoa, Guam, the Marshall Islands and the Federated States of Micronesia have different degrees of association with the USA; Pitcairn is still administered by Britain, the Torres Straits Islands by Australia, and the Cook Islands have close relations with New Zealand. These arrangements with former colonial powers or with Australia and New Zealand replacing Britain, often carry with them some of the economic consequences of colonialism, as indeed has been recognised in recent payments of compensation to Nauru for the desecration caused by phosphate mining. And indeed, Greenland, the Dutch and British West Indies, Hong Kong (until 1997) and many other overseas countries and territories are still colonies. In the decolonisation process France has not been notably out of step with the other European powers. In the Pacific, for example, the process started in 1962 with Western Samoa and has continued to the independence of the New Hebrides (Vanuatu) in 1980. The independence of the French African colonies, mostly taking place in 1960, followed approximately the timetable for independence of Britain's African possessions; Algeria predated Rhodesia by nearly twenty years; Vietnam followed only eleven years after India, even though Algeria and Vietnam saw more violence in the process.

Countries which have become independent since World War Two have not necessarily profited by the move, either. Even if one ignores the African débâcle, the independent Pacific islands are in difficulties. Vanuatu, the former New Hebrides, is recognised as poverty-stricken, and has been forced to resort to becoming a tax haven. The Marshall Islands have offered to store nuclear waste in an attempt to find a source of income. Politically, complete freedom and openness is unlikely to ensue: Fiji had two revolutions in 1987 and now has a racially based Constitution, which ensures that the 'ethnic' Fijians cannot be overwhelmed by 'immigrant' Indian or Chinese populations, and which was considered repugnant by the Commonwealth.

Neither is there much pressure for independence from the indigenous populations. Although independence movements exist, none of them has achieved success at the ballot-box and violence in favour of political independence is a rare feature of the *DOM-TOM*. If violence occurs - as in April 1994, when nickel drivers attacked the docks in New Caledonia - it is more likely to be in support of acquired rights or economic privilege than of political independence.

6. THE ECONOMICS OF FRANCOPHONIE

Organised Francophonie suffers from a number of problems in the realm of economics. The contemporary organisation was not founded as an economic grouping, and there is still much discussion as to whether and how far economic relations can, or should, be a major part of the relationships between countries. If, however, organised Francophonie wished to establish itself as an economic grouping or generate closer economic ties, a number of problems need to be considered. These include at least those we shall discuss in this chapter: the range and diversity of economies currently involved, the dispersion and distance which is characteristic of Francophonie, the franc zone and its future, the nature of international exchanges and policy on development aid, and the question of language and its relationship to economics. The list is by no means exhaustive. But the main question is to assess how far a Francophone economic zone exists or could exist. The 1994 French government report *Etat de la Francophonie* attempted to draw up a balance sheet in this area, but noted how strange the association between Francophonie and economics seemed - at least to France - in the light of the history of Francophonie, the values on which it was founded and the concerns of those who brought it into being. Is there any possibility that a Francophone economic region (*Espace Economique Francophone*), proudly advanced in the report, might emerge, and that it would show success if it did?

Diversity of Economies within Francophonie

The economies of the Francophone group range from the developed, wealthy and productive successes of France, her European neighbours and Canada, to the strangely false transfer economies of the *DOM-TOM* and the underdeveloped and generally collapsing social, political and economic structures of the Third World in Africa. The developed economies are among the richest in the world, while the Third World members of Francophonie are among the poorest. Francophonie thus represents the extremes: there are very few economies which occupy the middle ground. Table 6.1 shows the countries in Francophonie - including the main *grand absent*, Algeria, but excluding separate entries for the *DOM-TOM* or Provinces such as Quebec - in terms of their ranking in the High, Middle and Low categories of the United Nations Human Development Index. Table 6.1 also shows three other indicators: population, Gross Domestic Product expressed in terms of purchasing power per head (Purchasing Power Parity dollars), and the life expectancy of the total population.

Table 6.1

Economic diversity in Francophonie

Country	Population (millions)	GDP PPP $	Life expectancy	HDI world rank
Canada	26,552	19,320	77.2	1
Switzerland	6,712	21,780	77.8	2
France	56,315	18,430	76.6	6
Belgium	9,845	17,510	75.7	13
Luxembourg	384	20,800	75.2	17
Bulgaria	9,011	4,813	71.9	48
Mauritius	1,075	7,178	69.6	60
Dominica	83	3,900	72.0	64
Romania	23,200	3,500	69.9	72
St Lucia	151	3,500	72.0	77
Tunisia	8,180	4,690	67.1	81
Seychelles	67	3,683	71.0	83
Lebanon	2,701	2,500	68.1	103
Algeria	*24,960*	*2,870*	*65.6*	*109*
Morocco	25,061	3,340	62.5	111
Gabon	1,172	3,498	52.9	114
Vietnam	66,200	1,250	63.4	116
Vanuatu	147	1,679	65.0	119
Cape Verde	370	1,360	67.3	122
Congo	271	2,800	51.7	123
Cameroon	11,834	2,400	55.3	124
Madagascar	11,197	710	54.9	131
Laos	4,139	1,760	50.3	133
Ivory Coast	11,998	1,510	51.6	136
Haiti	6,486	925	56.0	137
Zaïre	35,562	469	51.6	140
Comoros	551	700	55.4	141
Senegal	7,327	1,680	48.7	143
Togo	3,531	738	54.4	145
Cambodia	8,246	1,250	50.4	147
Equatorial Guinea	348	700	47.3	150
Burundi	5,348	640	48.2	152
Rwanda	7,181	680	46.5	153
Benin	4,736	1,500	46.1	156
Mauritania	2,050	962	47.4	158
Central African Rep	3,039	641	47.2	160
Djibouti	409	1,000	48.3	163
Guinea-Bissau	965	747	42.9	164
Mali	8.156	480	45.4	167
Chad	5,679	447	46.9	168
Niger	7,732	542	45.9	169
Burkina Faso	9,001	666	47.9	172
Guinea	5,756	500	43.9	173

Source: HDR 1994. See also Appendix Table A2.

The Human Development Index (HDI) used here is derived from measures of three equally weighted dimensions: longevity, knowledge and income. Longevity is measured by life expectancy at birth. The knowledge base of a country is assessed by the mean years of schooling it provides and a measure of adult literacy. The usual measure of wealth is the raw Gross Domestic Product (GDP) - 'the total output of goods and services for final use produced by the economy, by both residents and non-residents, regardless of the allocation to domestic and foreign claims', or the Gross National Product (GNP) - 'total domestic and foreign value added claimed by residents...GDP plus income residents receive from abroad for services (labour and capital), less payments made to non-residents for services' (HDR, 1994, 220). The measure of wealth used by the United Nations is the Purchasing Power Parity dollar per head, also called the Real GDP per Capita: 'an internationally comparable scale using purchasing power parities rather than exchange rates as conversion factors, which is expressed in PPP dollars' (HDR, 1994, 221).

Among the 43 Francophone countries and regions listed in Table 6.1, 26 (60%) are in the lowest category of wealth and success. It is hardly surprising that among the HDI Low group almost every indicator of wealth, social stability and progress, education, and health shows poverty, deprivation and distress. Quite apart from the low life expectancy at birth shown in the Table and which drops to just over forty years in Guinea and Guinea-Bissau, almost every country in the group contains refugees, rising to 480,000 in Guinea and the astronomical numbers in Zaïre. The number of rural dwellers in absolute poverty ranges from seven million in Guinea to more than twenty-five million in Zaïre; 3.8 million people are without access to health services in Burkina Faso, while 2.8 million in the same country have no access to safe water and more than eight million have no sanitation. There are 2.4 million illiterate adults in Senegal, while malnourished children under five amount to 113,000 in the Congo (HDR, 1994, Table 3). By contrast, Switzerland, Canada, France, Luxembourg and Belgium are well above the world average and even above the average of the fifty-three countries of the High group. Canada leads the HDI High group, while Luxembourg, at seventeenth rank, is at the lowest position of the Francophone countries of this group. Of the nineteen countries whose income per capita exceeds 15,000 Purchasing Power Parity dollars, five are Francophone (Canada, Switzerland, France, Belgium, Luxembourg) - while four are Anglophone (Canada, Australia, USA, UK). Regionally, the same picture emerges: European and North American Francophonie is better placed than most; African and Asian Francophonie worst.

The disparities have been there for a considerable time, and if anything, are becoming greater. The realisation of the extent of the difference, and of the importance of the economic aspect of Francophonie, is however recent: it was not until the 1988 meeting of the *Haut Conseil de la Francophonie* that a serious study of the problem was presented (Guillou and Littardi, 1988, 36), and indeed, not until the 1994 *Etat de la Francophonie* that a section on the economics of Francophonie was included. The disparities did not suddenly appear, nor are they likely to disappear in the short term. Their origin lies in a range of factors: colonialism in some cases, the absence of natural resources in others, in the nature of the exploitation of these resources, the nature of international trade and of work practices in individual countries.

For the African countries, resources are generally derived from raw materials, agriculture and primary products, which, even in the case of minerals, are usually processed, refined and transformed elsewhere. Potentially, Africa is one of the richest regions of the globe: the continent has enormous reserves of petrol and gas (28 billion tons and 1,900 million cubic metres), minerals (96% of the West's diamonds, 60% of its gold, 40% of coal, 20% of iron, 97% of chromium, 44% of aluminium ore and bauxite), and 15% of the world's arable land (Djité, 1991). The exploitation of these resources has rarely been carried out in such a way as to benefit the inhabitants of the continent. Even agricultural production has been developed to satisfy Western tastes: coffee, bananas, cocoa have been sown and harvested in order to provide cash crops for others, while the rich agricultural and pasture lands have not produced sufficient to maintain life during the periodic droughts and crop failures. The blame for many of the Continent's problems can be fairly laid, historically, at the door of the colonial powers and the North generally: even the boundaries of countries across much of Africa bears little relationship to tribal, linguistic or geographical reality, and the colonial inheritance of languages adds additional problems to possible regional co-operation. Warfare, between colonial as well as indigenous powers, constant political, religious and tribal enmity, added to seasonal lack of food and the disorganisation of food production, has contributed to massive deprivation and death, unevenly spread across the continent.

Attempts to improve the lot of developing countries have often ended in unsuccessful or unfruitful development projects, themselves often funded through multilateral aid schemes for which money and technical assistance is provided by one or more of the 23 agencies of the United Nations, which had over 5 billion dollars available in 1995. The United Nations Development Programme (UNDP), formed in 1965 and responsible for the annual Human Development Report, is represented in 130 countries, helps 170 of the poorest, and manages the United Nations effort apart from peacekeeping; money is allocated according to a formula and the receiving government determines priorities. But thirty years of such assistance, particularly that from the World Bank following orthodox financial lines, culminated in a disastrous 1994 report by the Africa bureau of the UNDP, which concluded:

> Technical assistance has not brought to Africa the results expected of it...At present the feeling is widespread that it is more often misguided

than well used and frequently counter-productive (quoted in Guardian, 17.5.1995).

The World Bank has been attacked particularly for its concentration on programmes attempting to repeat the virtuous cycle of economic development typical of capitalism: private investment creates production through commercial activity, which creates profits which create investment. To make room for commercial activity, pursuing the ideology of free-market competition and the reduction of the State, Structural Adjustment Programmes have been funded, requiring governments to cease supporting bureaucracies, reduce public spending and force investment in industry, but it has proved very difficult to transform habits, ensure that investment is in fact channelled correctly and cope with the social chaos which has followed mass sackings, reductions in government purchases, and salary reductions. The World Bank now proposes to stress fewer free-market notions, support closer integration of employers and organised labour, fund infrastructure projects such as water and health, and improve the education of women, in what is a major change of priorities (reported in Guardian, 3.4.1995).

Blame must also be laid on a range of other factors, however: the greed of individual rulers, of whom the former 'Emperor' Bokassa of Central Africa is an archetype; undemocratic and dictatorial systems of government in many countries, ranging from the Guinea of Sekou Touré to the Rwanda of the Hutus; technological backwardness in every sphere of life, from agricultural production to diplomacy; the poor priorities of many governments - for prestige programmes rather than basic requirements. The lack of capital for development, and the inappropriateness of much development to the real conditions prevailing, are also responsible for the continuation of backwardness, although the definition of backwardness results from a comparison with the rate and nature of the economic development of the West.

Dispersion and Distance

It is a matter of pride that Francophonie, and French, are widely distributed throughout the world. Every continent and every ocean is represented by a French-speaking country, and the Summit meetings offer a cross-section of the countries of the world. But this dispersion has a negative side, too. The distance between French-speaking countries is often a barrier to trade, economic exchanges or merely to contact, and certainly represents the major barrier to the formation of a Francophone Economic Community. French Polynesia, for example, covers an area the size of Europe, and is located at about seven hours flying time from the nearest large land masses. Tahiti's direct trade relationships must come either from contact with other, comparatively small, Pacific islands, whether French-speaking or not, or from English-speaking partners such as

Australia or the United States. Dispersion means that there is a basic need for effective and efficient transport for goods and people. France has been at the forefront of State-led efforts to research, develop and manufacture advanced means of transport. Motor manufacturers such as Renault, Citroen and Peugeot have either been owned by, massively subsidised by or protected by the State since 1945, and the results are visible in the almost exclusively French lorries and cars in French *DOM-TOM*, colonies and countries within the French sphere of influence. Public transport has been in forms which are appropriate to France: the high-speed train (*TGV*) and urban light rail systems (the *métro* of Lille, after that of Paris). Systems such as these can be developed for use in regions such as the European Francophone partners, in Quebec and in some parts of the more developed and populated *DOM*. They would be of great use in Africa, but need greater political stability than is currently the case there. Their commercialisation throughout Francophonie would clearly benefit France and provide a tangibly Francophone link. Air transport is more open to joint Francophone activities, particularly in the creation or management of joint airlines. Air France is one of the world's more important carriers, but is in considerable difficulties in facing up to non-subsidised flying, fierce competition and European rules. Nonetheless there are examples of collaboration: Air Afrique is jointly managed by France and 12 African countries; Air France collaborates with Air Canada and Air Maroc, although such collaboration is dependent on the constant restructuring, code-sharing and other arrangements which underlie all airline financing. Air Calédonie, for example, jointly operates the Sydney-Nouméa route with Qantas, while British Airways and Air France hardly compete on routes between France and Britain.

More importantly, trade towards the end of the twentieth century is not limited to goods: services, particularly financial and media services, are less dependent on contiguity. The spread of the satellite broadcasting service, TV5, and the dissemination of media products - music, cinema, TV programmes - is accompanied by growth in electronic communication. But much of the technology for this is American or Japanese; the French Minitel service, massively expanded within France and initially provided through free distribution of French-made terminals, is suffering from comparison with the growth of devices like electronic mail and the Internet. Similarly, the explosion in the provision of services on Minitel is paling by comparison with the possibilities for global distribution through media empires such as that of Rupert Murdoch, and their potential move into cable and satellite broadcasting accompanied by the range of associated services.

The Franc Zone

In two parts of the world France has maintained a franc zone, in which the money (franc of the *Communauté Financière Africaine* (*FCFA*) or of the

Communauté Financière du Pacifique (FCFP)) has fixed parity with the French franc. Until 11 January 1994, the parity of the first of these was fixed at 50 *FCFA* to the French franc, the second at 0.55 of the French Franc. The second is in effect limited to the *TOM* where the Pacific franc is used, although with different coins, in New Caledonia, French Polynesia, and Wallis and Futuna. Pressure here is if anything to fully integrate the local currency with the French franc, and it is the avowed policy of the Tahiti Territorial Government - admittedly basically *RPR* - both to obtain more local control over finances, particularly over the maritime Exclusive Economic Zone, and, at the same time, to replace the Pacific franc by the French franc. This somewhat paradoxical approach is thought to improve chances of local investment from outside France: particularly from Japan, Australia and the USA.

The African franc has had a difficult history (Coussy, 1995). Established in 1960 for its former colonies, the purpose was to save foreign currency reserves and allow firms to invest in Africa, transferring profits and capital easily, and also to guarantee supplies for France and stabilise prices, but also to ensure stability and provide liquidity in times of need. The franc zone guaranteed a fixed parity between the French franc and the local one; the centralisation of the major part of foreign exchange reserves, held and managed by the French Treasury; guaranteed convertibility of money; and free transfer of capital within the zone (including to and from France). In effect, the system meant that monetary policy was decided by France, regulated by French experts, and was closely associated with France's aid policy, which depended on grants rather than loans. The overall system was decried by many as colonial in intent, its main effect being to ensure capital flows of public finance towards the zone and transfers of private capital (profits) out of it. Psychologically and socially, since its creation was predicated on 'anticipated failure...invariably likely to be self-fulfilling' (Coussy, 1995, 167), colonial attitudes were continued.

Reforms in 1972 led to a more successful decade. But this success also provoked problems: it permitted countries to get loans in other currencies, aggravating external debt; did not accompany this by internal financial rigour, and encouraged non-productive investment. During the 1980s these problems came home to roost: there was greater involvement by external financial institutions like the World Bank and the International Monetary Fund, imposing structural adjustment programmes; conflict between these aims and the essentially public-finance oriented aims (public investment, import substitution) of the franc zone intensified; the isolation of the zone from the world market made it more and more unreal.

On 11 January 1994, the African franc was devalued by 50% (to 100 FCFA for the French franc) for 13 of the 14 countries involved (Benin, Burkina-Faso, Cameroon, Central African Republic, Chad, Congo, Equatorial Guinea, Gabon,

Ivory Coast, Mali, Niger, Senegal and Togo) and by 33% for the Comoros. Pressure for the devaluation had come principally from some countries whose exports had become completely uncompetitive after the strong franc policy; the de-facto revaluation of the franc-dollar exchange rate by 70% in 1985; and the devaluation of Nigerian currency. The World Bank and the International Monetary Fund, considered by some as 'offshore finance Ministries' (*Le Monde Diplomatique*, January 1994, 5), had also pressed for the devaluation. Since the *FCFA* was, until 1st August 1993, freely convertible outside the region, the capital exodus had been enormous - some 8.8 billion francs in 1992 (Express, 7.10.1993). Structural Adjustment Programmes, proposed by the World Bank and followed by France implied increased fiscal revenue and reduction of wages. After the devaluation, in an agreed package to soften some of the social consequences, France cancelled or halved public debts up to 25 billion francs, the IMF will make available over three years 10 billion francs in credit and price maintenance grants, and the World Bank will make 4 billion francs available to prevent inflation.

L'Express welcomed the move (27.1.1994), commenting that 'the blindness and cupidity of African elites and the desire of Paris to maintain, whatever the cost, its imperial bloc (*pré carré*) have lost a lot of time'. Most African countries, despite the fact that discussions had been going on since September 1993, were ill-prepared. The Balladur Government had exercised considerable pressure for them to work with the World Bank, to the extent that, for some commentators (Leymarie in Le Monde Diplomatique, January 1994, 5), the 'Balladur approach' represented a rejection of the traditionally independent French policy. France could not continue to be 'Africa's paymaster'; aid would be tied to development projects; the policy of insisting on the protection of democracy and human rights would be modified: Balladur was following the line of thinking enunciated by Mitterrand at the Franco-African summit of 1990. Despite the generally positive evaluation by the French government (Etat, 1994, 38-41), the consequential price increases - 20-33% for rice, flour, sugar, cooking oil and milk in Senegal, for example - and reduction of expenditure on education and health were bad for Africa, and the effect of increased prices of French exports to Africa and the reduced inflows from the zone to French companies could not be ignored.

Francophonie in International Exchanges

Trade and investment

Despite the existence of the franc zones and the history of close economic ties between France and her former possessions, there is little evidence of a close relationship based on trade among members of existing organised Francophonie. Generally, external commerce is not conducted with Francophonie in mind, nor do the available statistics show a high proportion of trade being conducted with other French-speaking countries in preference to others. Partly this may be due to the difficulty of obtaining accurate statistics - 'We have complete and credible figures for 27 countries of the 43' (Etat, 1994, 351).

Table 6.2
Trade within Francophonie

Less than 5%	Canada (Quebec: 2%);
5-10%:	Bulgaria, Cape Verde, Romania, Seychelles;
10-20%:	Cambodia, Egypt, France, Guinea, Lebanon, Mauritius, Viet-Nam;
20-30%:	Gabon;
30-40%:	Ivory Coast, Madagascar, Morocco, Mauritania, Senegal, Tunisia;
40-50%:	Cameroon, Chad, Luxembourg, Niger;
over 50%:	Burkina Faso (65.2%), Central African Republic (77.4%), Mali (75.5%), Zaïre (68%)

Source: Etat, 1994, 351.

The general rule is that countries trade principally with their neighbours and take no or little account of whether these are members of organised Francophonie or not. 60% of France's trade was with the European Union in 1992; 70% of Canada's trade was with the USA. This regional rule is not altogether observed, but even when countries trade at a distance they do not show signs of any preference for Francophonie. Quebec for example trades more with Britain than with France, while Bulgaria and Romania trade more with Germany and Italy than with France.

Comparisons with other economic groups were shown in Bach, 1995, 206, where, in 1987, trade within the European Union accounted for 58.8% of the total exports of members. Equivalent figures were 17.7% for the Association of South East Asian Nations (ASEAN), 6.3% for the Caribbean Community (CARICOM), and 11.3% for the Latin American Integration Association (ALADI). On this basis, Francophonie seems as (in)effective an economic grouping as most.

Investments are equally difficult to identify: the 1994 report mentioned the Francophone proportion as 5.6% of Canada's investment, 20% of Romania's, 22% of Vietnam's, 35.5% of Morocco's, and 79.8% of Tunisia's. France alone provided 2.3% of Egypt's, 10.7% of Laos's, and 80% of Gabon's investment capital. One development, of comparatively recent date, is the relocation of production units away from high labour cost centres such as Europe or North America into areas of low labour cost: into the Maghreb or eastern Europe - or indeed Scotland. Such a development may increase French investment in such areas, and despite the social unrest such relocations may cause within developed countries like France, they have not been ruled out of court and have even been welcomed by a Parliamentary report published on 5th March 1994.

There exist nonetheless within Francophonie a number of examples of co-operation and partnership, of industries, municipalities and firms. Following the Mauritius resolution of 1993, the Quebec co-operative banking institution Desjardins has set up banking co-operatives in Africa and the Caribbean, although only small French banks and charitable funds seem to have made any similar effort. Partnerships exist around Air Afrique (Air France and African governments); between Quebec and France in printing, telecommunications, mineral waters and natural gas; with Quebec's Hydro-Québec, Electricité de France and Saur-Afrique to manage Guinea's electricity supply; between Marseilles and about 15 ports including Algiers, Tangiers and Alexandria. But even the government report bemoans the fact that 'small business is too weak; operations are concentrated in major towns; training and the exchange of know-how is often insufficient' (Etat, 1994, 356). The *Forum Francophone des Affaires* was nonetheless set up during the 1987 Quebec Francophonie summit meeting, at the initiative of Quebec businessmen concerned to ensure an effective economic activity within Francophonie. The *Forum* was approved at the Chaillot summit, and following the 1993 Mauritius summit set up information exchanges and information about opportunities, regulations and the availability of capital. The Forum organises bi-annual meetings aimed at facilitating commercial relations. 24 national committees, intended to expand to 40 during 1995, have started specific joint action projects such as arrangements to vet and subsidise Canadian-Senegalese partnerships. One of the oldest of the institutions of Francophonie and dating from 1970, the *Agence de Coopération Culturelle et Technique (ACCT)* was of course set up in order to establish economic relationships across Francophonie and particularly to foster aid. Its budget of some 30 million francs means it is principally a source of information and advice, but its work supporting the main institutions of Francophonie (it is the 'operator' for eight of the nine programmes agreed in Mauritius) means it is well placed to co-operate also with international institutions such as the United Nations.

It is difficult to be sure who gains most, financially, from the existence of Francophonie. There are clearly advantages for developing countries from their association with friendly wealthy countries, and they have generally welcomed the increasing concern with economics expressed in the official summits of organised Francophone: President Soglo of Benin, for example, preparing for the 1995 Summit in his country, was convinced that 'One cannot sensibly talk of culture on one hand and economics on the other, as though economics was not one of the main elements of culture...the Francophone space will be whatever its economy is' (Lettre de la Francophonie, 81, 5).

France's own foreign trade shows clearly that Francophonie, for her, is an economic success. To take the situation in mid-1994 (Appendix Table A5), France was in credit (more exports than imports) with both Francophonie in general and with the European Union. She was in deficit with Bulgaria, Niger, Cameroon, Gabon, Egypt, Madagascar and Mauritius, but with the exception of these countries, she was in credit throughout Francophonie. Her overall positive situation in Francophonie was some 47 billion francs - of which the *DOM-TOM* accounted for over half. These figures exclude military sales and purchases.

With Africa, it is not just in relation to the African franc zone that France's special relationship can be seen. As a result of decolonisation, Africa's share of world trade dropped from 2.4% in 1970 to 1.3% in 1987 (Coquet et al, 1993). Dividing Africa into three parts (North, Central and South) it is the central group which has suffered worst: North Africa has generally improved its relative position in trade with Europe, while the special position of South Africa and its strategic reserves, despite embargos until recently, has meant that it has not worsened its trade position.   France has seen major changes in its economic relations with its former colonies. In 1961-65, these provided 15% of France's external trade, and more than 80% of France's African trade. By 1985-90, these figures had dropped to 5.6% (French imports) and 7% (exports), and 67% of African trade. Because French trade with Algeria has dropped, the importance of Sub Saharan Africa has increased, so that North Africa and Central Africa are equally important. But France is still centrally important for Africa. In each of the three zones she is the principal European trading partner, accounting for about a fifth of imports by the twelve countries of the European Union and a third of exports. 'Two factors explain this relatively important French position:..the permanence of structured economic links within the franc zone...the second is a real political will based on a logic of international power relationships, while the economic, political and strategic importance of the continent does not seem to be recognised by other industrialised countries' (Coquet et al, 1993).

The arms trade

One particular type of exchange is worthy of closer examination: the French arms trade. France is one of the world's main arms exporters, coming third after the USA and the former Soviet Union over the period 1988-1992, when she sold a total of 9,349 US millions of dollars worth of conventional arms (at 1990 prices), by comparison with the 54,968 by the USA and 45,182 by the USSR, 8,190 by Germany, 7,658 by China and 7,623 by the UK - all, except for Germany, members of the United Nations Security Council. Arms sales took place to the developing world and to countries at war, the latter accounting for 23% of France's exports in 1980-89, as compared with 5% of US sales and 9% of the UK's (HDR, 1994, 54-55). French arms exports (orders taken) amounted to 34.2 billion francs in 1991, 45.7 billion in 1992 (Bénichou, 1994). Aeronautics accounted for 50%, military equipment 30%, while naval products accounted for only 5%. Sales have varied from year to year, peaking at 61.8 billion francs (current prices) in 1984 and dropping to 21.7 billion in 1978. About 60% of sales were of comparatively small items or refitting, with the remaining 40% consisting of larger orders over one billion and accounting for the peaks and troughs. Up to 1990, 4 countries were the main targets (48%): Saudi Arabia, Iraq, USA and Germany. Africa and Latin America accounted for 8% of sales, the Pacific for 9%. Since the mid-1980s, annual decreases of 5% in sales have been noted, both in reduction of French purchases and in drops in exports. The reduction in arms procurements by the USA, the US policy of arms donations (rather than sales) to follow political decisions and the increased aggressiveness of US arms salesmen has led to a potential rethinking of the need for an independent French arms industry. Increases in British arms exports (the UK now being the second world exporter) reinforces this position, as does the appearance of new producers - Japan, China - and destocking by ex-Soviet powers.

France and aid

Table 6.3
Bilateral aid flows in Francophonie in 1992

Donor countries: payments to Francophone recipients as % of total aid	
Canada	18.2%
Switzerland	20%
Luxembourg	25.8%
France	47.3%
Belgium	59.2%
Recipient countries: receipts from Francophone countries as % of total aid received	
Less than 10%	Cambodia, Cape Verde, Egypt, Laos, Vietnam, Zaïre
10% to 30%	Benin, Burundi, Guinea Bissau, Equatorial Guinea, Mali, Morocco, Rwanda, Seychelles, Tunisia, Vanuatu
30% to 60%	Burkina Faso, Cameroon, Central African Republic, Chad, Comoros, Djibouti, Dominica, Guinea, Haiti, Lebanon, Madagascar, Mauritania, Niger, Senegal, Togo
Above 60%	Congo (62.8%), Ivory Coast (66.3%), Mauritius (67%), Gabon (88%)

Source: Etat, 1994, 353
Note: Appendix Table A2 shows bilateral aid flows

Many countries of northern Francophonie are generous in their provision of financial aid to developing countries, and conversely, Francophone recipient countries are aware that they receive a large part of their aid from Francophone colleagues, as can be seen from Table 6.3. French foreign policy in particular has constantly stressed the intention to provide a high level of aid, associated with a global foreign policy: 'France intends to maintain an ambitious foreign policy in a rapidly developing international context' (Notes Bleues, 94-1, 63). This ambitious foreign policy requires that France participate fully in international action in and through the United Nations and its associated organisations, keeps its armament and nuclear capability up to date, maintains its network of foreign representation - despite the 1.3% drop in the budget for the Ministry of Foreign Affairs between 1993 and 1994 - support the teaching of French throughout the world, and provide aid to developing countries - including its own *DOM-TOM*.

The logic of Official Development Aid - i.e. aid from Governments - is to start the virtuous cycle by providing the capital that local saving has not yet produced. Unfortunately, public aid has not incited private investment in Africa and in recent years much has been siphoned off to non-productive spending or devoted simply to repaying interest on previous loans. In 1970, French aid was 857 million US dollars of which 13.5% was multilateral. Britain's was 629 million dollars (18% multilateral). In 1990, France contributed 7,779 million dollars (20.6% multilateral), while Britain's contribution was 3,088 billion (42% multilateral). France is the second largest donor after Germany, but has the lowest multilateral proportion: much aid (40%) is bilateral and is tied to specific agreements and former colonies (Coquet et al, 1993). France's record in providing aid, particularly to Africa, has been heavily criticised in recent years. 1990, the anniversary of thirty years of African independence, saw 'virtually every magazine in France dealing with political and economic affairs' making "universally negative" assessments of France's record (McKesson, 1993). The criticisms included 'tolerating the misuse of French aid, giving political and military support to discredited regimes, misguided economic priorities and administrative mismanagement, and not redirecting French efforts to more deserving and potentially rewarding partners'.

Ignacio Ramonet, in Le Monde Diplomatique (May 1993, 13), was categoric:
> France is still the main provider of funds and gives Africa about 26 billion francs every year. Indignation comes first from the realisation that scarcely 5% of this is spent on development. The rest returns, through various routes, to French banks or European tax havens...African leaders have amassed impressive fortunes: that of Mobutu in Zaïre is estimated at 4 to 6 billion dollars...Paris is content to keep the illusion that France is a great power worthy of its permanent seat in the Security Council. Secondly, French aid (like that of most

wealthy countries) is linked to orders on the French market, which leads to white elephants - gigantic infrastructure projects, out of all measure and often unusable. (Thirdly) a lot of the aid is military and helps France to equip and train armed forces to fire on unarmed citizens in Togo, Zaïre, Rwanda and elsewhere. Units of the French army, based in numerous African countries, keep in power non-elected leaders, surrounded by kleptocracies robbing State resources and scorning human rights...35 years of aid and 300 million poor...France finds herself with a bankrupt continent at her southern frontier when she no longer has the means to support ambitions of solidarity with Africa.

One should note that France has traditionally been selective in directing aid: more has gone to some countries than others. Cameroon, the Ivory Coast and Senegal received 11.4% of France's world aid in 1990, and France follows the pattern of other European countries in funding the former colonies or principal economic partners. Unfortunately, the bulk of French aid may have gone to the 'middle income countries such as Gabon and the Ivory Coast rather than to low-income countries such as Mali or Burkina-Faso' simply because they are the most in debt (McKesson, 1993, 66; Gaulme, 1994). Some commentators see other problems: 'The personalisation of relations, connected with the traditional clientism of French politicians and African psycho-sociology, has influenced judgements and behaviour in Rwanda, Togo and Zaïre, where arbitrary choices in favour of authoritarian Heads of State have been made, based on motives which do not bear scrutiny (*inavouables au sens littéral*)' (Gaulme, 1994, 47).

Aid to Africa has caused most discussion and represents the most difficult situation. The revision of French policy since 1990 has responded to a number of factors: the criticisms we have noted, the fact that the importance of Africa in the cold-war competition between the Soviet and Western powers has decreased since 1989, a reconsideration of the implications of conditionality in aid - why, for example, is so much French aid directed at the former French colonies when better 'prospects' exist, for example in South Africa and Nigeria, or indeed outside Africa altogether? In addition, increased immigration to France can best be reduced by aiding development abroad, so increased aid to countries from which immigrants now come to mainland France might help in reducing social tension in France as well as providing help to populations overseas (Gaulme, 1994).

In 1990, at a summit meeting between France and African leaders at La Baule, Mitterrand spelt out the necessity for African leaders to co-operate with international associations such as the World Bank and the International Monetary Fund, hinted at the likelihood of *FCFA* devaluation, foresaw that French aid would be conditional (i.e. on signing contracts with French partners, although the condition envisaged here was the requirement for greater democracy) and insisted on democratisation and respect for human rights (i.e. representative government, multiparty systems, free elections, freedom of the press and the judiciary, the end of corruption (McKesson, 1993, 58). Policy during the Balladur government followed much the same line.

Aid policy is currently based on conditionality, increased internationalisation (i.e. co-operation with World Bank and International Monetary Fund, but also with the European Union, the G7, the London and Paris Clubs and other international economic organisations) and structural adjustment. Aid is dispensed through the *Ministre de la Coopération*, despite various proposals for reform and for broadening this Ministry's remit to countries other than the former colonies (aid to Cambodia followed this route in September 1993); through the Ministry of Education, the Finance Ministry, Foreign Affairs, the Banque de France and the Presidency, where the responsible office was until recently run by the then President's son, Jean-Christophe Mitterrand.

During 1993 and 1994 aid to potential Asian 'tigers' has increased. Senior French politicians, including the President, went to Vietnam, Cambodia and Laos, and such visits followed by one by the Economics Minister, Edmond Alphandéry, in July 1994 resulted in major contracts to French firms in recognition of increased aid. 250 million francs were allocated to Cambodia for 1994, 1.2 billion francs of debt (half the total) was cancelled and additional aid of 425 million francs (1992: 180, 1993: 250) went to Vietnam. Vietnam, in fact, has been courted by a flood of Western delegations: 1,900 went there in 1993. France, as the 8th highest investor, leads the Western countries (Libération, 25.7.1994). These are countries linked by 'traditional and historic friendship'. Libération described the phrase as 'a diplomatic euphemism meaning "inherited from the colonies"'.

Aid to France's own *DOM-TOM* has also been increased - by 50% - through planning contracts, agreed in late 1993 or early 1994. These engage the State to partner expenditure by the *DOM* or *TOM* itself. Overall, the *DOM-TOM* budget has remained the same as in 1993, although general programme authorisations have dropped by 10% (Appendix, Table A4). It should be remembered that overall expenditure in the *DOM-TOM* passes through many Ministries, and the 1994 budget estimates that total civil grants in support of the *DOM-TOM* amount to 37 billion francs.

Language and Economic Development

Societies where societal multilingualism is extensive have been said to be necessarily underdeveloped: 'linguistically highly fragmented countries are always poor' (Pool, 1972, quoted in Coulmas, 1992, 25). The proof of the statement was updated by Coulmas in a table showing, for example, that France, with 10 languages and a population of 56 million, had a per capita income of 16,090 US$, while Papua New Guinea, with 849 languages, had an income of 810 US$. The African countries of Francophonie are notoriously multilingual, and also poor, but how far can the noted correlation be said to be a cause and a continuing contributory factor to this poverty? Counter examples exist: Rwanda, with its population of seven millions, has only two languages, but was not among the richest countries. France, in the original 1972 study, was counted as a monolingual country despite the presence of a number of regional languages, and an even greater number of immigrant languages actively spoken among the four million immigrants or their descendants: even the ten languages used by Coulmas twenty years later are an understatement. The USA, economically successful, is hardly an example of a monolingual country: not only is Spanish widely used in addition to English, but many of the linguistic minorities have retained the use of their language, although it is true that this use tends to be found in domains remote from economic (or political) life. Canada, the world leader in terms of human development, is officially bilingual rather than monolingual.

The correlation is perhaps greater between a reduced number of languages (and cultural identities) and a politically strong State, on the argument that Statehood requires a unique means of official communication, although even here Switzerland 'is the exception that proves the rule' (Coulmas, 1992, 26). Particularly significant is the need for the strong (economically or politically) State to have available a standardised means of communication which can ensure the rapid and effective deployment of labour, ensure instructions are implemented, and relate the providers of capital to the providers of labour, and both to the market. Without such a standardised tool, widely available, economies will underperform.

In any case, if economic development on the Western model is to take place, both social and cultural 'development' - or at least change, in order to accommodate to the required centralisation and standardisation of communication - are necessary, and this can only come about through the adoption and use of a reduced number of vehicular languages which enable development in the Western sense to take place. These languages are typically exogenous, and typically European. Coulmas (1992, 54) concludes his study of this aspect of the relationship between language and economy by stating that

> deliberate attempts at overcoming linguistic underdevelopment in order to turn a language into a suitable medium of modern communication take the form of one of the following three approaches:
> (1) adopting a Western language...
> (2) adapting an autochthonous language...by...incorporating words, structures and norms of Western languages...

(3) adapting Western concepts by providing them with native expressions, especially loan translations.

In examining the situation in Francophone Africa it is clear that a number of factors must be borne in mind. Economic development depends, not merely on the adoption of Western approaches to capital supply and use, but on urbanisation, on changes in distribution and marketing, on the nature of food supply, and on the nature of the goods and services available. As with World Bank projects, failure may come about because insufficient attention has been paid to local conditions, and because a guiding principle has been taken as uniquely important.

Studies of multilingualism, language planning and the use of vehicular languages were undertaken in Africa (e.g. Baggioni et al, 1992) in the late 1980s and early 1990s. In general, these found that languages tended to adapt to different functions - Wolof, for example, became more regular, losing a number of noun classes and standardising on a reduced set of oppositions as it adopted a vehicular role in towns. Studies of the use of languages in African markets (Calvet, 1992) tended to show that a reduced number of vehicular languages was employed, that, in multilingual towns, language choice was dependent on the nature of the interaction, and that there was no question of a common situation arising by agreement and even less by official planning: a variety of different vehicular languages was used, even in one town, and even on different days as different clients and goods came to the market.

Djité (1991) expressed a widespread attitude when he criticised exogenous languages such as English or French for the failure of economic and social policies, and for economic and political instability. He agreed with the major contention of Pool that multilingualism was a drawback to development, but, accepting that the only workable solution to African problems would be the decisions of Africans themselves, was sure that African populations would naturally gravitate towards the use of African linguae francae, used across the colonial frontiers, and that greater use of these would lead to more co-operation and linguistic and cultural tolerance.

Mauritius has also been extensively studied, as an example of a stable society which has made considerable social, economic and political progress (HDR, 1994, 45; North, 1994). The United Nations Human Development Report attributed economic progress to free education and health care, to a high level of social spending and very reduced expenditure on defence, and to diversification of the economy 'after a period of structural adjustment'. As a result, 'annual per capita income rose from 300 US$ in 1960 to 2,380 in 1991, while unemployment fell from 30% at the beginning of the 1980s to around 3% in 1992'.

This economic success was related to ethnic and linguistic harmony, and to the general use of French, Creole and English (Eriksen, 1993). But the recipe for success shows considerable reservations: although English is the official language it is 'equally awkward for everyone...no single group in the population has a linguistic advantage over any other group, so it works' (North, 1994).

For organised Francophonie generally, realisation that multilingualism and diversity is a fact of life has taken some time to emerge. For a considerable period not merely was the economic situation generally ignored but it was thought that economic relations could be based uniquely on French and all exchanges conducted in that language. As a consequence, relations would have remained tied to the French-speaking area, in bilateral exchanges with France, or in selective regional trade associations. The Caribbean and West Africa would thus have found themselves obliged to trade across and through English or Dutch-speaking areas, to mention only exogenous languages. For Africa, 'vertical' (North-South, bilateral with France) trade was characteristic of colonialism and could only perpetuate economic dependency, so the only solution was to develop regional trade. Unfortunately, countries such as Nigeria, Kenya, Uganda and South Africa use English, the most widespread cultural and economic language, and Francophonie finds itself unable to participate in regional trade unless it accepts that exports must often be made through English.

Francophonie: an Economic Community?

The nearest equivalent to Francophonie as a world community is the Commonwealth (cf. Toye, 1994), no longer called the British Commonwealth. In some senses the Commonwealth is an economic community: it has its own budget of about £35 million (1992), contributed by the 51 members for the Secretariat and for specific activities: the Commonwealth Fund for Technical Co-operation (CFTC), the Commonwealth Youth Programme and the Commonwealth Science Council. The CFTC, obtaining its funds by voluntary contributions from members, is mainly active in providing some 350 technical experts per year, training some 4,000 specialists annually, supporting 60 export promotion projects, providing 50 in-house consultancies, and subsidising the creation of 100 firms.

The Commonwealth's free-market principles and free-trade stance were reinforced by its review of principles (and of internal organisation) in the 1991 Harare declaration, and its support for privatisation and reduction in the role of the State meant that support from developed to developing countries had to be pragmatic: most important were debt relief and debt management - through the creation and dissemination of computerised systems (Commonwealth Secretariat Debt Recording and Management System (CS-DRMS) installed in 35 countries by the end of 1993. A similar practical action took place with missions from

Commonwealth Finance Ministers in the run-up to the GATT negotiations. But overall, the definition of the Commonwealth as an economic community depends on its roles and on its informality:

> a market-place - at least an informal one - where producers of raw materials can discuss. It does not undertake the role of the different raw material producer organisations in negotiation on these products, nor is it a regional organisation since it is so widespread. It is probable that the cultural community linking its members plays a role, for example in the ACP group of countries (Toye, 1994, 67).

Francophonie has not been as pragmatic, nor is it so far advanced, as the Commonwealth in defining for itself a role in economics. But there is a long history of regional economic links within Francophonie, particularly within Africa, and particularly with France. These have had a chequered history, and the value of the lesson to be drawn from them seems to underline the problems facing the prospect of Francophonie at some time developing a stronger economic base. France is dependent on Francophone countries, and particularly on ex-colonies, for raw material supplies:

> France's current rate of dependency on (strategic) materials from Africa is 100 percent for cobalt, 87 to 100 per cent for uranium, 83 per cent for phosphate, 68 per cent for bauxite, 35 per cent for manganese and 32 per cent for copper. France's rate of dependency on Francophone Africa is 35 per cent for manganese (Gabon), 32 per cent for chromium and 22 per cent for phosphate (Senegal and Togo)...France is at present actively prospecting for uranium in Senegal, Mali, Guinea, Mauritania and Zaïre, as well as in South Africa. Two major French parastatals...control most uranium exploitation and prospecting activities in the producing Francophone African countries   (Martin, 1989, 106).

The bilateral agreements made on independence secured such supplies of raw materials for France. These agreements

> contain special provisions concerning French privileged and exclusive access to oil and gas, uranium, thorium, lithium, beryllium and helium. These...must be sold to France on a priority basis - and restricted to third countries - as required by 'the interests of common defence' (Martin, 1989, 107).

The import of raw materials (77% of France's imports from Francophone Africa in 1986) and the export of manufactured goods (63% of France's exports to Francophone Africa in the same year) also still reveal the colonial pattern (Martin, 1989, 109). The old colonial trading companies (for example, the *Compagnie Française de l'Afrique Occidentale* and *Société Commerciale de l'Ouest Africain*) and shipping companies still operate.

During most of the 1980s France was in deficit in its external trade. With Francophonie, however, the reverse was the case, and in recent times the marked benefit to France's export trade of her relations with Francophone countries has become even more noticeable, with an overall balance in excess of 47 billion francs in 1993 (Appendix Table A4). Francophone countries are good customers for specialised exports such as arms and communications technology.

France is the principal economic partner of many African countries, is, for example, the principal Western investor in Vietnam, and is the more or less exclusive partner of the *DOM-TOM*. The franc zone is conducted mainly by France. However, in terms of international exchanges, the importance of Francophone trade to France is comparatively small. The proportion of her imports represented by trade with Francophone countries excluding the *DOM-TOM* (Appendix Table A5) is less than 11%, while that of exports is less than 15%. Belgium and Luxembourg are far and away her largest trading partners within Francophonie, and even they only account for 8.84% of imports and 8.61% of exports; trade with the African franc zone now accounts for a minute 0.92% of imports and 1.28% of exports. Furthermore, despite the beliefs of the colonisers in France, both in the first and in the second Empire, that the colonies would be of great economic benefit to France, the eventual result does not seem to support that view. French economic interests were dependent on the former colonies at the time of decolonisation in a large number of fields, particularly in raw materials from Africa, and indeed France has remained dependent on her traditional colonial suppliers in many fields, but these links can be broken as happened in the case of Algerian gas and petrol, or, indeed, for many years following the independence of Guinea, without causing major economic damage to France. The remaining *DOM-TOM* are if anything consumers, and indeed a financial drain on France rather than a source of wealth, while the trade and other links with Francophonie generally are not major elements in France's international trade relations.

Francophone economic relationships cannot of course merely be measured by trade between France and her partners. But trade between Canada and Francophonie shows a similar pattern: her largest partner is the USA, and Quebec trades more with the UK than with any Francophone partner. Trade between other Francophone countries, even regionally, is similarly poorly represented. Even within the African franc zone regional trade is small, while neither the Caribbean *DOM* nor the Pacific *TOM* trade with each other. Francophonie has traditionally not formed a close economic link, even regionally.

In Africa, the colonial federations - *Afrique Orientale Française* and *Afrique Equatoriale Française* - had centralised systems of tax collection, fiscal redistribution and common financial services. These were dismantled in 1959 -

according to Kazadi (1991) at de Gaulle's insistence in order to keep future African countries small and dependent, but according to Bach (1995) at the insistence of the two richest members, Gabon (in the *AEF*) and the Ivory Coast in the *AOF*, who could only lose if the Federation continued. The history of economic regionalism since shows constant changes, detailed in Bach, 1995, and little success. Some of the changes included the departure of Madagascar and Mauritania from the franc zone in 1972, of Zaïre, Congo, Cameroon, Chad, Madagascar and Gabon from *Organisation Commune Africaine et Malgache* at various times before its dissolution in 1985, the establishment of the *Communauté Economique de l'Afrique de l'Ouest* in 1973 and that of the Economic Community of West African States, including Anglophone States, in 1975. But despite increased trade until the early 1980s, by 1992, most regional organisations had more or less hit stalemate, and 'disinterest for Community objectives is quasi-general' (Bach, 1995, 204).

The failure of regional economic co-operation and interchange is clear from the small proportion of trade within the communities which still exist. By 1987, percentages of trade as a percentage of total exports were down to 7.7% for *CEDEAO*, 0.6% for the *CEPGL* and 0.9% for the *Union Douanière de l'Afrique Centrale*. But President Nicéphore Soglo of Benin could still mention that in the preparations for the 1995 meeting of Heads of State of Francophonie, the *Conseil Permanent de la Francophonie (CPF)*, the executive council of organised Francophonie, was encouraging 'increased efficiency and dynamism' in the regional economic groupings, listed as :

> *Communauté Economique des Etats de l'Afrique de l'Ouest (CEDEAO)*; *Communauté Economique des Etats de l'Afrique Centrale (CEEAC)*; *Communauté Economique des Pays des Grands Lacs (CEPGL)*; *Communauté de Développement de l'Afrique Centrale (CDAC)*; and the *Commission de l'Océan Indien (COI)* (Lettre de la Francophonie, 81, April 1995).

In North Africa the *Union du Maghreb Arabe (UMA)* was formed in 1989, uniting Algeria, Libya, Morocco, Mauritania and Tunisia. Plans for eventual integration have suffered delays, but a free-trade zone for Maghreb products, leading to an integrated customs union (both supposedly existing by 1995), a central bank, a common market and eventual political and economic integration have been outlined. The economic grouping in southern Africa: the Common Market of East and Southern Africa was agreed in 1993; the Association of Caribbean States was similarly formed in July 1994.

Indeed, it seems logical that the *DOM* and the *TOM* in particular should be involved in regional economic groupings. Judging by the relative tonnage of imports unloaded in Papeete, regional trade is important for Polynesia: 19.7% of imports came from Europe, 27.1% from (North and South) America, 6.7% from

Asia - mainly from Japan which is the principal partner - and 46.5% from Oceania (i.e. Australia, New Zealand and Pacific islands). But closer examination of the figures shows the problems we have already examined. Imports totalled 664 tonnes in 1991, while exports totalled only 27 tonnes. Europe (mainly France) is a main source of goods for consumption, with 75.1% of drinks, 48.9% of foodstuffs and 55.7% of vehicles, while Asian (mainly Japanese) cars account for 30.4% of vehicles imported and Oceania (mainly Australia) provides 84.9% of petrol products. America provides 64.2% of construction goods and 56.8% of animal foodstuffs. Integration has certainly not taken place into Oceania, despite the long-standing commercial relationships with Australia and New Zealand (statistics from (Polynésie Française, 1993, 23-27).

But regional and 'decentralised' co-operation does take place within Francophonie. Tunisia, for example, actively supplies expertise and key personnel for a number of international development schemes - not exclusively Francophone:

> Nearly fourteen thousand Tunisian experts are available for international work, according to the Director General of the Tunisian Technical Co-operation Agency (*Agence Tunisienne de Coopération Technique* (*ATCT*))...Set up in 1972, the *ATCT* is unique in the Third World...It works with the United Nations Development Programme...the American (US-AID), German (GTZ), Francophone (*ACCT*) and Arab (Saudi Arabia and Kuwait) Agencies prefer to use *ATCT* (Jeune Afrique, 1746, 23-29 June 1994)

The same Jeune Afrique article does point out, however, that of the 7,410 experts actually deployed on 31st May 1994, only 314 were working in Africa: '90% are working in the Gulf, where there is no lack of demand or of finance', although 'triangular aid' (Tunisian expert, African employer and foreign capital) is likely to develop further.

The 1994 *Etat de la Francophonie* report was very guarded as to the future for a Francophone Economic Zone. The negative points were clear: at the moment there was little activity that could show that Francophonie was taken into account by private industry at all, and only to a limited extent by States. If there was co-operative activity, it was generally undertaken by large groups and limited to major activities. Statistics were not maintained on this aspect of activities at all: those reported had had to be obtained specially. If there was joint activity, it relied on similarity of legal, financial, fiscal and educational structures and practices.

On the other hand, this similarity of structures and systems could bring about closer action, particularly at the regional level. Despite all the problems, the two largest groupings - the North American Free Trade Association (30% of world GDP) or the European Union (29.4%) - seem so large and threatening that in mere self-defence smaller organisations must either join them or combine to resist. It is probably to this that is due the renewed interest in 1995 in a possible Francophone economic organisation.

7. THE ORGANISATION OF FRANCOPHONIE

From 1945 to the First Summit Meeting

The concept of organised Francophonie, and the formal institutions through which it is organised, have developed slowly over the period since the end of Empire. Initiatives have been taken by a number of politicians, not necessarily French, in attempting to establish and then to broaden a formal grouping of nations and regions.

The 1946 French Constitution, following the Brazzaville meeting of 1944, and the *Union Française* it brought into being had outlined a number of ways in which close co-operation could take place between France and her former Empire. The 'Union' solution was considered too close to colonialism by the international community outside France, and indeed, was regarded by Roosevelt as hypocritical (Kazadi, 1991, 27). The 1958 Constitution and its *Communauté* needed major reconstruction in 1960 and 1961, as the African countries took the option of independence with association. After the independence of Algeria in 1962, the way became clear for establishing Francophonie as an organised international grouping of countries and regions based on co-operation and solidarity.

The African initiatives of the early 1960s, attempting to set up formal organisations within which contacts, aid and common approaches to world politics could be discussed have been documented in Kazadi (1991) and Deniau (1983b and 1992). African leaders such as Felix Houphouët-Boigny of the Ivory Coast, Leopold Sedar Senghor of Senegal, Habib Bourguiba of Tunisia, Hamani Diori of Niger, proposed different solutions: some like the British Commonwealth, some suggesting a more formal Federation of independent States, others aiming to create a series of concentric Francophone circles in which those with closest links would meet frequently, with outer circles meeting occasionally and restricting their contacts to cultural matters. France, under the leadership of de Gaulle, proved wary of formal multilateral organisations, preferring bilateral links with individual countries. The *AOF* and the *AEF* had been disbanded before independence, *Cartiérisme* - a generalised despair at the state of Africa, identified by the journalist Cartier - and *Afropessimisme* were rife. For De Gaulle, credited with deliberately avoiding 'impressing his personality' on Francophonie (Deniau, 1983a, 54), the priorities which indeed might be held back if France could not free herself from the weight of her past included the creation of Europe, the need to modernise France, the desire to release the energies of international capitalism, and investment in space. Apart from setting up the franc zone, ensuring that detailed agreements were in place to protect raw material sources, establishing defence agreements and technical military co-operation agreements - which together were tantamount to establishing a private fiefdom, the *pré carré* - the aim was to free France from responsibility if things went wrong. Nonetheless, in 1970 the first meeting which could properly be called the origin of present-day Francophonie took place in Niamey, with André Malraux attending for France, and established the *Agence de Coopération Culturelle et Technique*.

Broadening the arrangements to include countries outside the former Empire took time and patience. In 1968 Quebec's Minister of Education had attended a meeting of *CONFEMEN*, the international conference of Ministers of Education in French-speaking countries, without referring the matter to Ottawa. This was the time of de Gaulle's visit to Quebec, his speech ending '*Vive le Québec libre*' - viewed by the Canadian government as an open declaration of support to the autonomists of Quebec in their struggle for independence. Canada protested that international affairs came under its jurisdiction, and the matter was not resolved until a compromise noted the powers of the province over education and permitted both Quebec and Canada to attend Ministerial meetings on this topic. Thereafter, France 'could not participate in any Francophone meeting or summit of heads of government to which Quebec could not be invited' (Minister of Foreign Affairs, 9.11.1977). Agreement was not reached between France and Canada until 1985, allowing the first Summit of 'Heads of State and Government' to take place in Paris in 1986. Canada was eventually persuaded to permit this compromise both because of the country's need to obtain a higher profile internationally and because the cultural duality of the country had been more and more recognised since the 'patriation' of the Constitution in 1982 and the consequent rejection by Quebec of the proposed new Canadian Constitution. Part of the price which France had to pay was to allow discussion of Canadian concerns at the new Summit meetings: fishing rights on the Atlantic coast, particularly those claimed by France around St Pierre et Miquelon, and sales of uranium, which had been a sore point between the two countries in the 1960s (Thérien, 1993). Thérien is quite clear that the major characteristic of this first period of the organisation of Francophonie, from 1970 to 1990, was the competition between France and Canada for leadership, or at least for setting the agenda, both of wider Francophone co-operation involving countries outside the direct orbit of French domination and of ensuring the meetings did not restrict themselves to cultural and linguistic matters.

Contemporary Francophone Organisations and Associations

Official organisations

By the 1980s, a number of official organisations had been in place for many years, particularly the *ACCT* and the French *Haut Comité pour la Défense et l'Expansion de la Langue Française*, set up in 1966. Agreement had been reached in 1965 on Franco-Quebec shared 'responsibility' for the support of the language (Deniau, 1983a, 53), and Summit meetings of the French President and Prime Minister and African Francophone leaders had become a matter of routine.

Mitterrand's arrival in power in 1981 was the occasion for a review of the French governmental and international institutions. The mixed functions of de Gaulle's *Haut Comité de la Langue Française* were separated: the *Haut Conseil de la Francophonie*, with the President of the Republic in the Chair, was set up in 1984 with the intention of developing cultural and language interests across Francophonie as part of the Presidential concern with foreign affairs. The *Conseil Supérieur de la Langue Française*, the *Comité Consultatif de la Langue Française*, and the *Commissariat de la Langue Française*, under the Prime Minister, concerned themselves more centrally with the French language, particularly in France. Within the Foreign Affairs ministry, a *Direction de la Politique Linguistique* co-ordinated various aspects of language policy, while the Ministry for Francophonie was gradually established, at first as a Delegation or sub-Ministry and eventually in 1993 as a full Ministry in the Balladur Government, combined with Culture. Chirac's reorganisation in May 1995 nominated a *Secrétaire d'Etat*, Margie Sudre, in charge of Francophonie, but attached her to the Ministry of Foreign Affairs. The division of interest between President and Prime Minister, and between the language and cultural interests on one side and the political, foreign and economic interests on the other, reflected both President's responsibility for, and continuing interest in, foreign affairs. When cohabitation occurred in 1986-1988 and again in 1993-1995, the split of interests produced some fascinating conflicts. The strengthening of French Government interest in Francophonie in 1986-88, with the creation of a Ministerial post occupied by the flamboyant personality of Mme Lucette Michaux-Chevry from Guadeloupe, and her subsequent battle for control of all the language and Francophone policy interests, reflected simple rivalry between the Chirac government and the continuing Mitterrand presidency. The situation became tense again in 1993-1995, with Mitterrand's close interest in Foreign Affairs and Francophonie shown yet again by his 'irritation' at Prime Minister Balladur's interview (Le Figaro, 31 August 1994) on 'his' foreign policy, at Balladur's claim to have achieved success in the GATT negotiations and in the Rwanda intervention, after Mitterrand's supposed reluctance in both cases (Le Monde, 2.9.1994).

In mid-1995, the most significant governmental and intergovernmental organisations operating in support of the Summit meetings of Francophonie itself, and in some countries of Francophonie, were as follows, although it is to be expected that President Chirac's known interest in language and in Francophonie may lead to some reorganisation. The Table gives some additional information on each organisation.

Table 7.1
Organisations of Francophonie

International Organisation
Summit: *Sommet de la Francophonie.* Chair: host, by rotation and agreement.
Summit executive council - *Conseil Permanent de la Francophonie (CPF).* Chair: Mauritius (1994), Benin (1995).
Conférence Ministérielle de la Francophonie (CMF). Chair: Mauritius/Benin.
Operators for individual programmes: *ACCT, AUPELF-UREF, TV5.*
National Organisations
France
Haut Conseil de la Francophonie (1984). Chair: President. Secretary-General (1984 to 1995): Stélio Farandjis
To different degrees, all the following Ministries are involved with Francophonie:
Ministry of Foreign Affairs (1993-5: Alain Juppé. From 1995: Hervé de Charette)
Ministry of Coooperation (1993-5: Michel Roussin. From 1995: Jacques Godfrain)
Ministry of Defence (1993-5: François Léotard. From 1995: Christophe Millou)
Ministry of Education (1993 on: François Bayrou).
The Ministry centrally concerned with the range of Francophone activities was the Ministry for Culture and Francophonie between 1993 and 1995, when the Minister was Jacques Toubon.
Conseil Supérieur de la Langue Française (1989; new members 1994). Chair: Prime Minister. Vice-Chair: Bernard Quémada
Délégation Générale à la Langue Française (1989; replaced *Commissariat...,* founded 1984). Attached first to the Prime Minister, then (1993-1995) to the Ministry of Culture and Francophonie, 1995 on: Ministry of Culture. *Délégué:* Anne Magnant
Belgium (Communauté Française)
Conseil de la Langue Française (founded 1985).
Service de la Langue Française (founded 1985).
Canada
Official Commissioner for Official Languages
Quebec
Conseil de la Langue Française
Office de la Langue française

Sources: Lettre de la Francophonie; L'Année Internationale Francophone; Etat de la Francophonie; Bruchet, 1992

Outside and quite separate from the main organisations of Francophonie, other multilateral meetings continue to take place, particularly the Franco-African Summits between President and African leaders. This meeting has tended in recent years, particularly since 1990, to be an arena in which France can make clear her policy - for example on the allocation of aid as between Africa and the ex-Communist East, on the development of democracy and on the prevention of corruption - and ensure that African votes are still available to support French policies at the United Nations.

Associations and Non-Governmental Organisations

A number of pressure groups, semi-public and private associations, non-governmental organisations (*ONG*; NGOs) and International Non-Governmental Organisations (*OING*; INGOs) were operating in France and Canada during the 1980s and indeed well before (373 are listed in Bruchet, 1992; see also Offord, 1993). Indeed, for some observers, particularly in Canada (Tétu, 1987, 73-96) the whole Francophonie movement derives from such initiatives. Among the associations, it is difficult to identify which was first, which is senior, which has an organising and representative role; indeed, it is in general true that most associations are specific and concerned with their internal constitution and function. Nonetheless, some have been particularly active or have contributed to international Francophonie. Among the first were the *Association des Universités Partiellement ou Entièrement de Langue Française* (*AUPELF*), which was founded in 1961; the *Association Internationale des Parlementaires de Langue Française* (*AIPLF*), in 1967, the *Fédération Internationale des Professeurs de Français* (*FIPF*) in 1969. The *Association Francophone d'Amitié et de Liaison* (*AFAL*), founded in 1974, saw its role as co-ordination of the flurry of associations in Francophonie and contributed to the creation of the official lists and to the question of recognition. The Quebec stress on associations, opposed to the French desire for official organisations, has occasionally led to tension, while the lack of clarity, of effectiveness, of efficiency and of co-operation among them had been noticed by a number of observers. Indeed, to some extent the national characteristics of Quebec and France have led to disagreements between them, to attempts to systematise the associations and by contrast to retain their flexibility and enthusiasm (Deniau, 1983, 59; de Broglie, 1986, 225-30; Hagège, 1987, 248).

In 1995, a liaison committee for the INGOs was set up at the request of the *CPF* in order to try to systematise the groups. This brought together five representatives, with five alternatives, and Table 7.2 indicates the range of interests and origins which characterise the international associations. They are very varied, constantly changing and widespread, with very diverse aims, offices and constitutions.

Table 7.2
Liaison Committee of Francophonie INGOs

Members

Association Internationale des Femmes Francophones. Founded 1987. Office: Mauritania. Promotion of the role of women.

Union Internationale des Journalistes et de la Presse de langue française. Founded 1950. Office: France. Press professionals.

Association de la Presse Francophone. Founded 1992. Office: Senegal. Popularising the Francophone ideal through audiovisual means.

ENDA Tiers Monde. Office: Senegal. Independence of the Third World.

Union des Editeurs de Langue française. Founded 1960. Office: Brussels. North-South joint publishing.

Alternatives

Association francophone internationale des directeurs d'établissements scolaires. Founded 1983. Office: Montreal. Exchange and contact between establishments.

Association internationale de coopération pour le développement du Sahel. Office: Burkina Faso. Exchange of experience among southern partners.

Comité international des femmes africaines pour le développement. Office: Ivory Coast. Groups womens organisations from 17 countries; aims to promote income-generating activities.

Fédération internationale des professeurs de français. Founded 1969. Office: France. Federation of teachers' organisations.

Institut international de droit d'expression et d'inspiration françaises. Founded 1964. Office: Paris. Groups those interested in French law.

Source: Lettre de la Francophonie, 80. March 1995. (Date of foundation not always given).

The Summit Meetings

First

The first meeting, from 17-19 February 1986, took place in Versailles, and was mainly concerned with establishing a basis for the meetings and their support. The discussions centred around the indebtedness of the Third World, the economic disparity between North and South (which was agreed to be the major problem for Francophonie to tackle) and practical areas where work could be carried out. These were identified as education, health and communication (i.e. book publishing, computer- and screen-based communication, and the 'language industries'). In order to help the Summit implement its decisions, it agreed to use four associations: *AUPELF* for work in education, *AIPLF* and *AIMF* (*Association Internationale des Municipalités Francophones*) for work on communication and health, *CIRTEF* (*Conseil International de la Radio et de la*

Télévision d'Expression Française) for the development of audiovisual communication.

Kazadi (1991) felt that the first summit had enabled the African nations to prioritise the economic problem, but deplored their lack of preparation, while Thérien (1993) concluded that it had been somewhat of a battleground between Canada and France, with France resolutely trying to keep Francophonie on the cultural and language plane while Canada wanted the movement to tackle practical problems, and particularly to get to grips with the information revolution. Arnold (1989, 120) was convinced that the outcome was a backward move:

> The recommendations often corresponded to a sort of return to square one, particularly in understanding the objective reality of the linguistic situation in which French is situated. Some of the novel priorities were practically word for word those of the first Conference of the *ACCT* at Niamey in 1970...they returned to the identity phase of the Agency, with "everything in French" predominating and co-operation taking place on the North-North axis, specifically between France and Quebec.

Second

The second meeting, from 2-4 September 1987, in Quebec, specified the areas within which action could take place. Mulroney, Prime Minister of Canada, announced the cancellation of the foreign debt of the African nations present. The meeting also dealt with the *confusion des réseaux*: the network of groups and associations, all of which were vying with each other to act on behalf of Francophonie and each of which thought it owned exclusive rights to operate in this field or that. In the end, agreement was reached that a special study of the situation would be made by Jean-Louis Roy, Secretary-General of the *ACCT*, who proposed that there be 'operators' for each programme decided on, and that *ACCT*, as the longest established intergovernmental body, should be the principal operator.

Third

The third meeting, from 24-26 May 1989, in Dakar (Senegal), prioritised education and training among the various programmes. President Mitterrand announced the cancellation of the public debt of 35 African countries. Among the programmes for action was one for language planning - a ten-year plan for improvement, not just concerned with French but also with the other languages spoken within Francophonie.

Fourth

The fourth meeting, from 19-21st November 1991 - the 'summit of maturity' in Mitterrand's words - took place in the Palais de Chaillot, after the original venue, Zaïre, was decreed too dangerous and a meeting there too supportive of a non-democratic regime. It was this Summit that prioritised new conceptions of democracy, against a background in which democracy seemed to be under widespread attack: in Haiti, and in a number of African countries. This Summit also made the link between democracy and development, reinforcing the North-South contacts of Francophonie. In addition, the 1991 meeting created new organisational institutions and confirmed the methods of implementing decisions. Agreement was reached on the present structure: *Conférences Ministérielles* of the Ministers for Foreign Affairs and Francophonie; and retention of the existing Conferences of other Ministers, for example of Education (*CONFEMEN*) and of Youth and Sports (*CONFEJES*). The latter would continue to organise the *Jeux de la Francophonie*, the Francophone Games. To directly support the Summit Meetings, a *Conseil Permanent Francophone (CPF)* of 15 'personal representatives' of the Heads of State would meet, ensure follow-up and identify experts for specific projects. The *CPF* would report to the *Conférence Ministérielle* of Ministers of Foreign Affairs and Francophonie. Because of continuing pressure from the (600 plus) associations claiming interests in Francophonie, the Summit also agreed to instruct the *CPF* to establish criteria and conditions for the definition of appropriate NGOs, to accredit them, and to ensure that a forum for them would be held in conjunction with each Summit.

The main discussions established or confirmed nine programmes, eight of which were to be managed by *ACCT* as 'operator':
- culture and language planning;
- communication and audiovisual developments;
- agriculture;
- energy;
- environment;
- education, training, youth programmes;
- scientific and technical information dissemination;
- the law in the service of development and democracy, including specific programmes for the observation of elections in Djibouti, Senegal, Niger, and Romania.

The ninth programme, concerned with higher education and research, would be managed by *AUPELF-UREF (Association internationale des Universités Partiellement ou Entièrement de Langue Française - Université des Réseaux d'Expression Française)*. In addition, TV5 would report direct to the *CPF*, as would the Senghor University (*Université internationale de langue française au service du développement africain*).

Fifth

The fifth Summit was held in Mauritius from 16th-18th October 1993, with two themes: Unity in Diversity on the one hand, and Human Rights on the other. Again, the link between democracy and development was stressed, and again the finger was pointed at Haiti, while the coup d'état in Burundi and the murder of President N'dadaye immediately after the Summit stressed the immediacy of the problem. This Summit was notable for the emergence of a possible solution to the problem of the spokesperson: Mauritius, as the host country, provided a notable public figure in Ambassador Shirin Aumeeruddy-Cziffra, acting as President of the *Conseil Permanent de la Francophonie*.

Situation in mid-1995

After the Mauritius summit, the countries attending the Francophonie summits are as follows (Appendix Table A3):

> Belgium (*Communauté Française*), Benin, Burkina Faso, Bulgaria (admitted at Mauritius), Burundi (although the active participation of Burundi has been prevented after the assassination of Melchior N'dadaye, President, in October 1993), Cambodia (admitted in Mauritius), Cameroon, Canada, Central African Republic, Chad, Comoros Republic, Congo, Djibouti, Dominica, France, Gabon, Guinea, Equatorial Guinea, Guinea Bissau, Haiti, the Ivory Coast, Laos, Lebanon, Luxembourg, Madagascar, Mali, Mauritius, Monaco, Niger, Romania (admitted in Mauritius), Rwanda, Senegal, Seychelles, Togo, Tunisia, Vanuatu, Viet-Nam, and Zaïre.

Egypt, Guinea-Bissau, Morocco, Mauritania and Sainte-Lucie are 'associated States' within *ACCT*, while (the Kingdom of) Belgium, Cape-Verde and Switzerland participate in the Summits but are not members of *ACCT*. Quebec and New Brunswick are 'participating Governments' in *ACCT*. Of the countries involved, Canada, Seychelles, Mauritius and Vanuatu are also members of the British Commonwealth, and naturally, other countries participate in a number of other international groupings, from the non-aligned countries to the Pan-Arab States.

Official Francophonie: the Problems

The multiplicity of organisations

The first problem in this field is clearly that of the many organisations, groups, associations and even individuals who felt they had personally created

Francophonie and should therefore receive recognition, permanent membership of any national and international groups and considerable credit. Not all the credit they were seeking was limited to applause: the budget for practical work arising from the summits is considerable, and there is much need for consultants, research and development, and for studies of specific aspects of Francophonie. Little of this money goes anywhere except to France and Canada, however.

But there was one advance: the unification of the French Ministries of Culture and Francophonie in 1993 rendered it possible at that time to reduce one more of the complexities mentioned in Briand (1990). The elevation of Francophonie to a full French Ministerial post meant that its seriousness was unchallenged, and its alliance with Culture rather than with Foreign Affairs or Cooperation, was significant, too, in that it clearly underlined the French approach - i.e. Francophonie is primarily a language-based organisation, and the defence of the 'cultural exception' is the priority. In 1995 the post reverted to that of a *Secrétaire d'Etat*, and was again attached to Foreign Affairs. How this situation develops will be a matter of interest in what has to a certain extent become again problematic.

Membership

The definition of membership - who is entitled to join - leads to a major problem in defining Francophonie. We have noted above that the percentage of 'real' Francophones in the population of most member countries is quite small, ranging from half to less than one per cent of the total population.

The *grands absents* from the organised community of international Francophonie, too, are interesting: Ontario has 337,900 'real' Francophones but is not present. Algeria, with 30% 'real' Francophones, is another important country which does not have membership of the official organisation, and, like Ontario, shows little sign of wanting it. Andorra, with 'real' Francophones at 29% of the population, Israel with 11% and the Aosta Valley with 10%, are also not full members (cf. Appendix Table A3). But then there is no separate representation at the Summit meetings for the *DOM-TOM*, whose proportion of Francophones (except for Mayotte) is over 70%, whose total population represents a significant million and a half, and whose voice is potentially important in the Caribbean and the Pacific. The Summit meetings, and the *ACCT*, are only too aware of the difficulty of definition of a 'Francophone' country, and have attempted to redefine the criteria for membership, requiring applicants for example to demonstrate a real policy for the use and development of French (Etat, 1993, 19). But too strict a definition would leave most African countries outside, while many other countries would be eligible if mere numbers and a positive attitude towards French (for example, teaching it in schools) were the only criteria. The specific cases of Bulgaria and Romania, admitted as full members of Francophonie, highlight the problem of definition.

A second problem is that of the membership of official organisations by individuals. One of the interesting aspects of the *Haut Conseil de la Francophonie*, for example, is the number of former leaders it contains: Senghor as *Président d'Honneur*; Hélou, previously President of Lebanon; Cu Huy Can, former Minister of Culture in Vietnam; Michel Plourde, previously President of the *Conseil de la Langue Française* in Quebec; Philippe de Saint-Robert, previous *Commissaire de la Langue Française* in France. One may ask whether such a grouping has any more intrinsic interest or value than the Academy, whose technical role in relation to corpus planning for the French language is more and more transferred to the Terminology Commissions and the *Délégation Générale*. If prestigious organisations are regarded as meeting places for geriatrics, the importance of their activities may be called in question. But the *Haut Conseil* is a vehicle for the expression of French Presidential policy, not for that of the Government, and the *Haut Conseil* became more and more sidelined as a serious political forum in the later years of the Mitterrand Presidency.

Purpose of the meetings

The meetings are held in camera and followed by a formal statement. Much work has been carried out in preparation for them, and undoubtedly for those concerned it appears that a lot of ground has been covered, as the enthusiastic reports in *Lettre de la Francophonie* or in *L'Année Francophone* show. But Press comment, in both France and Quebec, remains as yet unconvinced of the value:

> Over eight years, from Paris...to Mauritius, there has been too much playing games: of declarations of principle, of resolutions subjected to interminable debate but which for the most part have remained dead letters of national sensitivities or personal concerns in the corridors, of limits on or extensions of the power of the 'operators', of hopes for subsidies from France or to a lesser degree from Canada. By playing such games, Francophonie is in danger of getting bogged down. Surely it's time to get on to the serious issues? (Le Figaro, 6.7.1994).

Representation

The fourth problem is that of bringing together and representing the role and function of the official and the unofficial organisations and associations. Who speaks for Francophonie? The Summit meetings are supported by the *CPF*, consisting of 15 'personal representatives' of Leaders of State and Government, chosen at each Summit and supposedly ensuring a distribution of membership. To counter fears that this group would be the real power-house of Francophonie, any country can also send a representative along to its meetings - and usually does! A 'Council of Ministers' (*Conférence Ministérielle de la Francophonie*), consisting of the Ministers for Foreign Affairs and Francophonie of member countries, meets regularly to oversee the work of the *CPF*. This Council acts both as a 'Follow-up Committee' (*Comité du suivi*) intended to ensure that decisions taken are put into effect, and also as the preparation group for the next Summit. It also acts as the regular discussion forum for matters arising between Summits.

Each Summit meeting has brought together between 40 and 50 countries or Governments, to discuss both the concerns of individual countries and to ensure understanding of how Francophonie can be of help. The agenda has been prepared and the follow-up to each meeting organised, in different ways, and even during and after the Mauritius Summit the organisation is subject to further readjustment. Partly this is due to the short life of the Balladur Government between 1993 and 1995. The Minister of Culture and Francophonie, M. Jacques Toubon, experiencing the meeting for the first time, showed he was quite ready for major reorganisation. In a speech to the *AIPLF* in July 1994, Toubon considered the response to the Rwandan crisis demonstrated the '*carences*'(lack of responsibility) of organised Francophonie, and proposed three solutions: meetings of 'certain' Heads of State to speak on behalf of Francophonie between the formal meetings of all; a legal structure, in the form of a loose Treaty, to unite Francophone States, perhaps retaining the *ACCT* formula of members, associated States and participating Governments; and an elected permanent Secretary General with sufficient authority to express, rapidly, the Francophone point of view. Toubon's concern about the inability of organised Francophonie to speak with one voice on important matters was echoed in Le Figaro (6.7.1994):

> Apart from France, what have the forty-six countries - mostly African - said since the Rwandan tragedy exploded? Nothing. What voice has been heard from this international institution, already consecrated by five 'Summits'? None. Why this surprising, even scandalous silence? Institutional structures are to blame...The 'Conference' has no General Secretary...the *CPF* has neither the powers, nor the people, nor the means...There is a vacancy at the head of the institution.

The main difficulty for organised Francophonie remains the plethora of official organisations, semi-public and private associations, NGOs and INGOs, and individuals who consider themselves as 'owning' Francophonie, and the consequential power struggles between them. Not least among these is the internal French problem of the unclear focus of power and responsibility between President and Government.

PART THREE: OPPORTUNITIES FOR FRANCOPHONIE

It has been generally accepted by official Francophonie that Europe and Africa are the continents where French stands the best chance of developing its role as a major language of communication, and where the values of Francophonie could be permanently affirmed (Guillou and Littardi, 1988, 259; Lafage, 1993, 215) - maybe simply because 89.9% of Francophones in the world live in these two continents (Etat, 1990, 38).

It is unlikely that Europe will be a French-speaking counterweight to America, as de Gaulle and even Mitterrand may at one time have hoped, and as even a professional linguist such as Hagège thought could still be 'reasonably advanced' (Hagège, 1987, 251). Although French is the official language of three European Member States, France must negotiate with partners who are similarly intent on obtaining national benefit, and whose culture and world influence are at least her equals, and English is after all the language of two members of the European Union. France must persuade or insist, rather than merely decreeing, that her language be used and her interests safeguarded by international civil servants who are not French; that her educational systems and the training of her diplomats be not ignored in developing new European systems; and that the realities of her economic and social situation be not submerged. Neither in Belgium not in Switzerland is French dominant, so she must capitalise on the support that she can gain from countries where French is often in a competitive situation. Nonetheless, there is a distinct and important opportunity for the language, values and practices of Francophonie in Europe. Francophonie has always been at the very heart of the European organisation, both geographically and historically, and Francophonie inspires many of the concerns and much of the practice of Europe.

Africa has the exciting potential for enormous wealth, growth and development, but also for the display of diplomatic skills in the context of humanitarian and universal assistance for some of mankind's most deprived populations. But a secure future for Francophonie in Africa is subject to a number of threats, as we have seen: instability in politics, economic diversity and underdevelopment, constantly changing relationships with the developed North, the fact that Nigeria and South Africa - the super-States of Black Africa - have an Anglophone past and indeed that English-speaking countries have a high profile, the policy of international agencies such as the World Bank or the International

Monetary Fund, and difficulties with the often self-centred international policies of many countries such as America. African Francophone countries may find in Francophonie, if not still in France, an amenable partner in maintaining or developing African cultural norms and practices in the definition of democracy, in the status of intellectual and creative life, or in approaches to social problems such as the treatment of Aids or the role of women.

Both France and Francophonie are aware that they cannot assume that these two continents are the only ones that matter. In particular, the explosive growth of Asia, and particularly of the Pacific Rim, may provide a new area for Francophonie to influence. The population of Vietnam alone is as large as that of the countries of the African franc zone, so there are immense possibilities for the growth both of French business and political links, and for mutual support for Francophonie as a separate geo-political voice (Gaulme, 1994, 52). Many of the commentators however are unclear whether such opportunities present themselves to Francophonie, or just to France. France must certainly maintain her influence if she is to continue to rate as a world power. But the legacy of colonialism has to be overcome, French influence must be constantly brought to bear and be adequately protected. For Francophonie, the potential is less defensive. Francophonie - in its linguistic sense, more so in its sense as a geopolitical organisation, and even more so as a cultural approach - could represent a different philosophy and practice for the Far East, provided that the idea of Francophonie can be kept clearly separate from the values and culture of the developed world generally.

In all three geographical areas the stakes are high for France. If she fails to maintain her separate identity in a significant world role, she will fall back to being one of a number of European States living on past glories and doomed to slow decline as her export markets dry up and her cultural distinctiveness is rejected as irrelevant. For Francophonie in all three senses - the French language, the idea of a cultural Francophone area and the organised geopolitical organisation - it is important that the world retains distinct characteristics and approaches, even if France herself plays a less significant role. Quebec - perhaps independently of Canada - Belgium's French-speaking region, Switzerland, although they depend to a certain extent on France and certainly on French, see the opportunities for increased world-wide status and economic influence. For African, Caribbean, Pacific and Asian Francophonie, the potential for a better life exists, whether simply in ease of communication, through membership of a structured international community and co-operative policies with a friendly group of like-minded nations, or through maintenance of an alternative mode of thought incorporating different and universal values.

8. AFRICA

The Opportunity in Politics

The main opportunities for Francophonie lie in possible transfers to Africa - of political experience, understanding of democracy, or of political understanding as practised elsewhere - and in working with Africa, seeing how far French can be used to link and unite, and clarifying the geopolitical role of a joint, multilateral Francophone organisation, operating on the basis of a common culture. France possesses immense advantages in these areas. She has knowledge of, and close and continuing contacts with many African countries, even though many of these started in colonialism. Since the time of de Gaulle, and quite outside the framework of world-wide Francophonie, the contacts have been systematised in both bilateral and multilateral Franco-African meetings on a regular basis. Personal contacts with African leaders have been a feature of this approach, during the Mitterrand years and throughout the cohabitation periods of 1986-88 and 1993-95. The 'African cell' operated within the Elysée after 1981 and under the chairmanship of Jean-Christophe Mitterrand until 1993, has been very influential in keeping African affairs at the forefront of Presidential thinking, although the principle of such Presidential exclusiveness had been attacked in internal reports in 1981 (the Cot Report) and again in 1989 (the Hessel Report) (McKesson, 1993), and both Chirac in 1986-88 and Balladur in 1993-95 established their own African think-tanks. France is, of course, an experienced player on the world stage, present in all the organisations and in all aspects of international relations across the globe. For organised Francophonie, too, the opportunities are immense. Francophonie could play a major role in world politics. Africa's huge population and enormous resources form one of the world's largest reservoirs for potential influence. Of its 52 countries, 24 already have close links with Francophonie and attend the Francophone summit meetings. The influence of French-speaking countries is well-established throughout the continent, and is not limited to one area alone: Francophonie affects the North (Algeria, Tunisia and Morocco); the Sahara and sub-Saharan Africa (Chad, Mali, Mauritania); Western Africa, where 12 coastal countries have or had links; the East, where significant outposts of French influence remain (Djibouti); and the Centre and Great Lakes area (Congo, Central African Republic, Rwanda, Burundi, Zaïre), where France or Belgium established major colonies during the nineteenth century.

There are hence at least five political opportunities open to France, to Francophonie, or to both: overcoming *Afropessimisme* in France and in the North generally; improving democracy and political life in Africa; working effectively with Islam; clarifying French policies towards Africa - and in particular overcoming colonialist or neo-colonialist attitudes and practices; and ensuring an effective role for the new international community of organised Francophonie itself.

Overcoming Afropessimisme

Cartiérisme and *Afropessimisme* seem to be endemic in French discussions of Africa (McKesson, 1993; Louvel, 1994). Much of this attitude derives from despair that, despite continuing aid and constant exhortation, close contacts between Presidents and the development of organised Francophonie itself as a new geopolitical force, little progress in economics or development seems to have taken place; there appears to be little gratitude on the part of Africans; and, if anything, French influence is being replaced by that of the USA. As a consequence, voices are constantly raised suggesting that France turns her attention elsewhere, and as we have seen, many investors and small firms have reduced their interest in Africa dramatically.

Afropessimisme peaked perhaps during the early 1960s, when independence was being achieved, and again thirty years later, after the realisation that the policy of supporting Africa in order to keep the Soviet Union from increasing its hold on hearts and minds was no longer necessary, that democracy needed to be redefined in Western terms and that aid should perhaps be directed at solving economic and social problems rather than at political prestige and the support of sometimes dubious regimes. The contrast between Mitterrand's 1981 speech at Cancun in Mexico in 1981, where clear support was given to the Third World and socialist idealism was the keynote, and his lecture to assembled African leaders in 1990 shows this increasing pessimism, even though the 1990 speech was characterised as 'softening-up' preparatory to a possible *FCFA* devaluation - which eventually took place in January 1994.

Louvel (1994, 8-26) devotes the whole of his first chapter to describing contemporary pessimism. He agrees that pessimism derives from French 'neurosis', but accepts that it is due mostly to the apparent failure of the aid programme, the constant changes in French policy towards Africa, the unreal ambitions and representations of what could be done, the lack of correspondence between policy and reality, and the enduring stereotypes of French representations, particularly those of the emotional 'native' and the rational 'white man'. The 'scenario' has remained the same since colonisation, and French behaviour is remarkably consistent; although vocabulary has changed - from 'exploitation' (*mise en valeur*) to 'humanitarian involvement' and then to 'development' - the reality is the same; the contrast between emotion and reason is so solidly entrenched in French ways of thinking that it provides the only clear basis for judgement of Africa; French myths and images of Africa are unconnected with the reality of the place; and although French ways of thinking, like African ones, seem solidly based, the two approaches do not coincide and lead instead to misunderstanding, lack of communication and despair.

From this point of view, the opportunity is poor, or at least long-term. Somehow France must 'think accurately' about Africa, and accept that the failure is not one of Africa but of France's understanding of Africa: 'Africa is above all a creation of our imagination, practically a virtual image arising from the prism of a Western view...the Negro has been created by the White Man' (Louvel, 1994, 194). *Afropessimisme* in France and the developed world generally has nothing to do with the success or failure of practical concerns but with French approaches to the African reality, and nothing will change until these change - which Louvel does not see as immediately likely. In this sense, *Afropessimisme* will continue unless Francophonie can develop a new set of views different from those of the French.

Improving democracy

From 1989 on, public pressure for political progress came to a head within the many African countries which had suffered single-party regimes and dictatorial systems since independence. Benin, Djibouti, Togo, Mali, Cameroon, Gabon, Zaïre, all saw large scale demonstrations, and in many of the countries of African Francophonie, the social unrest has increased in intensity and severity to the point of outright civil war or revolution.

In Sub-Saharan Africa, the colonial period had imposed frontiers and political divisions which bore no relationship to the realities of ethnic groups ('tribes'), nor to the well-developed cultural practices which had enabled the growth of large and well-organised indigenous empires, particularly in West Africa. Colonialism had destroyed local political structures by simply ignoring them, so when colonialism ended local populations were left with no history - or even simple knowledge - of how their local situations had been managed, and with administrations which required either sophisticated educational systems to provide the range of technical manpower needed, or which were dependent on a general consensus of the governed within a novel social structure. Yet independence took place generally around 1960, the colonial countries have changed in outlook since, and populations have had time to manage their own affairs. How far then has the transfer of modern political ideas been successful?

Political procedures and systems in many countries are apparently democratic, allowing periodic elections and governmental changes. Benin is the example most often quoted: President Kerekou - admittedly under French pressure - held elections in 1991 and was democratically replaced by President Nicephore Soglo. Elections - albeit held after violent protests - replaced the Presidents of Mali, Congo, and Madagascar, and major multiparty elections were held during 1993 in Burundi, Central African Republic, Congo, Gabon, Guinea, Senegal and Togo. Doubts must be expressed as to whether the retention of power in all the African countries could be called democratic. McKesson (1993, 60) listed Presidents Conté (Guinea), Eyadema (Togo), Compaoré (Burkina Faso), Cheiffou (Prime Minister of Niger), Koliongba (Central African Republic), Biya (Cameroon), Bongo (Gabon), Mobutu (Zaïre), Gouled (Djibouti) as being either one-party, manipulated or dubious election results. As one example, ex-President Carter, heading an international team of observers in Togo, left before elections were eventually held in August 1993, reelecting General Eyadema on the basis of a 15% turnout (Dabla and Lambert, 1994).

The undemocratic nature of African politics can be shown in at least four aspects: the role of the local military; constant external intervention; the role of strong individual leaders; and the 'tribal factor' - the nature of ethnic conflict.

The African military is often the only or the best organised group in the country, and unsurprisingly has imposed its will or attempted to oust political leaders since independence: in about two thirds of all cases of post-colonial violence according to Martin (1995, 78 - but written in 1988). Martin sees military intervention as following three phases: a first, moderate phase soon after independence when the military was concerned to stop civil maladministration and ensure technical competence; it generally stayed non-political, as in Zaïre, Benin, Togo and Gabon. A second, more radical phase, lasted from about 1975 to about 1985, when the military supported nationalism, changed countries' names (Burkina Faso, Bénin) and promoted what was often radical socialism and populism. In the third phase the aim was to re-establish constitutional order but also lessen the role of the State (Compaoré in Burkina Faso; Buyoya in Burundi in 1987). This third phase, roughly coinciding with Mitterrand's 1990 speech, should have spelt the end of the 'pretorian cycle' of military intervention. But Martin's caution - 'it is not possible to claim that this cycle is closed for ever' (p. 93) is well justified, with an attempted coup d'Etat in 1992 in Benin and in Togo in 1991. Burundi's President N'dadaye was assassinated in 1993 by political opponents assisted by the army. National strikes are sometimes an effective political weapon, and riots, whether for political or economic reasons, have political consequences as in the Central African Republic in 1992.

External military intervention is frequent, not always from the former colonial powers. Admittedly, some interfere frequently, not always openly, and France has been accused of providing or supporting mercenaries or secret service agents as well as intervening militarily. The Comoros, whose President (Ahmed

Abdallah) was assassinated while the Francophone summit meeting of 1989 was being held in Dakar, and which were 'helped' to re-establish order by French paratroops, had suffered particularly by the presence of European mercenaries as well as by the complexities of the local ethnic and linguistic situation, and have still not returned to any degree of political stability. But other powers intervene regularly, with the US, then the United Nations intervening in Somalia in 1994 and 1995 as only one of many examples. The purpose of intervention is the restoration of democratic processes, although often the definition of what is democracy and what is merely the support of one of the contending groups leaves much to be desired.

One characteristic of African politics is the change in the role played by strong individual leaders. In the establishment of Francophonie, in Africa as elsewhere, individuals such as Senghor, Houphouët-Boigny, Diori, Sekou Touré and others led their countries to independence and maintained a strong personal grip on the country's destiny. Charismatic leaders such as these, who made Francophonie and their relationship with France a main concern, are now rarer, but the strong leader is still a formidable figure. Houphouët-Boigny's case shows both the good side - stability - and the bad side - corruption and despotism - of such dependence on individuals. Dia Houphouët adopted the name Félix when he converted to Catholicism as an adolescent and added the family name Boigny at the age of 40. He had been a Minister in several French governments before independence; assumed the Presidency of the Ivory Coast in 1960, and was re-elected 6 times. French comments on his death show two sides of his character, as can be seen in two eulogies from the official organs of Francophonie and a less adulatory comment from Le Monde Diplomatique:

> The Miracle of the Ivory Coast, synonymous with economic prosperity and political stability, made of Félix Houphouët-Boigny a model for many Africans and for his northern partners (Lettre de la Francophonie, 68, 1994).

> This exceptional man, initiator of the peaceful decolonisation of Africa, the man of the Ivory Coast 'economic miracle', apostle of the pre-eminence of dialogue to solve social, political and economic problems, the mediator of Black Africa, the first statesman to open dialogue with South Africa, has given his name to the UNESCO international prize for peace whose first prestigious laureates were Presidents Mandela and de Klerck in 1993, Yitzhak Rabin, Simon Peres and Yasser Arafat in 1994 (Etat, 1994, 61).

> The clandestine publication of a list of '100 Ivory Coast millionaires' in 1991...associated the import-export quota recipients with major figures in the regime...the profitable import of foreign rice, allocated to the wife of the former Head of State...for several years the Opposition has

demanded the repatriation of the Presidential fortune, believed to be equivalent to the country's external debt...(Galy, M. in Le Monde Diplomatique, January 1994).

The close relationship of politics and economics was stressed by this latter article, which noted for example that:

The Ivory Coast miracle of the 1970s is no more than a distant memory: between 1986 and 1991, the rates for cacao and coffee - two thirds of Ivory Coast exports - dropped respectively by 59% and 72%...the Ivory Coast is the country most in debt in the world...because of its bankruptcy since 1991, money is provided only by the World Bank, with France paying sums due directly to it.

Significantly, too, Galy noted that the privatisation recommended by the World Bank had been profitable mainly to two French groups, Bouygues and Bolloré, rather than to any local enterprise.

An underlying component in many political changes is the ethnic identity (often referred to as the 'tribal membership') of the groups involved. Thus in Niger and Mali, 1992 saw revolts by Touareg; in Senegal separatists attempted to create independence for the Casamance area; in Chad the defeat of Hissen Habré by Idriss Deby can be interpreted merely as the victory of the northern over the southern tribes, as continuing armed conflict indicates. In Burundi President Melchior N'dadaye was assassinated in October 1993 in the fourth coup - and sixth series of ethnic killings - since the country's independence. Burundi was a particularly sad occurrence, with the assassination coming soon after democratic multiparty elections in June. These elections had removed Uprona, the party which had been in power for 31 years, to install Frodebu, the party led by N'dadaye. But Uprona was supported mainly by Tutsis, while N'dadaye and Frodebu were mainly Hutu. N'dadaye's successor, Ntaryamira, was also killed on April 6th 1994, in the same rocket attack which killed the President of Rwanda, Habyarimana.

Rwanda is the classic illustration of the descent into anarchy which characterises the African dilemma in the mid-1990s, of the role of ethnic groups, and of continuing French involvement in African politics. A Belgian colony until 1953 and fully independent from 1962, Rwanda, like Burundi to the south, contained a mixture of about 15% Tutsis (the traditional nobility and ruling class) and 85% Hutus (traditionally the peasantry). The two tribes speak the same language(s) and have the same appearance. The conflict, mainly but not exclusively between the two ethnic groups - who had been identified as such with identity cards during the colonial era - had caused refugee flows for more than thirty years between Zaïre to the West, Uganda to the North-east, Tanzania to the South-east, and Burundi to the South: 130,000 from Burundi and 25,000 from Rwanda to Tanzania in the 1970s, 300,000 from Burundi to Rwanda and a further 100,000 to Zaïre in 1993 after the assassination of N'dadaye. Indeed, the population movements to Goma in Zaïre go back to labour transfers by Belgian colonists in the 1930s, and the conflicts affect the whole Great Lakes area, although most contemporary commentators date the present Rwanda problem to the Hutu expulsion of Tutsis in 1959-61, when the Tutsi monarchy was replaced by a Hutu Republic.

War has characterised Rwanda, as has foreign military intervention. In 1963, soon after independence, Belgian troops saved the regime. In 1972 Tutsis were generally forced out in what was even then called genocide, ended by the Hutu Juvénal Habyarimana becoming President in 1973 after a coup d'état against the existing government. Habyarimina was accused of playing tribe against tribe, region against region and becoming ever more despotic during his rule, so those forced to flee came not from one but from many groups   (Le Monde Diplomatique, April 1993 - although it should be noted that this unsigned article was written by 'a Rwandan'). An ethnic quota system was supposed to ensure fair access to employment but was generally disliked. Refugees, mainly in the Ugandan camps, constantly claimed the right to return; Habyarimana's regime claimed they were more Ugandan than Rwandan, and played on the 'English' history of Uganda by contrast with Rwanda's Frenchness, in appealing to the former colonial power, Belgium, and to France. It was only after meetings in Belgium and then with Mitterrand at the Elysee on 18th October 1990, that Habyarimana referred the Ugandan 'invasion' to the United Nations Security Council.

Nonetheless, Rwanda had been quoted by many as a model new African State: economic development had taken place despite continuing poverty, many aid agencies were present, there were some Tutsi political figures, even though in a small minority: Le Monde Diplomatique (April 1993) quoted 2 Members of Parliament out of 70, one Minister and a diplomat, although there were no local mayors or army officers who had Tutsi origins.

In 1990 France intervened directly to save Habyarimana's rule when the *Front Patriotique Rwandais (FPR)* launched an attack from the camps in Uganda. The UN force which the Security Council agreed to - mainly French and Belgian - saw its role as an attempt to keep the peace, which essentially meant to broker a peace agreement between the *FPR* and Habyarimana. The Belgian paratroopers left when peace had been restored; until 1993, however, France actively supported the Hutu government led by Habyarimana, who obtained soldiers and training from France and arms from Zaïre's President Mobutu. The 300,000, mainly Tutsi, refugees in Uganda, who had both helped the President of Uganda to power and formed the *FPR* to regain power in Rwanda, also obtained their arms from French private arms dealers and on the apparently well provisioned arms markets in Zaïre, Sudan, Somalia and Ethiopia (Le Monde Diplomatique, July 1994). Other sources accuse Egypt of selling Habyarimana £4 million worth of arms, financed by Crédit Lyonnais, from March 1992 to June 1993; France of providing armoured cars and helicopters; and South Africa of selling a further £4 million of arms (letter in Observer, 9.4.1995).

Because the Tutsi refugees organised in Uganda, and particularly in the Ugandan refugee camps, English often became the language of external relations: for many leaders, the movement was the Rwandan Patriotic Front (RPF), and difference of language symbolised the ethnic conflict. Indeed, there were many accusations that Mitterrand and his African cell saw the conflict as a battle, not between Tutsi and Hutu, but between French and English for the future of Africa: 'until recently, France's choice was to repel the fantasy threat of 'Anglophonie' (Bayart, 1994). RPF support for Uganda's President Yoweri Musevenyi had enabled him to take power, although another English-speaking President, Daniel Arap Moi of Kenya, was opposed to Musevenyi and remained loyal to Habyarimana.

Dissatisfied with their lack of power, the *FPR* had attacked again in 1992 and 1993, entering the country in force at that point from the Ugandan frontier. The Arusha agreement of August 1993 between Rwandan Hutus and Tutsis was supposed to put an end to this war and to lead to the entry of the *FPR* to the Rwanda government.

The death of Presidents Habyarimana and Ntaryamira of Burundi, also a Hutu, in a rocket attack on their plane in April 1994 led immediately to what has been called genocide: the call to Hutus to massacre Tutsis. The Tutsi Prime Minister, Agathe Uwilingiyamana, and her Belgian paratroop escort were killed, provoking an immediate withdrawal by the remaining Belgian forces and civilians. As the *FPR* advanced across the country, the radio stations which had called for these massacres called for evacuation, and the flood of Hutus into Zaïre reached more than a million in a matter of weeks.

Operation Turquoise, launched by France in 1994, set up a 'safe zone' in the south-west corner of the country, temporarily preventing the further advance of the *FPR*. The intervention was supported by Senegal and Egypt with token military contingents, approved by the United Nations, 'just in time' and without notable enthusiasm, even though France was asked in August to prolong the intervention beyond that month but left on the 21st August.

The new, *FPR*, Government took over in 1994, establishing itself in the capital Kigali. The mainly Hutu refugee camps became more settled, and more and more the former Hutu Government took control of them, causing aid agencies to despair of helping: *Médecins Sans Frontières* (France) left the Zaire camps in

December 1994, the Spanish branch in April 1995, and others were 'quietly furious with the international community for putting them there and feel increasingly like political pawns' (Guardian, 5.4.1995). Hutu refugees in Nairobi, including Agathe Habyarimana, wife of Juvénal, together with the founder of *Radio Mille Collines* which broadcast the April 1994 calls for execution, and at least one former Minister, solemnly recalled Habyarimana's assassination at a memorial service in April 1995. It is probably only a matter of time before the next invasion - or return - to Rwanda takes place and before the next round of killing starts.

In these circumstances the opportunities, for France or for Francophonie to establish or to improve democracy seem slim. The most notable attempt by France to transfer Western and Northern notions of democracy to sub-Saharan Africa was the 1990 La Baule meeting between President Mitterrand and African leaders, where the French President went so far as to define the elements he expected to see present, and reinforced his message with greater conditionality for aid. While many countries quickly adopted the outward forms of multiparty elections, the net effect was not one of widespread change, and the African feeling of treachery and misunderstanding of their specificity deepened after the 1994 devaluation and the decision by the Balladur government to oblige African countries to work even closer to the World Bank norms.

Organised Francophonie has consistently taken the view that democracy without economic development is impossible, and hence that any political opportunity must be at least accompanied by economic improvement. The Mauritius Summit meeting in 1993 strengthened the political commitment of the group, its connection between democracy and economics, and its belief that the particular contribution of Francophonie lay in recognising and indeed celebrating diversity. In the final declaration the meeting declared its 'wish to strengthen the rule of law and support democratising political and civil society, (which are) conditions for durable development', and supported 'the courageous efforts by many countries of the South in their desire to achieve a fair economic system which will free energies and initiatives' (Lettre de la Francophonie, 66, 1993). Indeed, the declaration stated that

> Francophonie is a space for dialogue, co-operation and partnership in the most profound respect for its diversity. Its unity is founded on a community of values and languages, devoted to the promotion of peace, justice, security, solidarity, democracy together with respect for the rights of man and fundamental freedoms, which are universal and inalienable.

Organised Francophonie is clearly moving to take up the political opportunities its nature and status offer: to act as mediator between the Third World and the developed world; to ensure that the economic plight of African countries moderates demands for full political freedom; and that its values and approaches are recognised by all, including even France.

Working with Islam

In the North, in the Maghreb countries and in Egypt, the growth of Islamic fundamentalism appears to many people as an alternative to the lay Republics which replaced colonialism. For this analysis, the lay Republic - for example in Algeria - was itself conditioned by French Revolutionary ideals of universal human brotherhood, by French modes of thinking, and by concerns with international trade and diplomacy which were so coloured by French interests as to bear no relationship either to the nature of society as lived in North Africa or to the realities of the economic and social structures which could be regarded as appropriate. Islam offers the concept of a new brotherhood, more appropriate to Africa, and of a new simpler life based on recurring priorities: the family, daily prayer, duty to the community, coherence in the pursuit of a common ideal, and little reverence to the values of international finance. Islam is not confined to North Africa, but also represents a major religious force in many West African countries, and indeed throughout Francophonie.

But the Islamic *intégristes* are adopting violent methods in the attempt to impose their view, which often conflicts with that of Francophonie and indeed considers Francophonie - as well as France and the French language - as an enemy. Today, the growth of fundamental Islamic movements is a potential cause of tension for both Francophonie and France, since the majority of the countries of Francophonie - including France - have internal, large minorities or in some cases majorities of Muslims. French military action to restore order within the Islamic Republic of Comoros in the 1980s, the 'Islamic veil' affair at Creil in 1989, the role of the *Front National* and the changes in the Nationality Code of 1993, the moves in Algeria and France in mid-1994 to counter the growth of the Algerian *Front Islamique du Salut* (*FIS*) and the *Groupe Islamique Armé* (*GIA*), the hijacking of an Air France Airbus in December 1994 in Algiers by Islamic fundamentalists are examples of specific incidents of increasing conflict between Islam and Francophonie. Within France, North African immigration and the consequent social problems of integration have led to an association, in the public mind, of immigrants, the Muslim religion, North African ways of life and illegality or even criminality (cf. Silverman, 1992).

Algeria saw the resignation of President Chedli Bendjedid in early 1992. When his replacement, Ahmed Boudiaf, installed after elections were cancelled, was assassinated in June the government imposed draconian anti-terrorist laws aimed at defeating the *FIS*, increased austerity measures in an attempt to reduce the 25 billion US$ external debt and, while moving away from the stricter socialism of the 1970s, stoutly refused IMF prescriptions of devaluation. But 25%

unemployment and economic hardship increased political violence, and despite the capture of leaders and severe actions against them, the *FIS* is clearly not defeated - in fact targeting foreigners, educationalists, French speakers and working women in spectacular murders throughout 1993, 1994 and 1995. The Air France Airbus incident was said to be a specifically anti-Christian act, and the spirited release of hostages in Marseilles by French gendarmes showed that France was quite prepared to respond to violence with severe measures.

In Morocco (external debt: 20 billion US$) matters are less severe, although Tunisia (7 billion) has taken measures similar to those of Algeria in its attempt to reduce violence. In all three countries the post-colonial period saw deliberate policies of Arabification - of education, of the media, of public life. But these policies have been watered down in recent years - in Algeria, for example, the 1991 law imposing Arabic in most domains was placed in abeyance in mid-1992. In the Universities and in research, as in France, the importance of American English means that scientists must read and publish in English if they are to enable knowledge to grow - and if their own careers are to advance.

These actions are significant enough, but the battle between the values of Islam and those of Francophonie turns also on how each is represented. In 1989, one of the main rallying calls for the newly founded Algerian *FIS* was to finally achieve the aims of the 1962 war: to 'establish an independent State founded on Islamic principles' (Abbassi Madani, main *FIS* leader, quoted in Kepel, 1994, 220). France represented 'absolute otherness' and was constructed as the personification of evil and anti-Islam: during colonialism and afterwards she had followed a 'policy of cultural Westernisation, marked by a crusading spirit, aimed at destroying Islam'; she supported the emancipation of women, the destruction of Islamic family *mores* and secularism. Indeed, the French notion of democracy was anti-Islamic since it separated religion and politics. The sovereignty of the people contradicts the sovereignty of God: the law in Islam is the sharia, which is divine, and not open to intervention by individuals. (Political) leaders in the Islamic State might consult the representatives of the populace, but since there is no distinction between the State and religion, such consultation can bear on only some aspects of activity and is always subject to religious approval.

For Islamic fundamentalists, too, political institutions such as voting and Parliaments were means, not ends. The purpose of the *FIS* putting forward candidates for election in 1991 was to achieve the Islamic state: 'more radical activists, emerging partly from the ranks of Bouyali's companions and former Algerian fighters in the jihad against the Soviets in Afghanistan', considered the party's leaders impious (Kepel, 1994, 236).

The *FIS* obtained its support by picturing the Algerian *Front de Libération Nationale (FLN)* as led by *'enfants de France'*, brought up in the French tradition and supporting France, while only the *FIS* could ensure an Islamic solution. The technique led therefore to the 'diabolisation' of France, and diabolising a 'society, a State, a type of civilisation, a language' has much wider implications inside France and inside Francophonie. Apart from apparently approving violent methods of opposition, another way in which it could be said to affect the value system of the Francophone space lies in the notion of a (religious) community, interposing itself between the State and the individual. Traditionally, French citizenship is a matter for individuals who accept the social contract: the Republic makes no allowance for groups, communities or minorities, and justice is impartially available to individuals. To this extent, the establishment in 1990 by Pierre Joxe of the *Conseil de réflexion sur l'Islam en France (CORIF)* to act as a go-between can be said to affect one of the basic values of Francophonie, and although the *CORIF* disappeared in 1993, the Paris Mosque, set up by the French Government in 1926 to act as a channel of communication with Algerian Islam, remains, and is actively used by the French Government as though it were representative of the Islamic community.

For Francophonie, Islamic fundamentalism thus represents at least five threats: political, social, moral, rhetorical and global. It seems that for Islam, the concept of Western political democracy is simply unacceptable; violence is an acceptable means to an end; citizenship, traditionally individual on the French Republican model becomes subject to the existence of a politico-religious community 'which desires to negotiate its recognition by public authorities' (Kepel, 1994, 325). It considers such recognition to be a basic freedom, refused by 'anti-religious secularism'. Francophonie - or France, at least - cannot accept the externalisation of such a demand - for example by saying that the law of Allah is more important than that of France, as a Turkish imam did in 1993: he was simply exiled from France.

The second threat is social, rather than political. The charitable, community support fundamental to Islam may be a threat to society in times of exclusion such as those widespread today: French State grants which had been made available to Islamic support agencies but were not available to religious agencies were withdrawn on the basis that such agencies had demonstrated against the Satanic Verses and in favour of wearing the veil (Kepel, 1994, 314).

Islamic morals may also represent a threat: the sanctity of the family, Islamic laws on adultery and on the role of women are not those of French society. Islamic rhetoric, particularly in its representation of the West, is a fourth danger for Francophonie. If Francophone values are the work of the devil, and such beliefs are to be completely alien with no room for dialogue, Western concepts of negotiation, discussion, debate and compromise have no future. The main danger that Islam represents however is the totality of the global view it implies: not merely does fundamentalism see religion and the State as one and the same, it holds the view that countries may be of three types - dar el islam (an Islamic State), dar el harb (an enemy country, open to conquest and war) or dar el ahd (a country of contractual peace, where Muslims are not in conflict with authorities which do not combat them (Kepel, 1994, 207). Francophone countries upholding the values of the Francophone sphere are more likely to fall into the second than any other category.

Islam can however be regarded as a danger both to France and to Francophonie. Fundamentalists target teachers of French, particularly women teachers, because they introduce non-Muslim ideas and languages. On the other hand, the popular support for Le Pen and the National Front in France remains high - some 15% in the first round of the 1995 Presidential elections - and the prospect of France or Francophonie moving towards some common ground with Islam seems remote. But overcoming the danger of Islam and ensuring that Francophonie can work with believers in a productive future presents an opportunity: it will not be easy, despite the conciliatory attitude of some Muslims such as those of the Grand Mosque in Paris, which calls on all French Moslems to support the French State and to accept French laws and practices and reject fundamentalism. The political opportunity remains: Francophonie is well placed to be one of the few organisations which might enable a modus vivendi to be worked out.

Clarifying the role of France

France sometimes has difficulty in defining and implementing coherent policy towards Africa, and indeed, often towards Francophonie. The blame for this must lie partly in the number of different departments dealing with matters on the ground: the Presidency, the Foreign Office, the Ministry for Francophonie, the Ministry of Cooperation, the Ministry of Defence, and indeed the Banque de France with policy towards the franc zone, not to mention the involvement of many private or semi-private organisations such as the civil engineering firm Bouygues or the bank Crédit Lyonnais. But the blame must also lie with history: it has been very difficult for official France, as well as public opinion, to change and develop a new, non-colonial view. The consistency of the defence of Francophone Africa, and the fear of, and opposition to any encroachment by British, 'Anglo-Saxon' - particularly American - interests, is undeniable, and constant military interventions, the maintenance of military bases, and the domination of independent countries in the interests of France has marked much of the recent past.

Direct French involvement in the *pré carré* is undeniable. The Times (6.8.1994) somewhat sourly noted:

Unlike Britain, cash-strapped and weary of overseas engagement, or the United States, burnt by Somalia and absorbed by its own affairs, Paris has made the most of the vacuum left by the Cold War to bolster its long-standing domain in Africa and embark on a drive to project its influence world-wide by posing as a guarantor of peace.

The Times noted 'a dozen (military involvements since the 1960s) including forays into Gabon, Chad, Zaire, the Central African Republic, Togo and the Comoros'. The policy is cynical, too: 'French leaders make no bones about the *Realpolitik* behind their calculations'. 'In the interest of the Francophone family, France has used a combination of aid, military action, flattery and largesse towards leaders to prop up a string of unsavoury regimes'. As a result, France now has a calling to be a great world power: 'A century since Britain forced it to curtail its ambitions in Africa and four decades since its colonial defeats, France is emerging as the Western nation most eager to flex its military muscle and don the *képi* of gendarme to the world'.

Similar British dislike for French involvement was reflected by the Observer (9.10.1994):

France is undermining the new Rwandan government by blocking millions of pounds of European aid to the bankrupt Rwandan Patriotic Front administration. The French, who supported the previous Hutu regime in Rwanda and have been accused of training the extremists who led the genocide of a million Tutsis and moderate Hutus, are fiercely resisting what they perceive as British gains in the region... 'French policy is consistently anti-Anglophone', said Sharon Courtoux of the Paris-based human rights group Survie. 'French support for Sudan in its war with the South is an attempt to balance the supposed threat from English-speaking Egypt to the North. They're going crazy here about Anglo-Saxon influence in Africa'.

It is not just possibly jealous foreigners and journalists who condemn. Operation Turquoise in Rwanda was described as a colonial act by many French commentators, including Pierre Messmer, the former Gaullist Prime Minister, despite the protestations of the French government that its purpose was solely humanitarian. There is little doubt of French complicity with the Hutu regime both from 1990 to 1994 and well after its defeat. The list of accusations is long:

blindness of the Elysee towards the totalitarian and racist aspects of the Habyarimana regime...complicity in repression...outdated approach to the realities of African politics, fixation on an old anti-English complex (the Fachoda syndrome, which sees the Tutsis as 'Anglophones' used by an English-American plot to control the sources of the Nile!)...friendly and even family relationships between the two Presidential groups, the secrecy of military co-operation, the absence of any Parliamentary debate, the general silence over the genocide, spreading slogans from the secret services about the *FPR* who had been called Black Khmers since 1993 even though it was their adversaries who had developed *Khmer Rouge* anti-intellectual and exterminatory lines, the language of different journalists...strangely keen to defend the official line or even the Habaryimana family, and finally the ambiguity of the Turquoise operation which managed to save a few thousand Tutsis but collaborated with local administrators who had organised killing, before letting them go unharmed to Zaïre (Chrétien, 1995, 103-4).

'France will continue to play the Africa card' (McKesson, 1993, 67); 'the old colonial pact has survived for thirty years or more...France, after the withdrawal of Britain, then Portugal, has practised with finesse the art of going in order to stay' (Le Monde Diplomatique, May 1993). Le Monde Diplomatique in May 1994, on the same topic, noted:

Two of the petrol States have defence agreements with France (Cameroon, Gabon), others have military assistance agreements (Congo, Equatorial Guinea). Gabon has a permanent base, as have, elsewhere on the Continent, Senegal, Ivory Coast, Central African Republic, Djibouti and, in the Indian Ocean, Réunion and Mayotte. Long-term interventions are under way in Chad, Rwanda, Somalia, and in the shorter term and recently in Benin-Togo, Congo-Zaire, North-Djibouti, the Comoros...

Similarly, Leymarie in Le Monde Diplomatique (November 1994) commented that:

Despite the outrageous character of some of these accusations, the fact is that two socialist seven-year periods in power, accompanied by promises and hopes, have not allowed rejection of the practice of the 'reserved domain', of clientism, of conniving, of the dangerous links which have marked the nature of Franco-African relationships since the beginning of the Fifth Republic.

Up to mid 1994, French troops had been involved in 18 military interventions in Africa since 1962, many of them long-term. 15 military bases, including those in La Réunion and Mayotte off the African coast, are maintained to supply troops when needed (Le Monde Diplomatique, July 1994). France herself is nonetheless constantly reassessing her role. Leymarie (Le Monde Diplomatique, November 1994) thought the Rwandan episode and the consequential shift of the new regime towards the US and Britain:

was the most spectacular indication of the collapse of the old French 'private hunt (*chasse gardée*)'... The devaluation of the CFA franc last January, imposed by both Washington and Paris, had already been seen as 'treasonable'... The new attitude of the Balladur government since 1993... accounts for much in the feeling of abandon, of delivery bound hand and foot which many African regimes hold today; they know they can no longer count on the traditional political payoffs or on the politico-emotive blackmail which formed the web of privileged relationships with France.

Indeed, France had not neglected countries outside its traditional orbit, and although it may be alleged that self-interest is high, there is no doubt that South Africa and Nigeria have appreciated both the public and the private investment that has taken place. Nigeria, with 90 million inhabitants, is the most populated African country, and French investment in it 'is roughly equal to those in all Francophone Africa combined' (McKesson, 1993, 67).   The need to maintain military bases in Africa is lessening considerably now that Communism has ended and the former Soviet Union is no longer active in supporting client regimes, in Africa or elsewhere. The consequences, particularly economic ones, for the countries in which those bases were situated can be severe. And the progressive democratisation of South Africa, and the potential it provides for stable exchange with the rest of the world, means that France would be foolish to lose her chance to co-operate with the country which already provides 16% of African imports to OCDE countries. Similarly, the possible end to hostilities in Angola means that France must remain aware of possibilities to extend her influence to additional parts of the continent. There seems little likelihood that France will so far reconsider her role as to withdraw from the continent: if anything, the reverse is true. Nonetheless, for Francophonie in general it may represent a problem that France considers herself the 'world gendarme'. Constant intervention in pursuance of one country's interest may not necessarily suit all the countries of Francophonie, and the strains of supporting French policy represent one more burden for the international organisation.

The role of organised Francophonie

Many African States are conscious of their need for France: 'Africa has need of France more than France has need of Africa' (McKesson, 1993, 65). But for many, France is still too much of the ex-colonial and controlling power: there are great political opportunities for a new, multilateral political organisation which can incorporate the values of Francophonie and demonstrate that they are not, necessarily, those of France alone. Since for many African leaders the lack of political coherence across the continent is a major stumbling block in moves towards future development, membership of co-operative groups and integration are slowly being seen as a better way to improve than the previous reliance on unilateral contact with a European partner (Abdou Diouf in L'Année Francophone, 1992, 7). Before independence, African Francophonie was organised as two large regional federations: *Afrique Occidentale Française* and

Afrique Equatoriale Française. Regional unity may not now be a strong component in African Francophonie despite the creation of many groupings since: the *Union Africaine et Malgache (UAM)* from 1961 to 1965, the *Organisation Commune Africaine et Malgache (OCAM)* from 1966 to 1985 - both of which nonetheless perpetuated some of the bilateral links favoured by de Gaulle (Kazadi, 1991, 38). The problem is, if anything, the multiplicity of groupings: the Organisation for African Unity, the Commonwealth, the Francophone community, the African Economic Community set up by the Treaty of Abuja in 1991 and a variety of regional and sub-regional economic and interest groups.

The dependence of the African states on France is evident, and many African leaders are ready to sacrifice independence in return for aid, particularly when much of the aid enables them to salt away personal fortunes in the West or provides military defence for their own regimes. Nonetheless the European Union and its negotiations have required that the ACP (African, Caribbean and Pacific) countries co-operate, certainly in each region, and this has forced Anglophone and Francophone countries together: one result is economic groupings such as the Economic Community of West African States (ECOWAS).

If one opportunity open to Francophonie is to provide a framework to bring together many African States, the second is to ensure that such an international grouping finds friends and influence throughout the world, and persuades its own members to act collectively as a political, if not an economic, unity. A model might be the Commonwealth (Chapter 6), which effectively excluded South Africa from international respectability while apartheid was in effect, and which has forced Fiji to find new contacts and new friends after it insisted on instituting what was deemed its racist Constitution.

The political declarations of the Mauritius summit of 1993 were echoed by resolutions of the *Conseil Permanent de la Francophonie* on Rwanda on 4th and 5th July 1994, which:
- condemned with the greatest firmness the genocide and its instigators;
- called for an immediate end to the massacres;
- supported all international attempts to restore peace urgently;
- requested all conflicting parties to make an immediate cease-fire;
- requested its members to facilitate within their means the establishment of MINUAR II;
- desired the re-establishment of political dialogue based on the Arusha Agreement;
- welcomed the French decision to assist threatened populations within the framework of the United Nations mandate;

- decided to limit Francophone co-operation to humanitarian intervention, particularly through supportive funds, until a national reconciliation government is established;
- confirmed the availability of Francophonie for participation in re-establishing a legal State (Etat, 1994, 63).

Formal international statements of this type are effective only if followed - and if clearly differentiated from the policy of France. One might note in this declaration the degree of protection afforded to French policies for Operation Turquoise and for terminating aid to the new RPF government, so there remains some distance to be crossed before this is achieved. The opportunity for Francophonie generally to act in a coherent, systematic way in political questions in Africa is nonetheless helped by such declarations.

The Opportunity in Trade

(Francophone) Africa can be simply seen as a potential market, as trading partner or more frequently as a source for wealth for France. Even if such a neo-colonialist view is too simple and too cynical, economic contacts between France and Africa are more significant than for many of France's competitors. Potentially, the continent is rich, particularly in mineral resources, and the very process of its development should enable advanced countries such as France to provide know-how, the industrial base for advanced manufacture, and investment in local infrastructure. France, as an advanced country, has a well-established University and educational system which could provide an excellent service, if not a model for local developments; her administrative and management systems are extremely efficient; her experience in the economic aspects of international diplomacy is unrivalled. France could benefit herself economically, and in so doing pursue humanitarian ends. The same is true of the other developed countries of Francophonie: Belgium, Switzerland and Canada in particular.

The problems which have prevented increases in French interest in Africa are well-known at both the macro and the micro level. Macro problems are seemingly endemic: the chronic indebtedness of African countries; the marginalisation of African products in world trade; the policy of the World Bank in Structural Adjustment Programmes leading to privatisation, reduction of government bureaucracy and social expenditure; the difficulties of opening lucrative internal markets to external investment; the democratic deficit; and the population explosion. These factors, together with the increasing public indebtedness of the continent, do little to encourage private trade. The desperate public poverty of African countries colours the whole situation:

> Several countries have untenable financial situations...In the Cameroon, Senegal, and the Central African Republic, bureaucrats' salaries have

been reduced, sometimes to 20% and even farther. In addition, they are simply not paid...In the Central African Republic, back pay owed amounted to ten months (Dabla and Lambert, 1994, 212).

Nonetheless, anecdotal experience of the situation in many Francophone countries demonstrates the opportunities for private investment. Privatisation programmes give opportunities for large firms in the provision of services, for infrastructure projects in electricity, water and transport. Trade in arms, in specialist foods and drinks, and in aid-related activities continue. At micro level, the lack of (greater) interest by French investors is not for lack of opportunity, but is conditioned by political instability, lack of infrastructure, of credit, of trustworthy individuals and of trustworthy commercial practices (for anecdotal accounts, see for example Biddlecombe, 1993). Small-scale private sector investment in Africa is reducing except for specialised enterprises - of which, nonetheless, there were some 1,200 in 1992. Many of these smaller specialised firms have however been bought up by larger organisations, and it is unclear whether the same traditional relations will continue. Some of the larger groups are concentrating their effort in defined aspects of commercial operations, particularly of public services: Bouygues, for example, appears to be concentrating on buying up water distribution in the Central African Republic and electricity utilities in the Ivory Coast as a consequence of privatisation. Even the French banks (BNP, Société Générale, Crédit Lyonnais) seem to be reducing their activities in the continent (see Année Francophone, 1992, 7, 150-155). Overall, French investments in Africa were 3% of gross French investments abroad in 1989, and were concentrated in Sub Saharan Africa (80%), with the remaining 20% in North Africa. Towards the end of the 1980s, these investments decreased to become net disinvestments in many cases: 'only an exceptional investment of 450 million dollars in Nigeria maintained the average of the ten year period' (Coquet et al, 1993).

As official investments and the official economy decreases, the informal economy is increasing, 'defying the laws of Western economics and denying governments financial resources and means of action' (Dabla and Lambert, 1994, 212). As another way to avoid the problems of official economics, French and Francophone private sector links with Francophone Africa are being broadened to non-Francophone countries, as in the political sphere. Commercial contacts, particularly with South Africa, are increasing, and Nigeria, together with other countries of the oil belt, is increasingly receiving French investment. Informal banking systems, recalling the Bangladeshi Gramen Bank and linking the formal banks with rural development, have helped Burkina Faso rural development. British, German, Korean and other Asian countries are extending their involvement, although the presence of Russians has decreased massively since the demise of the Soviet Union.

The opportunities for Francophonie to develop special relationships in the economic sphere are, if anything, decreasing. The 1994 report on economics at the Mauritius Summit could end only on questions:

> Will a possible world economic upturn suffice to ensure an improvement in the economic situation of countries of the South?...the consequences of the *FCFA* devaluation could slow yet further the democratic process...countries of the South are concerned about the effect of the GATT proposals on themselves. ACP countries which are also members of Francophonie should look for support from countries which are members both of the European Union and of Francophonie. Support in the negotiations for Lomé IV will be particularly important. Will Francophonie be able to show its solidarity beyond mere cultural solidarity? (Etat, 1994, 20).

The Opportunity for French Language and the Associated Culture

The statistics of French speakers (Etat, 1990) show about 14% of 'occasional' users across Africa, as opposed to 7% in the Americas, Europe and Oceania.   While Quebec, at 6 million, is the country with the largest number of 'real' Francophones outside France, the total populations within reach of French speakers - that is, living in countries where there are already either real or occasional speakers, not just in organised Francophonie - are of the order of 235 million in Africa as opposed to only 52 million in the Americas, 73 million in Europe, 74 million in Asia, and 465,000 in Oceania. If the French language could become the lingua franca for Africa, its future would be assured. The arguments for and against such a future for French depend on past history, on a realistic assessment of the present linguistic situation, and on an understanding of the forces acting on those Africans who will eventually make the decision.

The past history is that of colonialism, among whose mixed aims was that of furthering the *mission civilisatrice* of France. This purpose could not be served by a language policy which gave any formal status to African languages, so the language policy which was implemented was that of simple substitution: French replaced local languages in every function. Not merely was the language to be used in government, commerce and education, but French methods, approaches and materials were also adopted. At the height of the colonial period, the only formal education a young African could obtain was that offered to a young Parisian: the same syllabus, the same methods, the same examinations, the same expectations in terms of spelling, linguistic correctness, range of vocabulary, reading and cultural baggage (Bokamba, 1991). The legacy that colonialism has left affects education and therefore social progress, the efficiency and effectiveness of internal government, and the relations of the African country with the outside world, including its immediate neighbours. Internal multilingualism needs to be managed, but so does the way in which the country communicates with the outside world. There are opportunities for Francophonie, in the sense of both increased use of French language and an understanding of the management of language diversity involving French.

The present linguistic situation shows a high level of societal bilingualism, as we have noted (Chapter 4). What is unusual is monolingualism. The use of French in this context represents therefore merely one more means of communication among a whole range of functionally differentiated ones, and one might expect few problems at the personal level in handling such diversity: there is no reason to attribute difficulties in economic development or in political stability to linguistic diversity. Among the most violently disrupted States in Africa, Rwanda and Burundi are also among the most linguistically unified.

The situation in many African countries is represented by a sociolinguistic 'pyramid', where the base is formed by the many ethnic groups using their languages for local communication, the second layer is formed from languages which are used by more than one ethnic group, often to respond to particular communicative needs such as commerce or political representation, the third layer is occupied by 'national' or 'semi-official ' languages - such as kikongo, kiswahili, lingala and ciluba in Zaire - and French occupies the summit as the official language of the whole territory (cf. Chapter 4; Chaudenson, 1991; Kazadi, 1991, 148). The situation is complicated by the use of French at other levels in some countries such as the Ivory Coast and Cameroon, where popular forms have developed, particularly in the urban centres, and by the widespread use of language mixing.

After independence, every African country within the Francophone orbit adopted French as its official language, with the exceptions of Guinea and Mali, where 'local' languages played some role in education. There were in effect three reasons for this, based on French tradition, on African desire for modernisation and on the fear of both some Africans and many French that tribalism would lead to political and economic disaster, and these three reasons remain as pressures on African decision-makers today.

French tradition in linguistic matters has always been to use the language to build a nation, by refusing to recognise linguistic diversity and organised or systematic diversity of any kind. Many African politicians, educated in France and, in some cases, having participated in French political life as *députés* or *sénateurs*, adopted the centralist and egalitarian politics of France, at least insofar as they affected language policy, and simply assumed that local languages had no place in independent countries whose government and constitutions were modelled on those of France. Indeed, even since independence, French-trained teachers found it difficult to abandon traditional French methods of eliminating 'patois' - wearing the *symbole*, punishments for speaking local languages in the school precincts. African desire for modernisation also saw French as the best vehicle for accessing the West's wealth. Societies which were essentially survival economies saw their future in development, and development aid, technology and knowledge were available in French and not in local languages. This view of French as the language of economic and social progress is not confined to politicians: some studies have found such a strong desire to shift to French that parents voluntarily ensure that their children learn only in and through French, not their maternal language (Breton, 1991, 168-170).

The third pressure also reflected the concerns of those in France who had considered language policy and its effects. During the rush for Africa, different European countries carved out territories as best they could, ignoring tribal, linguistic or even geographical groupings. The resultant political map of post-colonial Africa bears no resemblance to common sense, divides peoples using the same or recognisably similar languages or linguae francae, makes some new nations practically impossible to govern and others unable to support themselves. The fear was that tribal loyalties might prove greater than national ones, and that thus the use of a neutral language like French as the official language of a new nation could avoid making one of the national languages dominant, potentially offending any other tribal group and perhaps leading to warfare.

These three pressures on African decision-makers are comprehensively dismissed by some observers. Djité (1993b), for example, considers that 'Reliance and dependency on superimposed international languages to achieve development in Africa over the last three decades have proven to be a failure. Instead of leading to national unity, this attitude has significantly contributed to the socio-economic and political instability of most African countries' (149). His particular condemnation is reserved for the acculturation process involved in educating the elite in French: 'French has encouraged the acculturation of the elite and has produced intellectuals with split personalities and split societies in which there is an almost total lack of communicative exchange'. A language policy producing *tout en français pour que tout soit comme en France* (everything in French so that everything is as it would be in France) 'does not meet the basic survival needs of the majority'; and in fact, as the elite realises in the present world that French power and wealth cannot help them or their country, such a policy enables and in fact encourages that elite to turn towards a language with greater power and wealth - US English.

Kazadi (1991, 138) also notes the difficulties the African Francophone nations have had in following a consistent language policy, particularly in education. A 'new' Francophonie requiring French needs an extensive educational system. But universal education is in disarray in many African countries, and there is a great shortage of adequately trained teachers for French - as for everything else. Some disillusion about the role of French as a unifying national factor, the growth of influence of some national languages (Wolof in Senegal), the linguistic reality of multilingual states where language laws on the use of French are impractical, the question of political representation through what was in effect a foreign language - all these factors militated and continue to militate against the use of French as a simple official language in all administrative domains.

Even in demography, the population figures which show Francophonie at 140.5 million people, and actual and potential Francophones together at 235 million do not reveal quite so clearly the complex nature of the linguistic environment in which French has to survive. In most cases it is in competition with local languages, each of which identifies not merely an ethnic group but may also have functional value as a language of commerce or politics. French may also be in competition with other European languages such as English, in countries like Cameroon where colonial influence divided natural regions which are now reasserting their economic or political unity. More recently, French is in competition with Arabic, acting not merely as the vehicle for the greater influence of Arabic-speaking countries, but particularly as the 'new colonial language', according to some observers who consider that Islam's spread carries with it dangers, different but as serious as those which the nineteenth century commercial rush brought to Africa.

If Djité (1993b) is right, the complexity of the linguistic situation could be simplified if the African linguae francae regained their 'rightful' place in language policy. His argument is that the inter-communicability of many languages and dialects has not been fully recognised, and that a (comparatively) small number of languages could act across political boundaries as efficient and effective communication networks: Kiswahili in East and Central Africa; Bambara in West Africa; Pular in West and Central Africa; Wolof in Séné-Gambia; Ewe in Ghana, Togo and Benin; Hausa in Niger, northern Nigeria, Ghana, Togo, Cameroon, Benin, Burkina Faso. Such a coherent and systematic language policy could arise in the future, but would require a degree of political will and collaboration that is certainly not currently visible. The suggestion was also made in a number of earlier analyses of African vehicular languages (see Arnold, 1989, 128; Bokamba, 1991). But Arnold, along with Gueunier (1992), considers that 'French has become an African language' and in this role, as one language among many, it can claim some rights to being helpful for African development. French by itself, and certainly the European form of French, is not an adequate tool for Africans in their search for development.

Francophonie, particularly since the Mauritius Summit of 1993, has opted for 'Unity in Diversity', and most official discourse in Francophone circles now stresses the need for multilingualism, respect for other languages and use of French in those circumstances and domains where it can be of help. The opportunity for French is hence at a more moderate level than during colonialism: the expectation now is that cultural and economic Francophonie is of at least as much importance as linguistic Francophonie.

9. ASIA AND OCEANIA

There are a number of reasons why there seems to be a future for French influence and for organised Francophonie in the Pacific. Three countries of the former Indochina - Laos, Cambodia and Vietnam - were members of the empire and now attend the summit meetings of Heads of State and Government. In the Centre and South, France still maintains the Pacific *TOM*. France has a significant presence and a distinctive role in the area; there is potential for expansion and for organised Francophonie to make its values known.

Oceania

Francophonie in the Pacific Ocean is based on a scatter of small islands, the 'confetti' of the empire, often disregarded as mere dust lacking importance. But the distances are enormous: from one end of French Polynesia to the other is the breadth of Europe. This distance has led to isolation of the populations, both within the islands and from one island to another, although there is evidence that the Polynesian peoples had continuing contact among themselves, both by sending out colonising expeditions from settled islands and by travelling to assemblies. One consequence of spatial dispersion is the number and diversity of languages originally spoken: 27 indigenous Melanesian languages in seven groups in New Caledonia and the Loyalty Islands close by, and at least five languages spread across the five 'French' Polynesian island groups (Tahiti, the Society Islands, the Marquesas, the Gambier Islands and the Tuamotu archipelago) (Ruhlen, 1987, 351 and 353). The Austronesian languages, spoken across the immensity of the Pacific from Madagascar to Easter Island, and from Formosa to New Zealand, form one of the three families of island languages of the Pacific and Indian Oceans, and together account for 40% of the world's languages.

The immense spaces of the Pacific were populated by migration, starting (probably) about 1,500 BC, and originating in India, Malaysia or Indonesia. These original populations remained technically in the Stone Age, not using metal, until their contacts with European explorers during the 17th, 18th or 19th centuries. Their social organisations, based on oral culture and on family links, their understanding of their environment - its frequent cyclones, its vastness, the value of land as a resource - and finally their almost mystical imagery, rites and ceremonies, relating people to the natural world in intimate symbiosis, demonstrate complexity and sophistication. Their variety through this underlying similarity shows, too, how societies are conditioned by and relate to their environment. Faced with determined colonialists, European diseases and warfare, the survivors of these societies reacted differently: the Polynesians adapted quickly, while the Melanesians found it difficult to accept change and withdrew into isolation. The Melanesian revolts in the 1950s and 1980s, and the extent of their rejection of French domination in New Caledonia, shocked the French of the time who had simply not realised that the differences of culture and approach between themselves and the colonised groups remained significant. The Pacific, like Africa, became the site of colonialist competition in the 19th century.   Britain's treaty with the Maoris of New Zealand dates from 1840; New Guinea was divided in the 1885 Berlin conference between Britain, Germany and Holland, condominiums were set up in the New Hebrides (Vanuatu, divided between the French and British) and Samoa (at first British, German and American; then German and American). The Spanish influence (Philippines and Micronesia) decreased after 1898, while the American influence increased, culminating with the Second World War during which first the Japanese, then the American GI, American consumer society and customs had an enormous influence. The colonial powers, naturally, misunderstood the societies they colonised. The French in particular found it difficult to accept local organisations, assuming that 'chiefs' had powers they did not, and confusing local conceptions - for example of time and, particularly, of space. Distance was a fact which had not prevented regular travel, meetings of delegations from all the Polynesian islands in the Leeward Islands, nor the regular transmission of news. Despite the diversity of languages, populations were generally multilingual and Polynesian languages show a remarkable degree of uniformity, with some mutual intelligibility.

With progressive decolonisation France now stands as the only major colonial power in the Pacific - depending on one's view of American areas such as Hawaii and Guam. The Pacific, too, is the only part of the globe where France has retained more or less complete her 1930's Empire, although the status of many of the possessions has changed. The potential of this vast area for Francophonie as an international movement should be enormous, in both economic and geo-political terms, and whether or not the existing *TOM* become independent as did Vanuatu.

Economic potential

The Pacific has comparatively unexploited commercial potential. The natural resources of the islands ought not merely to support indigenous populations but to do so in comfort. To a certain extent this is so: the Polynesian population has expanded to 200,000 from 56,000 in 1946; that of New Caledonia to 170,000 as against 57,000 in 1931. But the Pacific *TOM* are transfer economies, supported by France, so there must remain doubts as to whether the economic basis could provide a foundation for Francophonie, and particularly on whether the commercial potential could ever be fully exploited - or indeed whether it should be (see also Chapters 5 and 6 above).

The 200-mile exclusive economic zone (EEZ) around each of the *TOM* and their dependent islands provides a vast reservoir for fisheries and sea-food. In total, the maritime zones around the islands account for eight million square kilometres, of which five millions are accounted for by Polynesia. These maritime zones represent 40% of France's world total, and make France the third largest sea power after the USA and the former USSR (Chesneaux and McLellan, 1992, 96). Japanese and Korean fishing vessels exploit the resources, while a European programme for increased tunny fishing is predicated on a new base in the Marquesas and the training of fishermen; most fishing is local, small scale and intended for local consumption (Belorgey and Bertrand, 1994, 88). In mineral resources, nickel mining in New Caledonia is the largest single possibility. Up to 1988, only 30% of the reserves had been extracted, and, despite fluctuations in market price and demand - which are likely to be affected by the decrease in production for the armaments industry - nickel remains an essential raw material for modern technology. Phosphates could be mined in Mataiva, but it has been necessary to compensate the islanders of Nauru for the resulting environmental destruction. Exploitation of the mineral and hydrocarbon resources of the coastal areas and the lagoons of New Caledonia and elsewhere could ensure continuing wealth, but the full commercial exploitation of both these resources - the sea and the minerals - is strongly opposed by environmentalists, whose influence is growing. The destruction of the environment that even the present extent of nickel mining has caused in New Caledonia is evidence of what might happen with full licence to extract, while the lagoons and their coral reefs are vulnerable heritage sites.

Other economic resources are however less profitable. Tourism in the Francophone Pacific has three main markets: the USA, Australia and New Zealand, and Japan. It has dropped heavily with the unfavourable exchange rate against the American dollar, and the market in Australia and New Zealand is not yet developed enough to sustain consistent profits - which, in any case, are often drawn off to international hotel chains based elsewhere. Tourism from Japan is again insufficiently developed. Agriculture suffices for only 25% of Tahiti's consumption, while the production of monoï (perfume oil) only received Paris approval and protection in 1992. The trade in cut flowers exported by air - to France, since exports to Japan are subject to strict hygiene controls and the American market has not yet been explored - is minute, black pearls (although accounting for 80% of Polynesian exports) have merely replaced copra and similar traditional trade (Dixit, 1992).

Very little of the economic activity in the *TOM* is taxed or contributes to the public finances of the *TOM* themselves. Quite apart from the lack of tax on incomes and capital, three activities which could contribute to public finances in Polynesia are the pearl trade (some two billion French francs in 1991), inheritance and capital gains taxes - on which statistics are difficult to identify - and services, on which VAT on the forty to fifty billion francs worth of activity could be considerable (Polynésie Française, 1993, 126). For the Polynesian *TOM* the transfer economy - some six billion francs in 1993 - although essential to survival,   gives a completely false picture of reality: the disaster scenario for the *TOM* generally is that quoted by Belorgey and Bertrand (1994, 108): 'down-and-outs managed by an overpaid bureaucracy' (*la clochardisation administrée par des fonctionnaires surpayés*). This falsity was underlined and increased by the creation in 1963 of the *Centre d'Expérimentation du Pacifique* (*CEP*), the nuclear test centre in Mururoa, and many of Polynesia's current problems are traced back to this period:

> The disturbance to Oceania's society was profound, destroying the local source of goods and services, providing a manna of public funds...Cultural and psychological balance was weakened at the same time as the Territory's economic base lost its foundation. The evils which dramatically characterise the contemporary disequilibrium of the territory can be dated from this time: the very weak local production compared with needs; hyperexpansion of the tertiary sector (commerce, vehicle sales, garages, all services); the explosion of imports by comparison with exports, sizeable financial transfers from the metropolis, the exaggeration of many wages and salaries and the absence of income tax (Belorgey and Bertrand, 1994, 86).

Belorgey (1993, 211) in analysing the future of the *TOMs* for the French Government, was more pessimistic than optimistic. The structural disequilibrium his group identified was made up of a range of handicaps: distance, climate, and the natural risks associated with geography, but also rising demography, where unregulated growth and lack of mobility would cause pressure on resources and social cohesion; the micro-market phenomenon, in which economies of scale were impossible; and the lack of regional co-operation, without which significant movement was unlikely. The suggestions for future French policy, as we have seen above, tied the *TOM* to four groupings: the franc zone, the French nation, the European Union, and the region. The two strategies of deconcentration of research and military units and the opening up of the *TOM* as free banking and fiscal zones both have drawbacks.

The fiscal advantages of free banking zones, and the type of investment they have attracted to Vanuatu and to some Caribbean islands, not to mention to European tax havens such as the Isle of Man and the Scilly Isles, represent a very dubious contribution to world stability and to public morality.

Deconcentration of military and research units would enable equalisation of the resources arising from the taxes levied on imports to support them, but would not help Polynesia, which learnt to depend on resources arising from the *CEP* and now is dependent on replacement handouts from France. Some resources might be devoted to the improvement of outlying islands in Polynesia. However, the stability of military and research units as a source of income for the foreseeable future must be questioned: there is nothing to stop France removing the testing site altogether, deciding to close testing permanently, or indeed, as happened in 1995 and following the military review, restarting nuclear testing for a comparatively short period and then closing it permanently after signing the Comprehensive Test Ban Treaty in 1996. Certainly, if internal autonomy were ever to become independence, France would remove the installations immediately, with instant and serious consequences for the local economy.

The matter came to a head in 1992 when France decided to halt nuclear testing. Gaston Flosse's government in Tahiti was faced, it claimed, by potential direct job losses of 5,200, indirect losses of a further 5,000, a shortfall of US$ 45 million in the budget and loss of revenue of 22% (Rapaport, 1994). After a panic-stricken Flosse met government representatives in Paris, a 'Pact for Progress' was drawn up, financed partly by France and partly by the European Union, with a share from the Tahiti budget, for spending US$ 3.2 billion between 1993 and 2003, in order to reduce dependence and to facilitate capital expenditure. As part of the deal, France 'suggested' the creation of a local income tax as an indication of the seriousness of local intentions, and a system was eventually agreed in 1993 for 'Contributions to Social Solidarity' ranging from 0.5 to 3.2% of (salaries and wages) income. The most important outcome from the situation however was that France assumed some responsibility for the local economic situation caused both by the existence of the *CEP* and by its possible closure. Some of the gloss of the agreement was later removed by the discovery in Tahiti that France had also increased payments to all the *DOM-TOMs* and set up agreements similar to the 'Pact' with them, and by the faltering institution of the tax itself, reported abandoned in mid 1994.

The lack of personal income tax, and indeed of any income-related taxes until 1993, together with both the high numbers of expatriate functionaries and the lack of a developed sense of financial responsibility and accountability by those managing the internal finances of the *TOM*, have provoked problems both with the financial basis for the *TOM* and also with the French administrators, only too painfully aware of the necessity to control but unwilling and, since decentralisation, legally unable to intervene except in dire circumstances. More, and more effective, intervention by the State, according to Belorgey, might go some way towards improving social justice and obtaining a more stable future - and, indeed, in attracting tourism and investment. Although the presence of the

French senior administrators and their capacity to take over control of internal economies is a responsibility which many participants in Belorgey's group wished therefore to see increased, unless the *TOM* themselves cope with corruption and take full responsibility for the management of their financial affairs they will be constantly attracted by a dependency framework and by the belief that France will not wish to see their situation deteriorate. But local income taxes, complete financial responsibility and a restructuring of relationships with France - necessary anyway, once the full consequences of European Union support are realised - would still leave the Pacific *TOM* in economic difficulties. Independence from France would, at least in the short term, and assuming a similar fate to Vanuatu, make the economic situation worse. Whatever opportunity may exist for Francophonie in the Pacific, a better economic future lies in close association and a necessary continuing economic dependence on France.

Strategy and geopolitics

French world strategy is predicated on the basis of being a medium-sized world power, and this aim was reaffirmed in the 1994 review of military strategy and defence capabilities and the 1995 report by Admiral Lanxade (Libération, 6.6.1995). Her global strategy requires that France maintain independent nuclear capability, under her own control, tested and perfected on French territory. 'France, as a power present in the Pacific, intends to make her own sovereign decisions there on matters affecting her national interests' (Mitterrand, 1985, quoted in Chesneaux and McLellan, 1992, 97). Mururoa, the nuclear testing site, is hence the key point for the whole of French global strategy, and denuclearising the Pacific would mean removing France from it. Independence for Mururoa (which was transferred to French sovereignty from being a dependence of Tahiti in 1964) might have consequences for the independence of other French possessions, particularly New Caledonia.

To maintain her presence, France deploys large-scale land and sea forces in the Pacific: the fourth largest fleet after those in the Mediterranean, the Atlantic and the Indian Ocean; units allocated to the *Force d'Action Rapide* (*FAR*), law and order forces (*CRS, gendarmes*). These are nonetheless sovereignty forces rather than an effective offensive or even defensive army, trained and equipped to repel any possible attacker - and who would that be, anyway?

Sovereignty forces, and those dedicated to internal control and police duties, are limited in size and equipment. In New Caledonia in the difficult period of 1986-8 French forces amounted to only 8,000 men for a total population of some 160,000, while Papeete brought in limited military forces from Nouméa in 1987 and 1991 to control independence movements. French naval units constantly patrol the Pacific, but the major units - the five aircraft carriers and the attendant battle vessels - are usually retained in the Mediterranean. Support arrangements (including a large-scale dry dock) exist in Tahiti, together with a large military airport on Hao. But the civil airports scattered throughout French Polynesia are intended for smaller aircraft, and even the major airport in Tahiti represents a tight landing for jumbo jets, as Air France found to its cost in 1993 when one of its 747s ended up in the lagoon.

Nuclear testing in the Pacific has been extensively condemned by the Pacific countries and regional organisations, particularly the South Pacific Forum. This group, formed in 1971 by Fiji, Tonga, Cook Islands, Nauru and Western Samoa, and later joined by Australia, New Zealand, and others, was set up in distinction to the South Pacific Commission which grouped the colonial powers. The Forum declared the Pacific a nuclear-free zone in 1985, and has supported independence for New Caledonia since 1986. Its continued opposition to testing was reaffirmed in June 1995, when the possibility of tests restarting emerged, and particularly in June 1996, when an official delegation including Australia, New Zealand and Japan tried to obtain a reversal of the decision in Paris and violent protests against French action spread through the South Pacific. France herself had tried hard to defuse such Pacific regional opposition, gaining Forum approval for the New Caledonia Matignon Agreements of 1988 and trying to gain support for its nuclear policy, by propaganda, public relations (New Caledonia houses a French Language Institute intended for Australian and New Zealand students) and by providing aid to the region to encourage collaboration with the *TOMs* and regional countries (Chand, 1993, 72). Fiji, for example, after its coup d'Etat in 1987 and its new racist Constitution, was barred from membership of the Commonwealth, and France almost immediately increased military and financial aid (US$ 1.9m in 1987, 10.2m in 1988), extending to a 1993 military exchange scheme and agreements for defence training. Joint naval exercises with Fiji, Tonga and the USA took place in 1993. Chand (1993) considers these moves by France to be outright attempts to purchase the co-operation, or at least silence, of the South Pacific nations, in the face of unchanged French policy - the 1992 suspension of nuclear testing came about in response to the US and Russian moratorium, not to the protests of the Forum, policy on *TOM* independence has remained unchanged, and President Chirac and the French government have remained unmoved at protests against resumption of testing. The increased aid to Forum countries, declared at US$ 42 million in 1994, half through the European Union (Le Monde, 5.8.1994), and increased investment in the *TOM* seem to be purchasing Forum approval for continued dependence of the *TOM* on France. As a result, New Caledonia's independence movement is in danger of being ignored by the Forum. The 1994 meeting 'barely mentioned France'; Mr Keating (Australian Prime Minister and spokesman for the Forum) said that New Caledonia's independence was 'not a matter for the Forum' (Le Monde, 5.8.1994), and the matter was not discussed in the plenary session.

Geo-politically, France retains the *TOM* in order to enable her to play a global role. The motivation is therefore essentially pursuance of the Gaullist design, or more cynically, one of glory and grandeur for French politicians. Whether more glory, and more grandeur, would come from independence for the *TOM* and their support as part of Francophonie for a global Francophonie, perhaps with a unified or at least agreed policy of international relations, is difficult to assess. Certainly independence in the British Commonwealth has not had a bad effect on worldwide 'Anglophonie', despite the longer existence and larger number of participating countries and populations in the Commonwealth. But international Francophonie would necessarily operate differently, and the presence of new, independent countries in its internal groups and in organisations such as the United Nations could provide greater credibility for Francophonie. At the moment, and as with the economic situation, the geostrategy of Francophonie is that of France, and it is difficult to see how it could be otherwise.

Vanuatu

Vanuatu is a member both of Francophonie and of the Commonwealth. As the New Hebrides, it was a condominium, controlled by both Britain and France, and its independence in 1980 was brought about mainly at the insistence of the British. Indeed, local French settlers petitioned Paris to remain French citizens after independence, and New Caledonia's French administrators - and the Melanesian politicians there - regarded Vanuatu as a dependence of New Caledonia itself and wanted to continue this relationship (Aldrich, 1993, 215). Prior to independence, and indeed since about 1960, both the Anglophone and Francophone authorities engaged in what can only be called manoeuvring in the hope that 'their' political party would take control of the new country. There had been increased educational spending, particularly by the French, the rival Churches were active - both political groupings were led by priests - and regional countries including both Australia and the French in New Caledonia expressed interest in the future of the country.

The Anglophone and Protestant party, Vanuaaku Pati (VP), led by Walter Lini, obtained power in 1979 just before independence, opposing the Francophone *Modérés* (Union of Moderate Parties). A group of French settlers and French-educated Melanesians, led by Jimmy Stephens and backed by an American libertarian group - and secretly approved by the last French Commissioner - declared the independence of the island of Santo, forcing France and Britain to send a joint military force there. This was replaced in late 1980 by soldiers from Papua New Guinea transported by Australian planes. Stephens was arrested (and only released in 1991) after the PNG soldiers attacked his camp. From 1980 to 1991 Lini was actively opposed to French influence. He 'was a supporter of Independent and Nuclear-Free Pacific, of Kanaks in New Caledonia, and expelled three French Ambassadors in a row for supporting the UMP' (Buckley, 1992).

> The VP approach to political life promoted discontent and disunity...the VP regime seemed to be systematically set on a course towards Anglicising the State...no more than ten per cent of the civil service was constituted of Francophones...no cabinet member was Francophone...external advisors were almost entirely Anglophone. A hostile foreign policy was projected against France's presence in the Pacific (Premdas and Steeves, 1994, 68).

Only in 1992 did the French officially return to Vanuatu after a new Francophone Prime Minister (Maxime Carlot) had been elected in 1991, in a coalition government then still containing Walter Lini. The 'return of the French', in a 'great grey warship' paying a courtesy call to the island of Santo 'from which hundreds of French residents were deported following the Santo rebellion' (Buckley, 1992) marked the return of Vanuatu to more normal relations with France: the new Prime Minister was welcomed to the Francophone Summit in 1991 with rather more warmth than that accorded to Lini; 'most political appointees are now French speakers'; and France, in return, allocated financial support (channelled through New Caledonia), cancelled external debt and promised the return of teachers and doctors. The Linis (Walter and Hilda) and their party left the coalition in August 1993, condemning the Carlot government for placing more importance on the link between Vanuatu, the French and the French Community in New Caledonia and Tahiti.

Vanuatu, although a small country, is a microcosm of the problems facing France in retaining influence and a global policy in the post-colonial world, and of the stress within Francophonie on the role of France. The opportunities - for economic development, for political influence, for support - are comparatively small, and it hardly seems worth while for a large independent, wealthy country like France to spend so much time and effort courting a small, remote island with few resources and little influence. For some commentators, as we have seen, the contacts with Vanuatu are merely reflections of a world-wide policy of opposition to Anglophone - 'Anglo-Saxon' - influence, whether this derives from Britain, Australia or the USA. For others, it is an indication of the importance France attaches to world influence, no matter how small the country concerned. For others again, the quarrel between Anglophones and Francophones shows how the effects of colonialism continue: 'the heritage of the Condominium, and the cross-currents of the colonial era, have not disappeared from Vanuatu' (Aldrich, 1993, 239). The opportunities for France are few; those for Francophonie seem to be brighter. Vanuatu has rejoined the Francophone community; Francophones are reinstated in public life and French influence is welcomed again.

Asia

The Pacific Rim has been recognised as an area of phenomenal growth for the last decade, and the 'Asian Tigers' have become a recognised category in economic statistics. The opportunities for French interests to capitalise on this economic growth, whether direct or through French Polynesia, should therefore be great, a point that was recognised by visits from senior French politicians, including the then President Mitterrand, during 1992 and 1993. On 3rd February 1994 President Clinton lifted the total embargo on trade with Vietnam, which had lasted for almost thirty years. International credits totalling 1.86 billion US dollars followed, as did private investment, visits from trade delegations and a general rush of potential economic activity - although much investment from Japan, Korea and Taiwan had already been made, and factories, golf courses and hotels built (Le Monde Diplomatique, April 1993 and April 1994).

The Vietnamese economy is growing rapidly: an increase of 8% in GDP in 1993 for the third successive year, a low inflation rate (5.2%) and a rise in the exchange rate of the dong to the dollar.   Vietnam's economic potential is significant. Petrol production - helped by Total and Elf Aquitaine, among others - is increasing and is intended to reach 30 million tonnes per year by the year 2,000. Reliance on exploitative industries, involving the destruction of forests and rare animals - and characteristic of Third World countries in desperation - is decreasing. The foundation of economic recovery has been the small agricultural exploitation, providing 95% of production. But the current boom is concentrated on rapid growth of the urban economy and on the modernisation of industry.

Vietnam is however not yet in the Asian Tiger league: despite massive redundancies in the public sector, the Army (as in China) still runs a large number of businesses, the public industrial sector is still large and increasing, and private businesses are still mainly joint ventures with the public sector. Despite Vietnam's history, labour conditions and the public sector are both comparatively unprotected, and indeed strikes took place during 1992 and 1993 in protest at the exploitation by Taiwanese businesses and at the reduction in monthly minimum salaries from 50 to 30 US$ equivalents. The main brake on development is the lack of appropriately trained Vietnamese key personnel, and recruitment of foreigners extends to middle management. Reform of the educational system, and increased investment in it (up by 10% in 1994), will eventually provide linguists, natural scientists and social scientists, all without ideological education in 'Stalinism', and all able to contribute to the new privatised economy. Vietnam is hence 'open' to external investment - 75% of the total 2.2 billion US dollars of investment in 1993 came from outside the country. The profitability of such investment is undeniable: shirts, retailing in France at 250 francs, cost 5 francs in Vietnamese labour costs. France clearly has a role to play in this scramble for profits, and the visits of politicians in 1993 underlined this. But for 1993, investment in Vietnam still came principally from Taiwan, Hongkong, South Korea and Australia. France was seventh in the list. From 1994, after the lifting of the US embargo, it is expected that the principal investors will be the USA, Japan and France.

Whether the Vietnamese response is other than cordial towards France is unclear. Contacts between France and Vietnam have always been marked by a strange love-hate flavour, quite unlike that which characterises relations between France and Africa. In the twentieth century, writers like Malraux ostensibly attacked the colonial system in Indochina but in fact supported widespread (and later, more specifically Gaullist) views of an ideological, culturally-based world approach to the dissemination of universal French/humane values. De Gaulle's advocacy of Vietnamese independence after French withdrawal in 1954 looked on Indochina as 'the last dramatic example of France's consistent effort to use her colonies to sustain a certain idea of France which is so important to the nation's self-esteem' (Raymond, 1991, 66). Despite the violence of the decolonisation process, and perhaps because France's later role in supporting independence from America and her refusal to wholly support American involvement, Vietnam has retained contact with Francophonie and indeed attended the Summits since their inception. More recent contacts with France have been close, although solicited more from the Vietnamese than the French side (Daniel, 1992), so renewed friendship with the USA may not mean reduced friendship with France. The potential for growth within Francophonie is great.

There remains the 'Anglo-Saxon' danger, and the danger from the possibility of excessively jingoistic French policy. Vietnamese relations with America are, perhaps surprisingly, cordial: Nguyen Duc Nhuan, writing in the Monde Diplomatique (April 1994), notes the revival of memories of Vietnamese-American co-operation in 1945 to remove Japanese invaders - and the remaining French (Vichy) occupiers - of the country. It is undeniable that in Vietnam, as in Cambodia, younger generations see relations with the English-speaking world as central, and sometimes resent being obliged to accept the conditions of French help:

> Some 250 Cambodian students demonstrated and burned tyres last week in protest at the use of French as the teaching medium at Phnom Penh's Institute of Technology...This is not the first time that Cambodian students have demonstrated against their French-language education. More than 1,000 took to the streets in 1993 to demand English-language courses...French support for the rebuilding of Vietnam, Cambodia and Laos is aimed at recreating a Francophone zone in South-east Asia of the type which formerly existed in French Indochina. Its support...came with the proviso that French be the main or sole teaching language (Times, 12.5.1995).

For some politicians this problem is not the fault of Francophonie. In 1993, Michel Guillou, head of *AUPELF-UREF*, the operator responsible for funding the Phnom Penh Institute, suggested that the protest was instigated by the CIA in order to counter French influence in the region. M. Toubon, then Minister for Culture and Francophonie, called for the Prime Minister to reprimand the French ambassador to Cambodia, who had been reported as agreeing that Cambodia was 'not Francophone'. Even Libération (27.12.1994), in reporting these matters, noted that

> business in Vietnam is mainly conducted in English...France has a tendency to confuse policy for Francophonie and policy for France...Wouldn't it be better to try and understand the Vietnamese - and more widely the South-East Asian - position, to implement a policy whether or not it was Francophone or French?

In Asia, the opportunities for Francophonie may still be fragile; they certainly still require considerable input from France, and it is by no means clear whether the countries of the former Indochina still see clear advantage in Francophonie.

10. EUROPE

With the exception of Switzerland, European French-speaking countries - Frontier Francophonie - all form part of the European Union, and France herself was a founder member, playing a central role in the creation and closer integration of Europe. Much of the work in creating Europe has been done in and through French, using French methods and traditions, drawing on French-inspired law and administrative practice. The European institutions, the approach and culture of European legislation, the priorities and concerns of European politics, derive from models, perceptions and structures which have been heavily influenced, if not formulated, in Paris. If Africa is one site which must be defended for French and Francophonie to survive, the other main one is Europe. Ideally, too, Europe, in order to underline its cultural difference from the United States (in particular) should use a European language in which all citizens would be competent. The 'cultural exception' of the 1993 GATT negotiations, applied to the totality of European culture, would thus make very clear European desires to be distinct from Anglo-Saxon - seen as non-European - domination. Hagège's view is that the role of French in the European Union will benefit from the 'development of cultural demands, in a reaction of lassitude in the face of the insolent madness of profit'. It could also act as a federating agent between the specific domains of interest of English and German. French could play the role of European language to perfection:

> The absence of any policy for domination on the part of modern France, added perhaps to its decreased power, imply guarantees, while at the same time they allow French to be something more than a convenient Esperanto. French, today, is at Europe's disposal, as a language well placed to give voice to a great shared design, since, despite the presence of Great Britain which renders the situation complex, the adoption of Anglo-American would remove much of the persuasive force of the Community in building its independent identity (Hagège, 1987, 251).

Not merely could French have this internal integrating role, but, because it is spoken on all five continents, 'is the only (language) which can be an alternative to English as a route to internationalisation' (Hagège, 1987, 208).

Enlargement of the Community, and potentially its transformation into a more Federal State or integrated Union, may damage this pre-eminent role. In addition, if present policies continue and if present-day linguistic nationalism prevails, the attempt to use a large number of working languages in the Union institutions will be so inefficient as to cause breakdown. Many Anglophones are content to leave the 'market' to operate, which will naturally advantage English as the main working language and possibly as the eventual lingua franca for Europe; in order to protect the future of French, French traditions of language planning and control assume that central direction is required in the institutions but possibly also more widely. In order to do this, France and Francophonie may have to support a policy not for French alone, but for a range of languages.

The Opportunities for French as the European Language

The role that French would apparently like is hence firstly, that of official language of the institutions and hence of the government of the Union; secondly, a role as language of international communication and foreign affairs; thirdly, a role as symbol of European identity; and fourthly, a role as vehicular language for communication by the population of Europe in commerce, tourism and in all contact situations. What other languages could play these roles? English is well established in the last; in the first, French was at least until the early 1980s the first choice but is now more and more attacked by English; in the second, English, French, Spanish and possibly Portuguese could be of major importance; in the third, Europe is only at the beginning of developing any concept of common identity.

An official language

French has been in danger of replacement by English in the first role ever since the entry of Britain to what was then the Common Market, in 1973, even though Prime Minister Heath is said to have agreed with President Pompidou that French should remain as Europe's main language and that for example all seconded British Civil Servants would use French. Still, in the 1990s, French retains the first position, but only just. Legally, all the languages of Member States are official languages; in practice, French and English are most widely used and some institutions have instituted linguistic regimes of their own. Practice varies according to the institution, although the cost of multilingual communication is high: 1% of the European Union budget is already devoted to interpreting and translation; 20% of Commission staff, 50% of the Parliament's and 80% of those of the Court of Justice are employed in language work (DGLF, 1994, 103). Even as late as 1991, French was essential for Civil Servants, even though recruitment did not require French. Normal career development was practically impossible without mastery of French. In communication with the Press and the public, language use was nonetheless evolving towards English.

> With the Press, in particular, the quasi-exclusive use of French is fragile after the arrival of journalists from third countries, particularly Americans and Japanese, and with increased interest from British newspapers (Etat, 1991, 225).

By 1995 the situation had become more difficult in the Commission. Jacques Delors as President of the Commission up to 1994 used his own language in speaking to the Press, and it is said that Mitterrand insisted his replacement had to be a Francophone to keep this public face French. Jacques Santer is notably less insistent on using French alone than was his predecessor. Official spokesmen have traditionally always used French and provided translations, and a March 1994 official request to use French and English on an equal basis was only just fended off at that point - 115 accredited journalists use French, 275 English, the 400 others markedly preferring English. At working level in the Commission, more than 10,000 meetings needed interpreters in 1993. Some significant Directorates have tended to use one language only - English (external relations, transport, science, research and development, telecommunications). Across the Commission, in 46% of official written documents French is the drafting language for 46% of written documents; 40% use English and 10% German. Written answers prepared for the Parliament in French have dropped from 72% in 1990 to 62% in 1994. English has mainly been used for new programmes directed at former Soviet bloc countries, and English is creeping into even such traditionally French domains as agriculture. It is unlikely the Commission will be able to stay Francophone for much longer.

The Court of Justice has always used all the official languages for documents and proceedings, but since judges must retire to consider their verdicts, without interpreters present, the exclusive use of French in this role is likely to continue: one inevitable consequence is that all documents must be translated into French. Council of Ministers' meetings and those of officials in preparation for them, particularly of the Committee of Permanent Representatives (COREPER), use mainly French and English, often to the disgust of those who must rely on interpreting services - which are not always available, and on some occasions have relied on interpreters using their third or fourth languages. But French retains a strong presence as drafting language for 66% of documents (against 78% in 1990). In the Parliament, in practice English is more and more used since it is the most widespread lingua franca, although the official regime uses all official languages and all documents are translated.

Further enlargement of the Community, its conversion to the Union, and integration of a range of policies, make the danger for French worse, as most French commentators have noted (cf. Hagège, 1992, 120; DGLF, 1994, 106). The policy of decentralisation for new Agencies enables them to determine their own policy, and work in the compliance field uses only five: English, French, German, Spanish, Italian. A 1994 French Government initiative attempted to apply this rule in all Agencies, in many cases expanding working languages from de facto English, and as part of a generalised onslaught to create a multilingual Europe. Vigorous Dutch protests mean there is some danger that the

Agencies may pronounce an official policy of using all the official languages but in effect limit themselves to English.

The *Délégation Générale à la Langue Française*, in its first report to Parliament in December 1994 (DGLF 1994) from which many of the statistics in this section are taken, was nonetheless reasonably content with the present position.

An international language

In the second role, that of international contacts and external communication, Britain's entry brought much closer to the decision-making centre of Europe her own contacts with English-speaking countries outside Europe, a tradition of internationalism, and a language of international diplomacy and above all trade. Spain, too, has claims to importance, an external reservoir of speakers greater than that of Francophonie and a world-wide spread greater than that of French, with local populations in South, Central and North America which have developed popular forms of the language and in which there is no question of the language being restricted to the elite.

But it is essential to remember the facts of linguistic development: a language of international communication is necessarily adapted and transformed by its users; it cannot remain monolithic and static. English will break up into a variety of regional and functional forms, and already shows signs of doing so in its US, Australian, Indian, scientific and commercial forms. In this process, the lack of a protectionist policy, or of a defensive attitude towards a monolithic, correct, form of English, is an advantage for the wide use of at least a form of English. But it also follows that, eventually, the creation of regional and functional forms, less mutually intelligible, will lower the value of standard British English as the international language for the whole of Europe. If French wishes to be a language of international communication it too could suffer the same fate. So the dilemma is clear: either French can remain standard French and necessarily remain a language of limited communication; or it can lay claim to wider use and accept both modernisation and regional fragmentation.

Calvet (1993, 142 - 69) assessed how far English really is a danger to French in international communication. He used two statistics: speeches in the United Nations and scientific communication. In United Nations debates English was used for 44.8% of time, French for 16.88%, Spanish for 12.98% and Arabic for 11.68%. Secondly, between 1800 and 1980, while scientific publications in English have risen from under 40% to nearly 80%, those in French have dropped from 30% to barely 5%. English is growing as the language of international communication: French, if anything, is maintaining its second position - growing, but not as quickly. But the legal situation in all international organisations is still favourable to French, where its situation as official language is nowhere in jeopardy, while 'French is spoken in debates in greater proportion than the proportion of speakers of French in the world' (Etat, 1991, 251). Although in informal meetings in the United Nations as well as in Europe, in situations where speed and practical utility demand instant communication, English is becoming the normal language of interaction, French still offers Europe the opportunity of being an alternative. The opportunity is strengthened by the opening up of Eastern Europe, where the recent admission of Bulgaria and Romania to Francophone institutions augurs well for the further spread of French. Significantly and despite this, Romania, along with Vietnam and Albania, has opted to communicate with the United Nations secretariat in English, despising their own preferred diplomatic language. Indeed, French is the preferred language for only 50 of the 184 UN national delegations.

In scientific communication, Calvet's pessimism seems equally justified. Quite apart from the fact that the prestigious *Annales* of the Pasteur Institute became 'Advances in Microbiology' in the mid-1980s, French science and scientists have mostly adopted the practical route to career progression and scientific advance by publishing in English. Despite the attempts of the 1994 Toubon law to punish those holding conferences in English on French soil by withholding official grants, and make publishing grants available to those publishing in French, the tendency seems set to continue.

An identity symbol

Most newspaper comment in recent times in France has stressed the unique contribution the French language makes to the awareness of French identity, and could make to a separate European consciousness. The arguments for the cultural exception to the GATT negotiations turned on this question, and particularly on opposition to the 'new world order' and American hegemony (cf. L'Express, 14.10.1993).

Opposition to American - rather than British English - is the corner-stone of the cultural identity argument. English is seen as merely a version of American: 'English is no longer the language only of England, it has become for the whole world the language of America' (President Pompidou, quoted in Le Monde des Débats, July 1993, 24). American is a symbol of the end of the identities of those who formed it; it conveys and imposes a foreign culture, represents a way of life which is not European, is a road roller compressing everybody in its way. The convenient label 'Anglo-Saxon', widely used in preference to either American or English, can thus apply as a blanket negative to language, policies and culture, and often seems to lead many French and Francophone politicians to both misunderstand the variety of English-speaking countries and their very different policies, and to condemn a non-existent, monolithic imagined identity, represented as a united, dominating presence. American culture thus can be condemned for its aims of standardising cultural productions - cinema, television, books - according to economic rather than cultural priorities:

> the key to this world conquest lies in American will to please the greatest number, to do everything possible to succeed and earn lots of money...to fabricate a best-seller, they have efficient recipes: (in writing schools) writers learn to keep interest high, to construct well-managed plots...we make art, they make shows (L'Express, 14.10.1993, 34).

'Anglo-Saxon' culture

> sees history and society as made up of singularities without any pretence at universality. It would be impossible to interest the English in the question of "a language for Europe". They do not need it, and perhaps do not understand the point of the question (Eduardo Lourenço in Le Monde des Débats, July 1993, 25).

Chapter 4 above traces the danger English language and culture represent for French, and the range of arguments French writers deploy against the 'invasion'. The same arguments are used in opposing the use of English as the European language. But in what sense could French be representative of European identity? It is, after all, only one of many languages which could apparently lay claim to represent Europe: Spanish, Italian, and certainly German have at least as much claim to be at the centre of the European ideal. Linguists and others have reviewed the arguments for one language against another (Coulmas, 1991) and Posner, for example, has proposed a mixture of English and Italian as interactional languages against a background of 'passive multilingualism with polyglot exchange' (Posner, 1994, 31). For the support of French, arguments tend to group into those which find in French a range of inherent qualities - of clarity, precision and subtlety - which render it a unique means of communication; those which lay claim to universality and humanism as innate qualities both of the language and of its culture; and those which see it as most representative of the European spirit. Confusingly, one such argument is based not on universality but on difference: the Mediterranean peoples, 'the natural representatives of Europe', are unique and different, and 'French is the ideal language of difference, the non-aligned language' (François-Bernard Huyghe in Le Monde des Débats, July 1993, 24). A number of similar arguments are also assembled by François-Bernard Huyghe in the same article:

> French is quite simply the most widely spoken mother tongue in the Europe of the Twelve...the Treaty of Maastricht was signed three times in French and twice in English...functionaries live in Brussels and Strasbourg...French has been a European language since the XIIIth century...we have a responsibility towards the 100 million speakers of French in Francophonie...French is a link between all the identities of the countries bordering the Mediterranean...French is a symbol of modernity and diversity.

Whether French - or any other single language - will eventually become 'the' European language in this role of identity symbol is far too early to tell. Before the question can have any real impact, European institutions will have to devise answers to the range of problems already posed: the role of regional languages such as Breton or Welsh, strongly supported as identity symbols in their own right; the role of immigrant languages - the Turkish of a German national, the Arabic of a French citizen, the Urdu of a British old age pensioner born in Britain. For Calvet, all too often questions of language policy at this level are

> attempts to use Europe to settle problems of States, to profit from the construction of Europe to tackle questions which it has not been possible to solve elsewhere: a sort of recognition of failure and postponement of decision-making (Calvet, 1993, 186).

A vehicular language

Europe needs to be able to communicate in such a way that the barriers caused by lack of comprehension are minimised. Within each country and language area, this is hardly a problem. With growing international trade and cultural contact, citizens of Europe should be able to communicate in at least one other language; but with the present pattern of language teaching in the Union, it is most probable that this vehicular language will be English, that children in non-Anglophone countries will learn no other language, and that English children will see no reason for learning any foreign language at all.

A vehicular language is one that enables comprehension

> in limited domains, which can be exchanged between languages without the objects changing in sense or content...a vehicular language requires precision in order to be useful and efficient...it is pragmatic and precise, intends to be objective, is reduced to a range of single meaning units which do not permit any simultaneous meaning...it knows only one reality, one truth. Man, in it, is one dimensional (Lens in Le Monde des Débats, July 1993, 13).

For some commentators (Minc, 1989; Calvet, 1993, 151; Hagège, 1992, 43) this is inevitable and the obvious consequence is that all European children should be encouraged, if not required, to learn two foreign languages at school: English - to act as this vehicular, and simple, means of communication - plus one other. If Britain and Ireland wish to retain their monolingualism, then national policies elsewhere in Europe - similar, for example, to the 'Toubon law', and requiring that the national language be used in working environments within the country - would give Britain and Ireland a motive for changing the policy if they wished to increase their European export trade.

Not everybody shares this view: Hagège (1987, 205) recommended that France simply dismiss many teachers of English in order to appoint teachers of other languages. Either way, and whatever the methods proposed, diversification of the languages taught in France is recommended, as is respect for the diversity of languages found in France (including those of her immigrant workers) and in Francophonie.

Is there any likelihood that French would be able to act as the European vehicular language? All the arguments in France tend the other way: towards decrying the nature of vehicular languages, and towards stressing the multidimensional nature of French and its richness, rather than its practical use. The belief, despite much work on the creation of *Français fondamental* during the 1960s and 1970s, is that 'basic French' does not exist and could not - or should not - be invented. The consequence is that French remains, for foreigners, difficult to learn, and Calvet (1993, 157) points out the contradictory nature of the position that tries to spread French and at the same time to protect its inherent difficulty. One can either have a monolithic standard French and defend its 'quality' or one can open French to the dangers of simplification and thus destroy its very genius. The history of languages shows that it is impossible to combine the two.

Rearguard Action or Real Opportunity?

Most of the discussion in this chapter has reflected the tenor of the discourse in France, which sees danger and attacks on French, and proposes a rearguard action to protect French, and hence France if not Francophonie. This Franco-centric approach, indeed, sometimes becomes almost frantic, so strongly are opinions held and defended against enemies, both real and imagined. The French Government report in 1994 saw an international plot, the affirmation of a 'veritable anti-Francophonie':

> A current of thought, attitudes and behaviour which criticise or condemn the construction of an international Francophone community and deride the desire of Francophones to pass linguistic legislation and defend their cultural identity, notably by their support for cultural exception in the free exchange of goods (Etat, 1994, 514).

The Anglo-Saxon press

> regularly produces venomous articles laughing at and ridiculing the supposed archaism and narrow-mindedness of Francophonie's vigilance and consistency...Such excessively free-market, globalist and uniformising conformity is shared by part of the French Press which religiously reproduces the slightest attack on Francophonie...we've even seen an Italian newspaper liken the Toubon law to Fascism! (Etat, 1994, 514).

Despite such paranoia, and the protectionism to which it leads, there remains the serious question of whether there is an expanding role for French in Europe, and what this role might realistically be. How far, too does a role for French imply a role for Francophonie, both as a set of values and as an international organisation? Europe, and indeed any international grouping, clearly needs a language of vehicular communication. Its officials need to be able to interact effectively and efficiently with each other - but there is no need for this to be in only one language. It would be useful if the amount of translation of official documents could be reduced - but it is not essential, and in today's paperless office, it is certainly not essential for all translated material to be printed on paper. It would be helpful - but again not essential - if its major leaders spoke the same language to the Press and the public. Europe needs, also, to be able to externalise itself in a language in which its major partners themselves communicate, and to play its part internationally.

Whether it needs a common language as a symbol of identity, and whether this common language needs to be managed, controlled and uniform, is a matter of debate. Even if one accepts that European culture - in literature, film, cinema - needs protection from the laws of the global market-place and hence from domination by the most efficient - it does not necessarily follow that it needs a single form of European culture: in fact, the logic of the argument is that the opposite is true, at least until such time as a common European identity can be distinguished.

Language policy experience elsewhere in multinational States seems to indicate that the most effective policy requires a decision on the interplay of three levels of language choice: that of the State language, that of the national language, and that of the regional language(s); and on the nature of the functional differentiation involved. If there is to be a language policy for Europe, and assuming that national language policies remain the prerogative of national governments, the supra-national decision must tackle both the supra-national and the regional policy, particularly since the regions are not confined to one nation (Catalonia in France and Spain), and that what is 'regional' in one nation is 'national' in another (Flemish in France and in Belgium and Holland). While Britain appears now to have solved her regional language policy by giving official status to Welsh and improving the educational role of Scottish dialects and Gaelic, and Spain, Italy and Germany have made considerable progress in this direction, France has remained resistant to any acceptance of extended official roles for her regional languages. Slowly, this is changing, with reluctant concessions in the educational sphere; but any question of semi-official status for Breton or Basque is highly unlikely.

It has taken organised Francophonie, and particularly France, some time to develop policies of 'Francopolyphonie' and plurilingualism for questions of functional interaction, and the suspicion must remain that both France and Francophonie see Europe not as an area of opportunity for multilingual and multicultural respect but as a fertile area for the propagation of one language in preference to others and of a European values of one type as opposed to alternatives. The 1992 Maastricht referendum and the often virulent anti-Europeanism notable during the 1995 Presidential campaign are only two indications that Francophonie and Europe are somewhat uneasy bedfellows.

CONCLUSIONS

Francophonie is a changing concept, becoming gradually better known in the Francophone world and outside it, but not yet clearly understood nor yet itself clear on its purposes. The term 'Francophonie' is defined here in three ways, as we have noted in the Introduction. It is firstly the French language and its future. Secondly, it is the values, ideals and identity of an imagined community of nations and peoples. Thirdly, it is a recently founded international organisation of the governments of some 50 countries or regions. How far all Francophone countries share the same views on each of these aspects is unclear, as is the extent to which the importance of each is changing under the pressure of events. Our conclusions, necessarily personal and, in a constantly changing world, subject to change in the light of events, and based on the situation in the mid-1990s, assess how far Francophonie has an independent existence and how far there may yet be to travel before the concept can be said to have achieved success, and at the same time, examine how the different disciplines on whose insights we have based our examination illuminate the conclusions we can come to.

Language

The demographic base: French speakers throughout the world

French is not the major world language, either as an official language or as the first language of a large proportion of the world's inhabitants. But it is one of the few languages spoken or understood throughout the world, by individuals living in a variety of countries and States. In terms of the world population of speakers of French, accurate statistics are difficult to obtain, and even the UNESCO figures (Appendix Table A1) are subject to caution. At best, it is accepted that there must be about 80 to 90 million first-language speakers, of whom more than half live in France itself. Elsewhere, French is spoken, as a first language, by only part of the population of particular States. The proportion might reach about half, as in Belgium, or as little as less than one per cent, as in most African members of Francophonie. French, as a second language, is used by many citizens in a variety of States as a means of functional intercourse - in commerce, in politics and diplomacy, in education, and in the business of government and administration. For some countries, French is the only language available in which communication between ethnic groups within the State can take place, and thus any sort of national community can be formed: it is an essential component in stability. French is also the only language in which many such States can form political relationships outside the State. Up to a further 100 million people may use French in this way and may possess a reasonable knowledge of it, although the official estimates are much more cautious, totalling, in the estimations of the 1990 Etat Report, about 104 million for both the first two groups. French is learnt as a foreign language by numbers of children, particularly in the Anglophone countries. For Britain itself, France is the nearest neighbour and it continues to make sense that French should be the most widely taught language. This logic does not apply to other Anglophone countries, and there is every likelihood that the tradition of French teaching in Australia and New Zealand will decrease: in fact, organised language policy in Australia foresees this but still allocates a major role to French as a language in which to externalise Australian trade (Lo Bianco, 1987). In the United States French retains some role as a language of education, being preferred to Spanish on elitist grounds, but Japanese and other languages have the major role. Overall, it may be that as many as a further 100 million children and students come into contact with French as part of their education. Overall, French is spoken by or known to between 130 and 200 million people in the world.

Monolingual French speakers are very much in the minority, and in no country apart from France is it possible for French speakers to avoid contact with other languages. On the other hand, awareness of French and of French culture is very widespread throughout the world: it is not possible for world leaders in politics, economics or commerce to be unaware of French. French is evenly distributed, too: it is spoken in most continents, even though by only 2.5% of the world's population. The conclusion must be that French is in a healthy position, with an assured present and an equally assured future. It is only in danger on a comparative basis: it is less spoken than many other languages - particularly, among European languages, English, Portuguese and Spanish - and its demographic base is less representative of the mass of the population than any of these.

French as an opening to world-wide communication

French is a world language. As such, it offers the possibility of gaining access to the cultural, scientific, economic and political exchanges which make the world of international contact possible. It is said by many supporters of Francophonie to offer an alternative - perhaps the only one - to English in this role. English itself is undeniably the most used language in the world, whether as first, second or foreign language.

For citizens of the world, access to French is comparatively easy - through the educational systems, through the *Alliance Française*, through French-language TV and broadcasts (although this is limited), and through the presence of *DOM-TOM* using French and which make it available regionally, as well as acting as regional showpieces for French culture. The migration of Francophones - from Haiti to New York, from Mauritius to Australia, from Algeria to Egypt - spreads French, and the prestige of French-language education (in Egypt, for example) does likewise and ensures its continuance. French is, and will remain, widespread. World languages such as Mandarin Chinese, Arabic, Hindi, Russian, or Bengali are said to be local, in the sense that they do not enjoy the same vehicular use in every continent that both French and English do. Up to a point this is true, and it is also true that Chinese, Hindi, Bengali and Arabic are languages which - so far - are more or less restricted to the ethnic group of their main use. Both these points are less true of Spanish, Portuguese and Russian, although the role of the latter is at present somewhat obscured by the collapse of the Soviet State and the consequential uncertainties about the future vehicular language of Eastern Europe and the ex-Soviet Republics. Spanish is gaining ground fast throughout the world, and particularly in the United States, where many States have passed laws to protect English as the official language precisely because it is under attack in this role (Dyste, 1989). It is, of course, the first language of Spain and of much of South and Central America; it is the first language of most immigrants to the United States, legal and illegal, since about 1960. As both first language and official language its reservoir of speakers outranks French, and it has the advantage that it is less a language of conflict than French. Despite its colonial past, Spanish is not much in evidence apart from these geographical areas, however, and is unlikely to compete with French or English as yet. It is not so prestigious a language as French, and is less used by the decision-makers of the world.

Using French it is possible to gain access to any aspect of international communication that is desired. Although data-bases (such as banking and credit-card information) are in many cases English-based, and the cost of using French accents and diacritics remains about 25% higher in terms of computer storage space than English, modern memory formats, screen representations and document-handling packages mean that there is no practical limit to the use of French in computer-based communication and language engineering applications. Minitel, the widespread French data-base, is now outdated and superseded by e-mail for correspondence and Internet for services, but it remains possible to access large-scale bibliographic and scientific French-language data-bases, and the future for French in these forms of communication must remain good. The conclusion must be that French does indeed offer an alternative means to English - and hence to the American approach - as a way of gaining access to the world, to business and to information, and is likely to retain this advantage. It is attractive in this role, as the applications for membership of the Francophone community by Bulgaria and Romania indicate.

French as an official language

French has high status as an official language, both of a number of countries far in excess of its demographic base - where the total of populations affected amounts to some 300 million (Appendix Table A1) - and also in prestigious international organisations. It is of prime importance that it retains this role if it is to be advantageous for potential new recruits to Francophonie to join, and for those States where French is now spoken by an infinitesimal proportion of the population to retain its use as their own official language.

But the cost of maintaining French is high. Some costs are associated with the attitudes it provokes - the social costs of the protection of an elitist language, the cost of maintaining its corpus through such institutions as the French Academy, the French Terminology Commissions and the Quebec language protection institutions , and hence the cost of maintaining one norm of usage which is the prerogative of one member country of Francophonie. Other costs are more direct: the cost of education in Africa, for example, needed to ensure the availability of the language, is high. The future for the use of French in Africa has been much discussed (Dumont, 1986; Gueunier, 1992) and remains unclear, since statistics are notably lacking. Despite the growth in the number of primary schools (73,000 to 169,000) and pupils (11.9 million to 51.3 million) from 1960 to 1980, the drop in this growth rate and in the quality of education during the 1980s and 1990s has had severe effects in many African countries (World Bank, quoted in Kazadi, 1991, 169). Although the apparent decline has much to do with the increase in births, with the lack of adequate manuals, and with increasing access to education and does not necessarily indicate an immediate collapse of the educational structures supporting French, there remains a danger. If African countries cannot guarantee that their speeches in French will be received in international fora such as the United Nations, the Olympic Games or the World Health Organisation, they will see little point in maintaining their own support for Francophonie. Equally, if French is not a prestigious, officially recognised language in every international organisation of which France is a member, it may appear to them easier to adopt English as the easiest route to world understanding. On a cruder level, it is to the advantage of French that aid, both bilateral and multilateral, is distributed to Third World countries from French-speaking sources and through French-speaking agencies. Seeing French as the medium through which salvation might come to depressed economies and to desperate populations is a positive factor in the continuing world use of French.

In Europe, French will remain as one of the official languages, and as a preferred language of education. But the price of its retention is that it remains as one of a number of languages: it will never replace, as English potentially could, all the other languages as the practical and sole language of Europe for official and interactional purposes. A policy of multilingualism is essential to French, but necessarily it entails support for other languages too, each of which has a potential base for further expansion. Italian may be preferable for linguists as a mean average for Romance languages; Spanish is becoming more and more the language of the North American underclass; German has a potential role as lingua franca for the new Eastern Europe. All of these have to be supported if French itself is to be supported. Overall, maintaining French at the forefront of the official role is expensive, in social and financial terms. But Francophonie is likely to find the cost acceptable.

French as the language of conflict

Conflict with English
French is perceived as a language of conflict: with English - although this is mainly the result of the aggressive defence of French in Quebec and France - and also with 'local' languages, ranging from Flemish in Belgium to a number of vehicular and vernacular languages in Africa. On a linguistic basis, the conflict with English is somewhat illogical, in that the role French wishes is that of vehicular language - of science, of economics and of diplomacy - and yet most of the official arguments deployed against the use of English condemn it as being precisely a vehicular language with minimal cultural content. Attitudes suggest that it is not the nature of French to harbour a reduced form of the language, a sort of basic form, which might play such a role. Many supporters of French take glory here also from the fact that French is a difficult language, with a long and complex cultural history, and a strong normative tradition which is unforgiving towards mistakes and does not easily accept modernisation, regionalisms or alternative expressions. In the tensions between stability, polyvalency and elasticity (Thomas, 1991, 53) French falls clearly into stability, while the major characteristic of a vehicular language is its ability to accept and adopt new terms, and to be usable in a range of social settings and subject domains. The battle in which French is engaged with English is less a battle of languages than one of power. Vehicular English is a tool, used by those with the most power. At the moment those with the most power are citizens of the United States, which is not about to cede economic, scientific or diplomatic power to anyone. A time will come when the power of the United States will proportionately decrease, when some other nation or group of nations will occupy the leading position; at that point the standard international vehicular English used in these domains will be replaced by some other international standard vehicular form of expression. Fighting vehicular English on the language basis is a battle lost in advance, and its only consequence is to disarm Francophone scientists, diplomats and politicians.

Quite apart from this pointless conflict with vehicular English, special considerations apply to the conflict with English in Quebec and perhaps in

France. The Quebec situation - in which the awakening of consciousness was nearly too late, and in which consistent language policy, associated with economic and political moves, over a period of nearly thirty years has had notable effects and may indeed delay language shift for a considerable time - is special and particular, caused by the physical nearness of the United States and the domination of the Quebec economy by American interests, and holds no lessons for Francophonie generally.

In France, the battle against English is confused and unclear in its aims. If the intention is to (judicially) prevent French people from using borrowed English terms, it is unworkable; if its aim is to raise awareness and pride in Frenchness, it conflicts with the construction of supra-national Europe and with the European policy of governments since 1948, and, as an undesired byproduct, gives comfort to xenophobes and racists; if its aim is to preserve the past and maintain French consumers in a protected (commercial and linguistic) market to which foreign goods (and languages) have limited access, it is subject to retaliatory action by others.

It is however in this latter aim that the battle against English holds most hope. There is a chance that France, and Francophonie with her, can withstand the imposition of American English, and with it American cultural products - particularly TV - on Europe and elsewhere by pursuing the idea of the cultural exclusion, and extending it to language. But it is a very small possibility, unless Francophonie, paradoxically, agrees both to attack English as it has and also accepts the necessity to change and modernise both French language and French culture. When Francophonie prizes popular culture (as opposed to high culture) more, or Europe develops a common popular culture which can compete with the American market on the same terms; and when Francophone speakers are prepared to adopt new terms for new ideas and better adapt the language to changing circumstances, French culture and language will be stronger. Static resistance to change merely provokes revolution rather than evolution. From this point of view, Francophonie stands a better chance than French: the openness of Caribbean, African and Pacific cultures to other influences, and their ability to absorb and modify them, means they are better able to withstand. Similarly, social categories which can adapt and modify the pressures on them and render Anglophone and American imports their own are better placed to retain their own culture than categories which simply refuse imports and take refuge in denying the existence of change.

Conflict with other languages

It is the norm throughout Francophonie that French is used in multilingual situations, where many languages compete for a functional role. The usual functional role assigned to French in Francophonie is that of official language - the language of education, of the administrative and governmental processes, and of the elite. In this function the strong normative characteristics of French play in its favour. It is the ideal bureaucratic language: not the subject of play or irony, not the language of romantic creativity, not a language in which fantasy and imagination find easy expression. But the multilingual situations bring conflict, and in social conflict particularly the mass of the population can easily characterise French as the language of domination. This is particularly dangerous for the continuing *DOM-TOM*, where independence movements naturally tend to condemn French; for areas of Francophonie where the colonial history of exploitation is not yet forgotten; and for Francophonie in the Third World generally. French speakers and Francophonie tend to actively participate in language competition, and such expansionism may be offensive. French can also be seen as the vehicle for inappropriate 'Western' religious or social practices. Francophonie is seen in countries under Islamic law as bringing undesired attitudes and practices - uncensored TV and literature, a different conception of democracy - and may be rejected for these reasons.

The image of French

French has an image as an elitist language, difficult to learn, and one whose speakers deride both foreign accents and inadequate mastery. It is a vehicle of social progress, a necessary accomplishment for future diplomats and politicians; but what has to be acquired is a specific form of the language, the international norm jealously protected by Paris and the French Academy. Although Terminology Commissions and dictionary publishers work hard to accept forms of the language from Africa, Canada and elsewhere, it is not lost on the international community that the French Academy can publicly regret a Belgian decision to adopt what it regards as non-sexist usage (applicable from January 1994), that official conferences on the quality of language can identify as mistakes what many would regard as the normal developments of any language over time, and that spelling contests are public entertainments, enabling the public to be amazed that a language can be so difficult. Attitudes which regard French as the property of the French, immensely difficult and therefore to be revered, take time to disappear.

French is therefore strongly characterised as a language deserving of protection: a venerable monument to be defended as it is. Indeed, the Francophone countries, and particularly Quebec, Belgium and France, are vociferous in constantly reminding themselves and the world audience of the need to defend French against attack, both externally against English, and internally, against decadence and corruption. The strength of this defence, and its open orchestration through official means, may provoke a negative reaction and make the price of defence too high. Indeed, in France itself the amount of negative newspaper comment on the protective measures of the Toubon law, and the comments of the judges of the Constitutional Council in July 1994, together give the impression that the point might have been reached when legal support for (stable unchanging) French seems to constitute an attack on human rights to free expression. The counterproductive nature of what is described as the defence of French, but which often appears to be offensive in all senses of the word, could not be clearer than when it is necessary for the Minister of Culture to defend himself against a judgement which quotes freedom of expression as the most precious of the rights of man, and he attempts to define that judgement as more restrictive than the text of his own law.

Unfortunately, too, active support for French language - through efficient cheap publication of books, music, teaching materials, films, TV programmes - does not adequately follow the rhetoric. Active support for the language industries - translation, publishing, informatics, even language research - is not yet on a high enough level to compete with English in disseminating the language. And research whose purpose is to discover ways of defending a policy - rather than identifying for example how far the policy is justified in the first place - is flawed research.

Identity and the Values of Francophonie

The colonial past

France's colonial past will in due course be forgotten by members of Francophonie, particularly in Africa. However, there is no doubt that France's own African policy has too many reminders of colonialism to be altogether ruled out as a negative factor affecting Francophonie generally. The values of contemporary Francophonie have to clearly differentiate themselves, perhaps more clearly yet, from the past. The Rwanda episode, one of 19 armed interventions by France in the internal affairs of former Francophone colonies since 1960, and the maintenance of military defence agreements and bases, together with the one-sided control of strategic materials and minerals, mean that Francophonie is still somewhat suspect as a free meeting of independent States with common values and a common language. The full truth about France's involvement in Rwanda has not, and probably never will be, revealed, in the same way that French secret service involvement with the Rainbow Warrior affair is now common knowledge. But there is sufficient doubt about the purposes and policies to mean that French colonialist attitudes and actions remain a factor in France's role in the world (Braeckman, 1994; Chrétien, 1995). The same is true of other areas of the world: France's role in the Caribbean and in the Pacific retains much of the dominance and dependence associated with an earlier time. Opposition to colonialism has nonetheless decreased as its reality disappears. Bilateral neo-colonialism, too, is less opposed than it was as the Third World comes to see world organisations such as the World Bank or the

International Monetary Fund in a changing light, and as the desperation of the state of Africa comes home to many in the North.

A middle course - between Coca-cola and Ayatollah

The two dangers for Francophonie are represented - at least by France - as being the Americanisation of world values - commercialism and consumerism - and the growth of fundamentalism, particularly Islamic fundamentalism. If Francophonie is to represent itself as a middle way between the extremes, it will have to respond to the needs which these two 'religions' satisfy: the desire for modernity and the desire for spiritual fulfilment. But Francophonie is neither a religion nor an economic miracle, and the values it proposes - in essence those of the French Revolution and the Enlightenment - are hardly likely to attract the poor, the young, or those who are currently attracted by demagogues and dogmatism. At least Francophonie does present an ideal - of personal freedom, of democracy, of human rights, of a way of life and a style of being - which is recognisable, which in some ways (music, dance) can accept different cultures, and which can be presented as universal, although this last point is debatable.

Francophonie's official disdain for consumerism smacks more of the politics of envy than of sincerity. Much of it, too, reminds the observer of aristocratic contempt for trade. In this respect, the official discourse of politicians and diplomats may lag behind the realities of the business community. Consumerism and commercialism can live with Francophonie. French TV producers can produce just as much mass entertainment as the Americans; fast food outlets can serve croissants and baguettes just as quickly as hamburgers and hot dogs; cheap clothes can be produced with French style just as well, and probably with the same Third World manufacturers, as American. If anything, Francophonie just hasn't been as quick into the mass youth market as the Americans have; there is nothing inherent in Francophonie to prevent such a development.

But it is towards Islam, and fundamentalism generally, that Francophonie is most vulnerable, and most opposed. To draw a distinction between Islam and the Arabic-speaking countries is not easy, particularly when France, the largest country in Francophonie, is host to millions of Arabic-speaking immigrants and when Islam is the second religion of France. Racist and xenophobic attacks in France, the slide of integrationist policies towards assimilation, and the determined pursuit in France of militants of the Algerian *FIS* give Francophonie a poor image in Arabic-speaking countries, where it is often characterised as 'associated with lack of religion, with loose morals, with female emancipation, with the rape of Arab cultural identity' (Etat, 1993, 512). Islam has a similarly poor image among most French citizens. Within Francophonie, in which Islam is the religion of many African States, the topic is not often - or not openly -

discussed. But relations between Islam and Francophonie are uneasy, and generally difficult.

The values of Francophonie

Francophonie defined its own (political) values in 1993 as the 'promotion of peace, justice, security, solidarity, and democracy; respect for the rights of man and fundamental liberties which are universal and inalienable' (Lettre de la Francophonie, 66). These are the humane values of the contemporary West, and it would be difficult to find a Western country which did not subscribe to them. The interpretation placed upon them by Francophonie lies in the concept of solidarity - among Francophone nations; democracy - defined in a particular way by Mitterrand at La Baule in 1990; and the universality of the rights of man and the fundamental freedoms, together with their particular Francophone connotations.

It is not necessarily a positive factor for contemporary Francophonie that these political values are interpreted in different ways by different member countries. Solidarity is often prevented by restrictive immigration policies, and is not evident, yet, in joint declarations on matters of moment nor in joint action - although Senegalese troops did join with the French military in Operation Turquoise in Rwanda in July 1994. Democracy, in the Western interpretation, is notably absent from any number of the African countries - whose defence, at least as expressed in the Mauritius Summit, was the impossibility of guaranteeing democratic rights in conditions of absolute penury. Much of the discussion at the 1993 United Nations world conference on the Rights of Man, held in Vienna in June 1993, turned on the relationship between democracy, development and the rights of man. The Francophone countries, represented by the chairperson of the *Conseil Permanent de la Francophonie*, pointed out that democracy 'cannot survive without a minimum level of development'; that rights to democracy and to development are universal and cannot be dissociated one from another; and that rights of women, children and minorities must be safeguarded (Lettre de la Francophonie, 62). Such pronouncements are rare.

Apart from the political values, Francophonie is 'a cultural, humane and modern supplement' to the world (Guillou and Littardi, 1988, 257). The cultural values of Francophonie depend on the recognition of the individual and an opposition to uniformity. Humanism, too, means tolerance of others and freedom of the individual: going beyond particularisms towards the universal. Cultural preferences however are necessarily personal and circumscribed by context. The cultural practices which are defended in organised Francophonie are those of an elite: Mozart rather than Motown, Racine rather than rap, ballet rather than bop. There is no sense in which such a universal cultural absolute can exist, in which Islamic art can be preferred to Italian, or the leisure pursuits of the rich be convincingly presented as inherently 'better' than the pursuits of the poor. The defenders of Francophonie do not say why Francophone culture is superior to Americanophone culture, why the American soap opera is to be rejected as an art form, or why the Astérix theme park is preferable to Disneyland Paris. If the future of Francophonie is to rest on its cultural preferences, and at the same time it is to be presented as a universal movement, there will have to be better comparative arguments which can defeat the charge of both xenophobia and elitism.

Francophonie faces the fundamental dilemma in its declaration of values, whether political, cultural or humane, that the universal has to be realised in concrete contexts. The conflict between the discovery of the universal in the individual, and acceptance of the individual's right to be considered a member of socio-cultural groups and regional or ethnic communities, presents a major difficulty for the Francophone values. Without being cynical, one can say also that the argument that Francophonie - and Francophonie alone - is a vehicle for ideas of tolerance amounts to hope rather than realisation. Those thinking within the French culture are so used to believing that the values of the Revolution and the Enlightenment are superior to others and universally applicable that it is impossible to convince some Francophones that these 'universal' values are themselves relative: that tolerance has to be applied to other ways of being as well as other ways of thinking. The Rights of Man were, originally, the Rights of the eighteenth century bourgeoisie; in their present international formulation they are those of the world of 1948. Their universality is a matter of discussion, not fiat. Indeed, the Senegal delegate to the World Conference on the Rights of Man noted that there was necessary complementarity between universal rights and their regional realisation: that the universal was relative, but that practical realisation had to take note of general aspirations. It is perhaps in this light that Francophone 'universality' can be seen.

The recognition of diversity

The culture of Francophonie hence means multilingualism and a multilingual policy: the enemy is not English, but uniformity. Diversity, and hence the defence of all languages, is essential to the survival of Francophonie, as most Francophone leaders pointed out in the Mauritius summit meeting (Lettre de la Francophonie, 66) and as many commentators have indicated (Guillou and Littardi, 1988, 257; Tétu, 1987, 297; Hagège, 1992, 118). The accepted formula for discussion in Mauritius was 'Unity in Diversity', claimed as a special characteristic of Francophonie. Throughout the gradual realisation of such an approach, however, lies a fundamental problem: if Francophonie is special and different, Francophonie cannot be a universally applicable movement with the same appeal for all: Francophonie cannot be both specific and universal; Francophonie as the language must be diverse and accept different manifestations. The solution - for organised Francophonie - stressed by the new formula of countries 'sharing French', turns on the idea of partnership, and underlines a weakening of the idea of universality within Francophonie. This paradox has a number of practical outcomes: the defence of French is key, but it must lie through the acceptance of other languages within Francophonie, together with their cultures, as integral parts of Francophonie. Is Francophonie then to be defined as a grouping which can accept any language, any culture? What is meant by a 'coherent framework' if Francophonie accepts any language, from Wolof to Tahitian, as an integral component? How unified can Francophonie be?

The Francophone Community

The strength of associations

The Francophone community is not made up merely of the formally organised Summits. Indeed, the strength of international relations lies more in the innumerable Francophone associations and non-governmental organisations in which writers, parliamentarians, chemists, computer scientists and mayors exchange ideas and experiences. The strength of these associations was recognised at the very first formally organised Summit, and indeed presented somewhat of a difficulty for the initial organisation. But it is a recognised strength and positive advantage to Francophonie that the associations continue and flourish, and that they see themselves as a necessary and fundamental component of successful Francophonie.

There is a further strength in Francophonie in the growth and development of popular festivals, meetings and celebrations, of which the most obvious example is the annual *Francofolies* bringing together musicians and performance artists across international Francophonie. While Francophonie, like the British Commonwealth, did not start as a widespread popular movement and there have been major difficulties in finding ways to involve the general population, events such as these may help greatly in ensuring more widespread support for the political and cultural values associated with Francophonie.

Devolved co-operation

Co-operation, meetings and exchanges take place between towns, schools, newspapers and sports organisations, and this has been recognised as an encouraging sign of the growing practical realisation of a Francophone Community (Etat, 1993, 506). Similarly, tourism, co-operation in TV and audiovisual production means that members of French-speaking countries are gradually realising their common partnership. Individual countries are establishing contracts and relationships between themselves without France as an intermediary: Canada and Quebec, in particular, offer direct support and interaction with members of Francophonie in a number of domains. But too much should not be made of this 'positive' sign. Business - private business in particular - shows very little awareness of partnership across the Francophone community: in France, awareness of the existence of other countries speaking French is still low, and self-centred concerns of local importance still generally take precedence over international relationships. The French Press is generally poor in prioritising news of Francophonie.

The weakness of organised Summits

The Summits have only been organised since 1986, and it was inevitable that teething troubles would prevent the operation of a fully integrated, efficient and smooth-running organisation in the initial stages. But the nature of the Summits, their organisational substructure, the aims and purposes of the meetings, and the follow-up to decisions taken, are all at the moment subject to improvement. At present, the organisation is a loose two-day meeting of Heads of State and Government, held behind closed doors, with a semi-structured agenda supported by a range of prepared items but with considerable flexibility to adjust and respond to events.

Francophonie at this level is a place for dialogue and discussion, not for action. This was probably inevitable at the beginning, but there are signs that some members at least would prefer concrete outcomes. Third World States would clearly like Francophonie to be an alternative channel for multilateral aid, without strings. The northern countries do not yet seem to have agreed on their aims and purposes: while for some the purpose of Francophonie is to support their particular policies, for others it is a market-place in which new technological inventions can be sold or ideologies disseminated.

The importance of the organisational problem within France itself should not be underestimated. The awkward division of responsibility for Francophonie between President and Prime Minister, and the multiplicity of responsible Ministries within Government, lead to uncertainty over who is ultimately responsible for the coherence of policy. The 'buried' Hessel report of 1990 recommended the creation of a *Haut Conseil de la Coopération et du Développement* in order to obtain advice from independent experts, moving away from too close contacts with individual African leaders, stricter controls on aid and greater stress on human rights and democracy (McKesson, 1993, 57). Most of the recommendations have been carried out in practice, but Rwanda is a demonstration of the problems involved. With the constitution of the Juppé government, and with Chirac as President, Francophonie appears firmly attached to Foreign Affairs; but the multiplicity of vested interests remains, and the relationship of the cultural, linguistic, economic and diplomatic strands remains to be clarified.

The weakness of economic links

The lack of inter-Francophone trade, the lack of preferential investment, and the lack indeed of any preferential economic relationships within Francophonie mean that it is at present a toothless tiger. Stronger economic links would clearly present problems for Francophonie, however. France is a founder member of the European Union, and although she has fought valiantly for preferential market arrangements for her ex-colonies, and indeed for the *DOM-TOM*, she owes her primary economic responsibility to the Union rather than to Francophonie. Canada, similarly, is a member of the North American Free Trade Association, and looks to protect her interests in trade with the United States. The African States are variously members of regional trade associations, and again do not see their economic future at the moment except in terms of increased aid. From this point of view, Francophonie is a negative link: countries in Africa, the *DOM-TOM*, are linked to France because they have to be, not because they want to be.

The lack of North-South understanding

The constant complaint of African leaders at the summit meetings is that their problems are little understood by northern, wealthy countries: 'how can democracy take place when one third of the world's population owns two thirds of its wealth, and two thirds lives in poverty?' (Cameroon delegate, Lettre de la Francophonie, 62). It is particularly on the question of democracy in the countries of the South that the northern countries of Francophonie find themselves unable to understand and sympathise. The general reaction of French or Swiss citizens is that democracy does not exist in the African Francophone countries; that they are ruled by despots or by military commanders, and that the basic freedoms are not available - hence the *Afropessimisme* and the despair noted by commentators. This lack of understanding is revealed at every Summit, and in many of the agencies, and represents a negative feature of contemporary Francophonie.

Guillou and Littardi (1988, 255) concluded their review of Francophonie with the belief that the economic development of Africa would be the touchstone for Francophonie, and the confident belief that 'this continent can, in two generations, cease being underdeveloped and dependent on international aid and enter the group of 'newly industrialised' countries'. The argument for the centrality of Africa in the future of Francophonie rested on two main points: (1) if French were to disappear from Africa, French (and France) would be replaced, but there would be no reason for French to replace other languages elsewhere; (2) although France needed the support of others, and particularly of Europe, to maintain her presence in Africa, it is because of her presence in Africa and her 'co-operation' policy that she can influence the main players on the world scene: the IMF, organised markets for products, European aid for less developed regions. France and Francophonie needed both Europe and Africa, and the need was interdependent. Nearly ten years later, these arguments have lost some of their force. Africa is not making steady - or even any - progress towards industrialisation and a triumphant entry into Western ideas of industrialisation and progress. Africa is more and more abandoned by Europe; at worst two irresponsible attitudes confront each other: 'African dependence and lack of initiative; European egocentricity and short-sightedness' (Guillou, 1993, 29). Even the Asian tigers who have made the move into the economic future are beginning to count the social cost. But Africa is still central to France, if not to Francophonie - and the distinction is worth making. So much discussion of Francophonie tends to confuse the two: what is good for France is good for Francophonie - that it has become difficult to separate the arguments and to identify what is good for Francophonie. But is France - or even Francophonie - essential to a better future for Africa? Continuing paternalism and continuing dominance have not led to independence.

The lack of democracy

President Mitterrand used the occasion of a meeting with African leaders in 1990 to spell out what was meant by conditionality in aid to be awarded to countries in which democracy was seen to be operating. Although it was effective in making clear the principles on which France would contribute to the economies of African partners, it did not support the concept of Francophonie as a free meeting of independent equals. Here again, the northern concept of democracy is not well understood in the South, nor even in some of the *DOM-TOM*, where the norms of democratic behaviour are not always followed. This negative factor has surfaced at many different times in France, and in the mid-1990s seems to be a strong element in general French disappointment with Francophonie.

The *DOM-TOM* as an unused resource for Francophonie

The diplomatic power of organised Francophonie is as yet an unexploited resource. Apart from considerations of general politics, cultural matters and specific projects, the discussions at the Summits to date have concentrated on two major areas: internal organisation; and the possible - but somewhat unlikely - potential for internal economic relations (sale of TV5, communications technology, Francophone broadcasts and art). Despite co-operation in preparation for the UN World Conference on the Rights of Man in 1993 and for other UN meetings in 1994 and 1995, there is little attempt to establish joint policy, to attempt to influence world decisions or actions through a Francophone point of view.

Since the *DOM* are an integral part of France, and the status of the *TOM* does not allow them any separate voice on the international scene apart from that of

France itself, Francophonie loses part of the overall value of the immense political support which might come from this range of countries in different parts of the world, and loses the additional UN votes from a range of different situations across the world which would come from the independence of these countries. The isolation of these *DOM* and *TOM* from their regional setting also loses them credibility. Although some do participate in regional meetings - France has attempted to establish a Polynesian Community; Tahiti-Nui is welcomed to meetings of South Pacific leaders - in general the falseness of the transfer economy and the clear desire of the French settlers and expatriate bureaucrats to have nothing to do with the local situation prevents these potential allies from being represented by their 'own' people in international exchanges. This is a pity, and an open invitation to those who would see the continuation of the *DOM-TOM* as proof that France is interested only in her own advantage, in the status quo and in what for many people are outmoded ideas of grandeur and glory for the home country, bought at the expense of those abroad. From this point of view, organised Francophonie is a sham: when neither the Caribbean, the Indian Ocean nor the Pacific Ocean countries are even present at Summit meetings, the discussions are necessarily false.

The problem of France

France, naturally, pursues her own foreign policy in pursuance of what is seen as advantageous to France. But in some circumstances what is advantageous to France is disadvantageous to Francophonie. French foreign policy is made and implemented in a rather more tortuous fashion than in most countries (Lequesne, 1993). The President takes control without opposition when the Government is of the same political persuasion; when cohabitation is operating, there is a constant battle for the right to establish and implement policy. This in itself is not a major difficulty - it is, after, all the normal procedure in the United States too. French foreign policy, in fact, has been remarkably consistent since the inception of the Fifth Republic in 1958, and perhaps for even longer. It generally follows the line of implementing the Gaullist grand design: France has a particular identity, consecrated in the special bond uniting all citizens and making them unique bearers of their mission, which is to utilise resource power (i.e. most frequently the power of myth, but also that of economic might and even, on occasion, of military dominance) in the pursuit of the grandeur of France. This grandeur is realised in the bond between France, democratic freedom and humanitarian ideals, and expressed in boundless rhetoric. In the real world, however, French foreign policy, like that of any country, is a matter of seeking advantage for one's country in a network of alliances. Sometimes the alliances can be dubious: Francophonie has suffered from a series of French policy initiatives which appear to be based on little other than the preferences of one President for another, as in the case of Zaïre, or for one ethnic group rather than another, as in the case of the Hutus and the Tutsis in Rwanda. Such alliances place great strain on Francophonie.

Although Francophonie is not France, France plays a major role in its success. Without France, Francophonie would be unthinkable, in a way which is not true of the British Commonwealth, which could perfectly well remain as a world force without Britain. But France is no longer alone in her relationships even with those countries to which she was closest in the immediate post-colonial era, in Africa. Her role is subject both to the range of multilateral organisations in which both France and other countries participate, and also to the fact that her partners have established bilateral links with countries outside Francophonie. The European Union, although it is far from establishing a centralised and common foreign policy, makes co-ordination of policy a strong point. It is after all, European money and not French money alone which enables France to continue supporting her overseas possessions. In economic relations, multilateral organisations such as the World Bank, the International Monetary Fund, the Paris Club, the London Club and the Group of Seven, co-ordinate their actions. In military intervention, even France is moving towards closer collaboration with the United Nations.

The Future of Francophonie

Francophonie has a past and a very varied present, and events in the contemporary world must always affect the prospects of any country or group of countries. Traditionally, Francophonie is regarded as suffering from two 'drawbacks', as seen from the Anglo-Saxon point of view: its excessive concern with language and cultural matters, and the second-rate political and economic position of its formal members by comparison with the Anglo-Saxon world. Its 'comparative advantage' is that it is less associated with economic dominance than other organisations, provides an alternative route avoiding political dominance by the superpowers, and has a cultural and linguistic core. In the contemporary world, such an analysis may have missed the point. Two questions are central for the future of Francophonie: the future of Francophone Africa, and the future role of France in Francophonie. Both questions have political, economic and cultural relevance, and both are necessarily and intimately concerned with questions of language and communication. Both are dependent, too, on how the new President and his Government handle overseas affairs. It is significant therefore not merely that Chirac's interest in and concern for language matters during his periods as Prime Minister are known, but that two key figures in his 1995 Government - Juppé and Toubon - have direct knowledge of all four aspects. It is impossible to investigate the future of French, of the organised international community of nations meeting as Francophonie, or of the values of Francophonie, without examining the essential interdependence of language, politics, economics and cultural values.

APPENDIX

Table A1
Major languages of the world

Language	Potential speakers	Real speakers	Total speakers	% of world population	Population of countries concerned
Arabic*	206,380,300	(same)	(same)	4	218,419,500
Bengali	177,609,100	(same)	(same)	3.4	948,429,800
Chinese*	1,077,548,100	(same)	(same)	20.9	1,165,974,500
English	137,591,700	456,328,300	593,920,000	11.5	1,818,816,800
French	42,759,100	88,658,300	131,417,400	2.5	308,110,100
German	88,800	88,997,600	89,086,400	1.7	101,547,000
Hindustani*	48,386,800	363,927,300	412,314,100	8	954,167,200
Japanese	122,846,200	(same)	(same)	2.4	(same)
Bahasa M & I*	49,441,700	63,852,200	113,293,900	2.2	197,612,000
Portuguese	2,629,500	158,447,900	161,076,200	3.1	184,517,200
Russian*	285,077,900	(same)	(same)	5.5	(same)
Spanish	3,309,500	308,075,300	311,385,300	6	317,685,800

Source: UNESCO 1989, quoted in Asher, 1994, vol 8, 4346
Notes
1.   * Arabic and Chinese are both treated as a single language
      * Hindustani includes Hindi, Urdu and Panjabi
      * Bahasa M&I: Bahasa Malaysia and Bahasa Indonesia are treated as a single language
      * Russian: statistics apply to the former Soviet Union
2. Potential speakers include those who have
  (a) learned the language in countries where it is an official or national language and
  (b) learned the language where it is a compulsory subject in officially multilingual countries.
3. Real speakers include those who have
  (a) acquired the language as a mother tongue in countries where it is an official or national language
  (b) learned the language in countries where it is an official language or a language of instruction
  (c) learned the language where it is a compulsory subject in officially multilingual countries.

Table A2
Francophonie in the world

Country	Population (000)	Francophones %	Official languages	Summit?	GDP PPP$	Life expectancy at birth	HDI rank/ group	HDI	Bilateral aid flow
Algeria	24,960	30	F, Arabic		2,870	65.6	0.553	109 M	16
Andorra	52	29	F, Spanish						
Argentina	32,322	0.1	Spanish		5,120	71.1	0.853	37 H	9
Belgium	9,845	45.5	F, Flemish	Yes	17,510	75.7	0.916	13 H	-165
Benin	4,736	10	F	Yes	1,500	46.1	0.261	156 L	55
Brazil	153,322	0.07	Portuguese		5,240	65.8	0.756	63 M	2
Bulgaria	9,011	0.1	Bulgarian	Yes	4,813	71.9	0.815	48 H	-
Burkina Faso	9,001	7	F	Yes	666	47.9	0.203	172 L	47
Burundi	5,348	3	F, Kirundi	Yes	640	48.2	0.276	152 L	54
Cambodia	8,246	0.1	F, Khmer	Yes	1,250	50.4	0.307	147 L	1
Cameroon	11,834	18	F, English	Yes	2,400	55.3	0.477	124 L	59
Canada	26,552	25	F, English	Yes	19,320	77.2	0.932	1 H	-96
New Brunswick	730	33.6							
Ontario									
Quebec	6,780	82.9	F	Yes					
Cape Verde	370	0.1	Portuguese	Yes	1,360	67.3	0.474	122 L	311
Central Afr Rep	3,039	5	F	Yes	641	47.2	0.249	160 L	56
Chad	5,679	3	F, Arabic	Yes	447	46.9	0.212	168 L	42
Chile	13,386	0.1	Spanish		7,060	71.9	0.848	38 H	10
Comoros	551	8	F, Arabic	Yes	700	55.4	0.331	141 L	82
Congo	271	35	F	Yes	2,800	51.7	0.461	123 L	48
Costa Rica	2,994	0.03	English		5,100	76.0	0.848	39 H	43
Djibouti	409	7	F, Arabic	Yes	1,000	48.3	0.226	163 L	250
Dominica	83	1.1	English	Yes	3,900	72.0	0.749	64 M	196
Egypt	53,153	0.4	Arabic	Yes	3,600	60.9	0.551	110 M	64

Country	Population	%	Language	Status					
Equ Guinea	348	0.1	Spanish	Yes	700	47.3	0.276	150 L	170
Ethiopia	50,974	0.008	Amharic		370	46.4	0.249	161 L	24
France *	56,315	98	F	Yes	18,430	76.6	0.927	6 H	-262
Guadeloupe	387	80		DOM	4,500				
Guyana	115	73		DOM	2,340				
Martinique	360	80		DOM	4,500				
Mayotte	94	33		Coll Terr	?				
New Caled	164	80		TOM	4,500				
Polynesia	189	80		TOM	6,000				
Réunion	598	80		DOM	4,500				
St Pierre et Miq	6	100		Coll Terr	?				
Wallis & Fut	14	70		TOM	920				
Gabon	1,172	30	F	Yes	3,498	52.9	0.525	114 M	56
Greece	10,269	0.1	Greek		7,680	77.3	0.874	25 H	-
Grenada	85	0.5	English		3,374	70.0	0.707	78 M	131
Guinea	5,756	5	F	Yes	500	43.9	0.191	173 L	75
Guinea-Bissau	965	0.1	Portuguese	Yes	747	42.9	0.224	164 L	106
Haiti	6,486	9	F, Creole		925	56.0	0.354	137 L	16
India	843,941		Hindi, English		1,150	59.7	0.382	135 L	3
Pondicherry	900	0.2							
Iran	58,031	0.09	Persian		4,670	66.6	0.672	86 M	3
Iraq	18,920	?	Arabic		3,500	65.7	0.614	100 M	10
Israel	4,659	11	Hebrew, Arabic		13,460	76.2	0.900	19 H	405
Italy			Italian		17,040	76.9	0.892	22 H	-126
Aosta Valley	120	10							
Ivory Coast	11,998	30	F	Yes	1,510	51.6	0.370	136 L	59
Laos	4,139	0.1	Lao	Yes	1,760	50.3	0.385	133 L	39
Lebanon	2,701	27	F, Arabic	Yes	2,500	68.1	0.600	103 M	28
Luxembourg	384	80	F	Yes	20,800	75.2	0.908	17 H	-98
Madagascar	11,197	9	F, Malagasy	Yes	710	54.9	0.396	131 L	28
Mali	8,156	10	F	Yes	480	45.4	0.214	167 L	45

Country			Language(s)						
Mauritania	2,050	6	F, Arabic	Yes	962	47.4	0.254	158 L	98
Mauritius	1,075	25	English	Yes	7,178	69.6	0.778	60 M	43
Monaco	29	90	F	Yes	20,000				
Morocco	25,061	18	F, Arabic	Yes	3,340	62.5	0.549	111 M	38
Niger	7,732	7	F	Yes	542	45.9	0.209	169 L	44
Poland	38,180	0.1	Polish		4,500	71.5	0.815	49 H	-
Portugal	10,525	0.1	Portuguese		9,450	74.4	0.838	42 H	-44
Romania	23,200	4	Romanian	Yes	3,500	69.9	0.729	72 M	-
Rwanda	7,181	3	F, Kinyarwanda	Yes	680	46.5	0.274	153 L	47
St Lucia	151	1.4	English	Yes	3,500	72.0	0.709	77 M	51
St Vincent/Grenadines	116	0.5	English		3,700	71.0	0.732	69 M	28
Sao Tome & Principe	121	0.7	Portuguese		600	67.0	0.409	128 L	433
Senegal	7,327	10	F	Yes	1,680	48.7	0.322	143 L	87
Seychelles	67	7	F, English, Creole	Yes	3,683	71.0	0.685	83 M	277
Spain	38,959	0.1	Spanish		12,670	77.4	0.888	23 H	-34
Switzerland	6,712	18.5	F, German, Italian, Romansch	Yes	21,780	77.8	0.931	2 H	-142
Syria	12,116	0.1	Arabic		5,220	66.4	0.727	73 M	12
Togo	3,531	20	F	Yes	738	54.4	0.311	145 L	60
Trinidad & Tobago	1,227	0.5	English		8,380	70.9	0.855	35 H	6
Tunisia	8,180	30	F, Arabic	Yes	4,690	67.1	0.690	81 M	48
Turkey	57,326	0.02	Turkish			66.7	0.739	68 M	6
USA			English		22,130	75.6	0.925	8 H	-44
Louisiana	4,500	2.2							
New England	14,000	1.4							
Vanuatu	147	31	F, English, Bislama	Yes	1,679	65.0	0.489	119 L	286
Venezuela	19,735	0.1	Spanish		8,120	70.1	0.820	46 H	2
Vietnam	66,200	0.1	Vietnamese	Yes	1,250	63.4	0.514	116 M	8
Zaire	35,562	5	F	Yes	469	51.6	0.348	140 L	7

Notes

1. France*: the population figure for France excludes the *DOM-TOM* and Territorial Collectivities.

2. Population: in thousands. Sources: Phillips Atlas, 1994; for France, *DOM-TOM* and Territorial Collectivities: 1990 census, as noted in Madinier, 1993.

3. Francophones: The figures are percentages of 'real' Francophones in the population. Source: Etat, 1990

4. Official language(s). Source: Calvet, 1993, 72; L'Année Francophone, 1992, 242; Katzner, 1986, 333-63

5. Summit?: Indicates Yes if the country concerned attended the Mauritius Summit in 1993. Source: *Lettre de la Francophonie*, 66 (nov 1993)

6. Countries or regions marked with an asterisk are not separately listed in HDR 1994. Data source for GDP for *DOM-TOM - L'Année Francophone*, 1992, 240 (figures are in US $).

7. GDP: Real Gross Domestic Product per head of the population, expressed in Purchasing Power Parities dollars (ie eliminating the effect of exchange rate conversions - cf HDR, 1994, 221). * indicates PPP figure not available; figure given is raw GDP per capita in US $ if available. Figures are for 1991. Source: HDR 1994 Table 1.

8. HDI: The Human Development Index is 'a composite measure of human development containing indicators representing three equally weighted dimensions of human development - longevity (life expectancy at birth), knowledge (adult literacy and mean years of schooling, and income (purchasing power parity dollars per capita)' (HDR, 1994, 220). The index provides a raw figure (0 to 1) and a ranked list of the world's countries (1 to 173). The figures given here show the index, the ranking of the country, and whether the country concerned is in the high group (H), the middle group (M) or the low group (L) of countries:

	High H	middle M
	HDI above 0.649	HDI above 0.355
life expectancy	above 68 years	above 55.8
literacy	above 80.4%	above 47.4%
average years		
of study	above 4.8	above 2
GDP per capita		
(PPP $)	above 3,420	above 1,170

Source: HDR 1994 Table 1.

9. Bilateral aid: the figures show inward or outward (shown as -) flows of Bilateral Official Development Assistance per capita in US $ for 1992. Source: HDR 1994, Tables 19 and 41.

Table A3
Summit meetings

Country	ACCT Status	CPF member
Members		
Belgium (Communauté Française)	FM	CPF
Belgium (Kingdom of)	PC	
Benin	FM	CPF
Bulgaria	O	
Burkina Faso	FM	
Burundi	FM	CPF
Cambodia	O	
Cameroon	FM	CPF
Canada	FM	CPF
New Brunswick	PG	
Quebec	PG	CPF
Cape Verde	PC	
Central African Republic	FM	
Chad	FM	
Comoros	FM	
Congo	FM	
Djibouti	FM	
Dominica	FM	
Egypt	AS	CPF
Equatorial Guinea	FM	
France	FM	CPF
Gabon	FM	
Guinea	FM	
Guinea-Bissau	AS	
Haiti	FM	
Ivory Coast	FM	CPF
Laos	FM	CPF
Lebanon	FM	CPF
Luxembourg	FM	
Madagascar	FM	
Mali	FM	CPF
Mauritania	AS	
Mauritius	FM	CPF
Monaco	FM	
Morocco	AS	
Niger	FM	
Romania	O	
Rwanda	FM	CPF
St Lucia	AS	
Senegal	FM	CPF
Seychelles	FM	
Switzerland	PC	
Togo	FM	
Tunisia	FM	
Vanuatu	FM	
Vietnam	FM	
Zaïre	FM	

Non members	% Francophones
Algeria	30
Andorra	29
Israel	11
Guadeloupe	80
Guyana	73
Martinique	80
Mayotte	33
New Caledonia	80
Ontario	?
Polynesia	80
Réunion	80
St Pierre et Miquelon	100
Wallis and Futuna	70

Source: *Lettre de la Francophonie*, 66 (November 1993)
Notes
ACCT Status: This column shows whether the country or region has joined *ACCT*, and its status therein:
FM: Full Member of *Agence de Coopération Culturelle et Technique*
AS: Associated State
PG: Participating Government
O: Observer
PC: Participating Country

Table A4
French 1994 Budget provisions as at January 1994. Allocations and extracts from Budget documents on selected Ministries and programmes.

a) General

Ministry	Recurrent	Debt	Investment	1994	1993
Foreign Affairs	6,863	7,469	367	14,699	14,890
Cooperation	947	4,801	2,022	7,770	8,095
DOM-TOM	874	311	1,087	2,272	2,480
Education	211,472	38,826	1,005	251,303	241,608
Total non-military	498,311	599,566	89,111	1,186,988	1,170,689
Total military	147,643		94,915	242,558	239,440

Note
1. The Table shows finance available (*crédits ouverts*), for a selection of Ministries as at January 1994. Figures are in millions of francs. 'Recurrent' includes costs of operations; 'debt' includes net public debt plus interventions (ie adjustments); 'investments' includes capital and is otherwise known as Payment Credits.

b) Co-operation

	1993	1994	1994/1993
General	3,834	3,534	-7.8
International contributions	3,475	3,873	11.5
Cultural actions supporting development	3,531	3,159	-10.5
Aid to least developed countries (*pays moins avancés - PMA*)	1,170	1,000	14.5

c) France's external action: Aid to developing countries

Expenditure on Official Development Assistance (ODA) (*Aide Publique au Développement* - *APD*) intended for countries of the southern hemisphere and *TOM* (5 billion francs) amount to 46.9 billion francs, or 0.64% of GDP as against 0.63% in 1993. This effort places France again among the leaders of the great industrialised nations.

30.8 billion francs will be allocated to bilateral aid, of which 16.6 billion in gifts. France intends fully to contribute to improving the financial situation of its partners. This aid takes the form of debt cancellation (4.3 billion) and adjustment gifts (1 billion). Budgetary effort in favour of principal debtors is maintained: 14.3 billion, of which approximately 10% can be regarded as *APD* in the OECD definition.

Within bilateral aid, the budget of the Ministry of Cooperation reaches 7.8 billion francs of which 7 billion can be counted as OECD *APD*. Intervention grants available to this Ministry represent 4.8 billion, principally in the form of technical assistance (2 billion) and financial cooperation (1.2 billion). Investment grants (2 billion) are intended essentially for the *Fonds d'Aide et de Coopération* (1.3 billion) and gifts to finance projects in the poorest countries (0.6 billion).

11.9 billion is devoted to multilateral aid, of which 5.9 billion will be delivered through the European Union budget and that of the European Development Fund. Contributions to Banks and Multilateral development funds amount to 4.3 billion francs.

d) The *DOM-TOM*

The budget for the *DOM-TOM* Ministry amounts to nearly 2.3 billion francs. The continuation underlines the desire of the State to take forward the economic development of the *DOM-TOM* and support conditions for harmonious social development. State provision for the *DOM-TOM* includes grants from all Ministries, which amount to more than 41 billion francs for 1994, of which 37 billion is for civil expenditure.

Economic development of the DOM-TOM.

Effort in favour of the economic development of the *DOM-TOM* remains high (1.2 billion francs in programme authorisations and 1.1 billion in payment credits).

• *FIDOM* (Investment fund for the *DOM-TOM*) benefits from global provision of 540 million in programme authorisations and 503.5 in payment authorisations, which allows the State to work with local overseas collectivities and the European Community in the economic development of the *DOM*. The State is thus supporting the efforts of local collectivities in the framework of the new program of planning contracts in the *DOM*, which will cover the period from 1994 to 1998 and for which State-provided grants have increased by 50% by comparison with the 10th Plan. In addition the State is to increase to a very significant amount the grants it provides for investment eligible for Community structural funds, in order to take advantage of the decision of the European Council of Ministers at Edinburgh to double the allocation of those funds for ultra-peripheral regions of the Community.

• The general section and the territorial section of *FIDES* (Fund for investment for economic and social development), intended for the *TOM*, is granted 202.3 million francs in programme authorisations and 125.8 million in payment credits. This allocation will permit increased sums for French Polynesia in pursuance of the State's obligations in the Orientation Law on the development of French Polynesia approved in January 1994.

• Total grants for New Caledonia, not including *FIDES*, reach 380 million francs in programme authorisations (+ 7%) and 342.5 million in payment credits (+11.4%), ensuring the application of the State's effort on behalf of this territory, decided on the negotiation of the second generation of planning contracts.

Search for harmonious social development.

The objective of social equality must not be taken in a narrow sense to mean parity of incomes with those of metropolitan France, which would contribute to isolation of the

DOM-TOM from their regional environment; on the contrary it is intended to support better economic and commercial integration (*insertion*), which is the only guarantor of future prosperity.
• The increase in contractually agreed funding for New Caledonia allows the placing of social cohesion at the heart of the plans; in this way, supplementary grants benefit:
- costs of primary education and free medical assistance: + 50 million francs;
- training of Caledonian key personnel and youth training periods: + 47.25 million francs.

e) Francophonie.
The budget for the Ministry of Culture and Francophonie prioritises the development of the territory, training and public awareness of culture, and Francophonie.
Action for Francophonie will take place through the sums made available to the *Délégation Générale à la Langue Française*, of 111 million francs. This delegation is henceforth attached to the Ministry of Culture and Francophonie.
Source for Table A4: *Notes Bleues*, 94-1

Table A5
France's external trade by country in 1993

Country	Imports	%	Exports	%	Balance (exp-imp)
Belgium/Lux	100,273	8.84	100,956	8.61	233
Canada	6,652	0.58	8,527	0.73	1,875
Romania	1,605	0.14	2,614	0.22	1,009
Bulgaria	758	0.07	728	0.06	-30
Morocco	10,868	0.95	11,387	0.97	519
Algeria	7,784	0.68	11,898	1.02	4,114
Tunisia	5,906	0.52	9,114	0.78	3,208
DOM-TOM	2,888	0.25	29,135	2.49	26,247
Franc zone:	10509	0.92	15,060	1.28	4,551
Mali	52	0	677	0.06	625
Niger	807	0.07	570	0.05	-237
Senegal	874	0.08	2,271	0.19	1,397
Ivory Coast	3,291	0.29	3,513	0.30	222
Togo	53	0	336	0.03	283
Cameroons	2,134	0.19	1,943	0.17	-190
Gabon	2,525	0.22	2,255	0.19	-270
Congo	419	0.04	1,274	0.11	855
Others franc zone	355	0.03	2,221	0.19	1,866
Egypt	1,674	0.15	362	0.03	-1312
Madagascar	852	0.07	472	0.04	-380
Mauritius	1,619	0.14	55	0	-1564
Zaïre	89	0.01	9,063	0.77	8,974
NB					
Total EEC	666,772	58.52	700,720	59.78	33,948
Total Francophonie (ie countries included above, including *DOM-TOM*)					
	151,477	13.3	199,371	17	47,894

Source: *Le Nouvel Economiste*, 950, 8: 17.6.1994 (itself based on statistics from the Customs service).
Note
This is an extract from the full table. Figures are in millions of francs. Excludes military equipment. The balance figure for Egypt, Madagascar, Mauritius and Zaïre has been recalculated from the import and export columns given.

Table A6
Elections in the *DOM-TOM*. 1993 and 1995
French legislative election results for the DOM-TOM, March 1993.

DOM	previous party	new party (1993)
Guadeloupe	PS, PPDG, PS, RPR	PS, PPDG, div d., RPR
Martinique	div g., PPM, PPM, div g.	UPF, RPR, PPM, RPR
Guyane	PSG, RPR	div g., RPR
Réunion	div d., UDF-CDS, div d., PCR, UDF-CDS	PS, PCR, UPF, RPR, UDF-CDS
TOM		
New Caledonia	RPCR, RPCR	RPR, RPR
French Polynesia	div g., div g.	RPR, RPR
Wallis and Futuna	MRG	MRG
Collectivités territoriales		
Mayotte	UDF-CDS	UDF-CDS
St Pierre et Miquelon		
	UDF-CDS	UDF-CDS

Source: *Le Monde*, 23 & 30.3.1993
Notes
div g - divers gauche - other parties of the Left
div d - divers droite - other parties of the Right
Right-wing parties
CDS - Centre des Démocrates Sociaux
RPCR - Rassemblement pour la Calédonie dans la République
RPR - Rassemblement pour la République
UDF - Union pour la Démocratie Française
UPF - Union pour la France
Left-wing parties
MRG - Mouvement des Radicaux de Gauche
PCR - Parti Communiste Réunionais
PPDG -Parti Progressiste Démocratique Guadeloupéen
PPM - Parti Progressiste Martiniquais
PSG - Parti Socialiste Guyanais

Presidential elections, 7 May 1995
Overall result in France including *DOM-TOM*
                    Jacques Chirac: 52.64%   Lionel Jospin: 47.36%

DOM		
Guadeloupe	Jospin: 55.1%	Chirac: 44.9%
1st round:	Chirac: 38.23%, Jospin: 36.13%, Balladur: 14.48%, Hue: 3.57%, Le Pen: 3.06%, Laguiller: 2.25%, Voynet: 1.41%, Cheminade: 0.95%; Villiers: 0.91%	
1988:	Mitterrand: 69.41%	Chirac: 30.59%

Martinique	Jospin: 58.89%	Chirac: 41.11%
1st round:	Jospin: 36.4%, Chirac: 29.14%, Balladur: 23.58%,	
	Hue: 3.54%, Laguiller: 2.67%, Le Pen: 1.65%,	
	Voynet: 1.27%, Villiers: 0.9%, Cheminade: 0.85%	
1988:	Mitterrand: 70.89%	Chirac: 29.11%
Guyane	Chirac: 57.43%	Jospin: 42.57%
1st round:	Chirac: 39.84%, Jospin: 24.15%, Balladur: 16.88%,	
	Le Pen: 8.08%, Laguiller: 3.76%, Voynet: 2.63%,	
	Hue: 1.9%, Villiers: 1.87%, Cheminade: 0.9%	
1988:	Mitterrand: 60.39%	Chirac: 39.61%
Réunion	Jospin: 56.07%	Chirac: 43.93%
1st round:	Chirac: 35.18%, Jospin: 30.36%, Balladur: 13.53%,	
	Hue: 10.54%, Le Pen: 2.89%, Laguiller: 2.42%,	
	Villiers: 2.23%, Voynet: 1.91%, Cheminade: 0.94%	
1988:	Mitterrand: 60.26%	Chirac: 39.74%

TOM

New Caledonia	Chirac: 74.1%	Jospin: 25.9%
1st round:	Chirac: 42.97%, Balladur: 26.57%, Jospin: 15.87%,	
	Le Pen: 8.17%, Villiers: 1.85%, Voynet: 1.72%,	
	Laguiller: 1.51%, Hue: 0.7%, Cheminade: 0.65%	
1988:	Chirac: 90.29%	Mitterrand: 9.71%
French Polynesia	Chirac: 60.98%	Jospin: 39.02%
1st round:	Chirac: 51.63%, Balladur: 24.93%, Jospin: 12.51%,	
	Le Pen: 3.12%, Villiers: 2.68%, Laguiller:1.63%,	
	Voynet: 1.54%, Hue: 1.23%, Cheminade: 0.72%	
1988:	Mitterrand: 54.47%	Chirac: 45.53%
Wallis and Futuna	Chirac: 55.3%	Jospin: 44.7%
1st round:	Chirac: 43.53%, Jospin: 29.88%, Balladur: 21.8%,	
	Le Pen: 1.21%, Cheminade: 0.87%, Laguiller: 0.87%,	
	Voynet: 0.7%, Hue: 0.6%, Villiers: 0.55%	
1988:	Chirac: 73.48%	Mitterrand: 26.52%

Collectivités territoriales

Mayotte	Chirac: 63.35%	Jospin: 31.65%
1st round:	Balladur: 47.16%, Chirac: 39.23%, Jospin: 5.22%,	
	Voynet: 1.72%, Hue: 1.61%, Cheminade: 1.52%,	
	Le Pen: 1.32%, Villiers: 1.2%, Laguiller: 1.04%	
1988:	Mitterrand: 50.33%	Chirac: 49.67%
St Pierre et Miquelon		
	Chirac: 60.87%	Jospin: 39.13%
1st round:	Balladur: 23.48%, Chirac: 33.97%, Jospin: 17.31%,	
	Voynet: 3.35%, Hue: 4.78%, Cheminade: 0.41%,	
	Le Pen: 7.51%, Villiers: 2.78%, Laguiller: 6.41%	
1988:	Chirac: 56.21	Mitterrand: 43.79

Source: Le Figaro, 8 May 1995

REFERENCES

ABOU, S. and HADDAD, K. (eds) 1994, *Une Francophonie différentielle*. Paris: L'Harmattan.
AGER, D. E. 1990, *Sociolinguistics and Contemporary French*. Cambridge: Cambridge University Press.
AGER, D. E. 1995, Immigration and language policy in France. *Journal of Intercultural Studies*.
ALDRICH, R. 1993, *France and the South Pacific since 1940*. London: Macmillan.
ALDRICH, R. (ed) 1991, *France, Oceania and Australia: past and present*. Sydney: Department of Economic History, University of Sydney.
ALDRICH, R. and CONNELL, J. (eds) 1989, *France in World Politics*. London: Routledge.
ALDRICH, R. and CONNELL, J. 1992, *France's Overseas Frontier*. Cambridge: Cambridge University Press.
ANNEE FRANCOPHONE INTERNATIONALE. (L'Année Francophone Internationale). Annual. Issues of 1991, 1992, 1994. Québec: L'Année Francophone Internationale.
ARNOLD, T. 1989, Le multilinguisme facteur de développement ou le paradoxe francophone en Afrique. In R. CHAUDENSON and D. de ROBILLARD (eds) *Langues et développement*. (Vol 1, pp. 115-31). Aix-en-Provence: Didier.
ASHER, R. E. 1994, *The Encyclopedia of language and linguistics*. Oxford: Pergamon Press.
BACH, D. 1995, Francophone regionalism or Franco-African regionalism? In A. KIRK-GREENE (ed) *State and Society in Francophone Africa since Independence* (pp. 200-12). London: Macmillan.
BAGGIONI, D. and ROBILLARD, D. de. 1990, *Ile Maurice: une francophonie paradoxale*. Paris: L'Harmattan.
BAGGIONI, D., CALVET, L.-J., CHAUDENSON, R., MANESSY, G. and ROBILLARD, D. de. 1992, *Multilinguisme et développement dans l'espace francophone*. Paris: Didier.
BAYART, F. 1994, Rwanda: les ambiguités d'une intervention. *Esprit*, 204, 187-9.
BEAUGE, F. 1994, La Belgique en ses habits fédéraux. *Le Monde Diplomatique*, February 1994.
BEBEL-GISLER, C. 1981, *La Langue créole, force jugulée*. Paris: Nouvelle Optique-L'Harmattan.
BELORGEY, G. (ed) 1993, *Outre-mer: le défi des singularités*. Rapport du groupe 'Outre-mer', Préparation du XIe Plan. Paris: La Documentation Française.
BELORGEY, G. and BERTRAND, G. 1994, *Les DOM-TOM*. Paris: La Découverte.
BENGTSSON, S. 1968. *La défense organisée de la langue française*. Uppsala: Almqvist and Wiksells.
BENICHOU, M. (ed) 1993, *L'avenir des industries de la Défense. Rapport du groupe Défense, Préparation du XIe Plan*. Paris: La Documentation Française.
BENICHOU, M. 1994, Les exportations d'armements. Annex to M. BENICHOU (ed) 1993. *L'avenir des industries de la Défense. Rapport du groupe Défense, Préparation du XIe Plan*. Paris: La Documentation Française. Reprinted in *Problèmes Economiques* 2, 383, 11-15.

BENOIT, J.-P., BESSONNAT, D., MASSERON C., PRIVAT, J.-M and VINSON, M.-C. 1991, L'Evaluation nationale en français: l'exemple des 6e en 1990. *Pratiques* 71, 27-68.

BENOT, Y. 1994, *Massacres coloniaux, 1944-1950: la IVe République et la mise au pas des colonies françaises.* Paris: La Découverte.

BENRABAH, M. 1992, La modernité passe par l'arabe algérien. *Hebdo libéré* 63, 64 and 65. (10-30.6.1992)

BENRABAH, M. 1995, La langue perdue. *Esprit* 208, 1, 35-47.

BERRENDONNER, A. 1982, *L'éternel grammairien. Etude du discours normatif.* Bern: Lang.

BIDDLECOMBE, P. 1993, *French lessons in Africa. Travels with my briefcase through French Africa.* London: Abacus Travel.

BOKAMBA, E. G. 1991, *French colonial language policies in Africa and their legacies.* In D. F. MARSHALL (ed) *Language planning. Festschrift in honour of Joshua A. Fishman* (pp. 175-213). Amsterdam, Philadelphia: John Benjamin Publishing Company.

BOURDIEU, P. 1982, *Ce que parler veut dire.* Paris: Fayard.

BOURHIS, Y. 1984, *Language conflict and language planning in Quebec.* Clevedon: Multilingual Matters.

BRAECKMANN, C. 1994, *Rwanda, histoire d'un génocide.* Paris: Fayard.

BRETON, R. 1991, *The handicaps of language planning in Africa.* In D. F. MARSHALL (ed) *Language planning. Festschrift in honour of Joshua A. Fishman* (pp. 153-74). Amsterdam, Philadelphia: John Benjamin Publishing Company.

BRIAND, S. 1990, Un labyrinthe encore trop cloisonné. *Geo* 138, 74-7.

BROGLIE, G. de. 1986, *Le français, pour qu'il vive.* Paris: Gallimard.

BRUCHET, J. 1992, *Organisations et associations francophones. Répertoire 1992.* Paris: La Documentation Française.

BUCKLEY, A. 1992, Return of the French. *Pacific Islands Monthly* (March 1992), 34.

CALVET, L.-J. 1987, *La Guerre des langues et les politiques linguistiques.* Paris: Payot.

CALVET, L.-J. 1992, *Les langues des marchés en Afrique.* Paris: Didier.

CALVET, L.-J. 1993, *L'Europe et ses langues.* Paris: Plon.

CHAND, G. 1993, France and South Pacific. Regionalism in the 1980s and 1990s. *Journal of Pacific Studies* 17, 57-81.

CHAUDENSON, R. 1979, *Les Créoles français.* Paris: Nathan.

CHAUDENSON, R. 1989, *Créoles et enseignement du français.* Paris: L'Harmattan.

CHAUDENSON, R. 1991, *La Francophonie: représentations, réalités, perspectives.* Paris: Didier.

CHAUDENSON, R. 1993, La typologie des situations de Francophonie. In D. de ROBILLARD and M. BENIAMINO (eds). *Le français dans l'espace francophone* (Vol 1, pp. 357-69). Paris: Honoré Champion.

CHAUDENSON, R., and ROBILLARD, R. de (eds). 1989. *Langues et développement.* Aix-en-Provence: Didier. (2 vols)

CHERRAD-BENCHEFRA, Y. 1989, Les Algériens et leurs rapports avec les langues. *Lengas* 26, 45-56.

CHESNEAUX, J. and MCLELLAN, N. 1992, *La France dans le Pacifique. De Bougainville à Moruroa.* Paris: La Découverte.

CHRETIEN, J.-P. 1995, Rwanda 1994. *Esprit,* 210, 99-110.

CHRISTNACHT, Alain. 1987, New edition 1990, La Nouvelle Calédonie. *Notes et Etudes Documentaires* 4839.

CLYNE, M. (ed) 1992, *Pluricentric languages. Differing norms in different nations.* Berlin: Mouton de Gruyter.

COMRIE, B. (ed) 1987, *The World's Major Languages.* London: Croom Helm.

CONAC, G, HERTZOG, R, CORBEL, J-C. and DESOUCHES, C. 1990, *Francophonie et coopération communautaire internationale.* Collection Coopération 4. Paris: Economica.

CONNELL, J. and ALDRICH, R. 1991, The last colonies: failures of decolonisation? In C. DIXON and M. HEFFERNAN (eds) *Colonialism and development in the modern world* (pp. 183-203). London: Mansell.

COQUET, B., DANIEL, J.-M., and FOURMANN, E. 1993, Les relations économiques entre l'Europe et l'Afrique depuis le début des années soixante. *Problèmes Economiques* 2333 (July 1993), 16-24.

COULMAS, F. (ed) 1991, *A language policy for the European Community - prospects and quandaries.* Berlin: Mouton de Gruyter.

COULMAS, F. 1992, *Language and economy.* Oxford: Blackwell.

COUSSY, J. 1995, The franc zone: original logic, subsequent evolution and present crisis. In A. KIRK-GREENE (ed) *State and Society in Francophone Africa since Independence* (pp. 160-80). London: Macmillan.

CZERNY, P. G. 1980, *The politics of grandeur. Ideological aspects of de Gaulle's foreign policy.* Cambridge: Cambridge University Press.

DABLA, J.-J. S. and LAMBERT, F. 1994, Afrique. In *Année Francophone Internationale,* 1994 (pp. 205-24).

DANIEL, V. 1992, *La Francophonie au Vietnam.* Paris: L'Harmattan.

DELOIRE, P. 1994, La France, Maastricht et l'Europe des Régions. *Regards sur l'actualité* 197, 41-52.

DENIAU, X. 1983a, *La Francophonie.* Paris: Gallimard.

DENIAU, X. 1983b, 2nd edition 1992, *La Francophonie.* Paris: Presses Universitaires de France.

DGLF (Délégation Générale à la Langue Française). 1994, *Rapport au Parlement sur l'application de la loi du 4 août 1994 relative à l'emploi de la langue française et des dispositions des conventions ou traités internationaux relatives au statut de la langue française dans les institutions internationales.* Paris: Délégation Générale à la Langue Française.

DIALLO, A. M. 1993, Le français en Guinée: une situation en plein changement. In D. de ROBILLARD and M. BENIAMINO (eds) *Le français dans l'espace francophone* (Vol 1, pp. 229-42). Paris: Honoré Champion.

DIXIT. 1992, *Polynésie Française.* Tahiti: Jeune Chambre Economique de Tahiti.

DIXON, C. and HEFFERNAN, M (eds) 1991, *Colonialism and development in the modern world.* London: Mansell.

DJITE, P.G. 1990, Les langues africaines et la francophonie. *Language Problems and Language Planning* 14, 1, 20-32.

DJITE, P.G. 1991, Langues et développement en Afrique. *Language problems and Language Planning* 15, 2, 121-38.

DJITE, P.G. 1992, The French revolution and the French language: a paradox? *Language Problems and Language Planning* 16, 2, 163-77.

DJITE, P. G. 1993a, Francophonie: gain d'humanité ou perte d'identité? *Language Problems and Language Planning* 17, 3, 254-64.

DJITE, P.G. 1993b, Language and development in Africa. *International Journal of the Sociology of Language* 100/101, 149-66.

DORAIS, L.-J. 1980, Diglossie, bilinguisme et classes sociales en Louisiane. *Pluriel Débats* 22, 57-91.

DUMONT, P. 1986, *L'Afrique noire peut-elle encore parler français?* Paris: L'Harmattan.

DUMONT, P. 1993, L'enseignement du français en Afrique: le point sur une méthodologie en crise. In D. de ROBILLARD and M. BENIAMINO (eds) *Le français dans l'espace francophone* (Vol 1, pp. 471-80). Paris: Honoré Champion.

DYSTE, C. 1989, Proposition 63: the California English Language Amendment. *Applied Linguistics* 10, 3, 313-30.

ERIKSEN, T. H. 1993, A future-oriented, non-ethnic nationalism? Mauritius as an exemplary case. *Ethnos*, 3-4, 197-221.

ETAT. (Etat de la francophonie dans le monde). Annual. Issues of 1985, 1986, 1987, 1988, 1989, 1990, 1991, 1992, 1993, 1994. Haut Conseil de la Francophonie. Paris: La Documentation Française.

EXPRESS (L'Express). Weekly. Issues of 7.10.1993, 14.10.1993, 27.1.1994.

FARANDJIS, S. 1994, *La Francophonie et l'Europe. 10e session du Haut Conseil de la Francophonie. 22, 23, 24 mars 1994. Vol 1: Actes. Vol 2: Dossiers et Documents.* Paris: Haut Conseil de la Francophonie.

FERGUSON, C. A. 1959, Diglossia. *Word* 15, 325-40.

FIGARO (Le Figaro) Daily. Issues of 6.7.1994, 31.8.1994.

FINEGAN, E. 1987, English. In B. COMRIE (ed) *The World's Major Languages* (pp. 77-109). London: Croom Helm.

FRANCARD, M. 1993, Entre Romania et Germania: la Belgique francophone. In D. de ROBILLARD and M. BENIAMINO (eds) *Le français dans l'espace francophone* (Vol 1, pp. 317-36). Paris: Editions Champion.

GAULME, F. 1994, France-Afrique. Une crise de coopération. *Etudes* 3801 (janvier 1994), 41-52.

GIRARDET, R. 1986, L'idée coloniale en France. *Pluriel* 78.

GRILLO, R. D. 1989, *Dominant languages: language and hierarchy in Britain and France.* Cambridge: Cambridge University Press.

GUARDIAN. (The Guardian). Daily. Issues of 2.5.1991, 6.2.1995, 3.4.1995, 5.4.1995, 17.5.1995.

GUEUNIER, N. 1992, Le français langue d'Afrique. *Présence francophone* 40, 99-120.

GUEUNIER, N. 1993, Les Francophones du Liban: 'fous des langues'. In D. de ROBILLARD and M. BENIAMINO (eds) *Le français dans l'espace francophone* (Vol 1, pp 263-79). Paris: Honoré Champion.

GUILLERMOU, A. 1964, La Fédération Internationale pour la sauvegarde et l'unité de la langue française. *Culture Française* 2, 16-28.

GUILLOU, M. 1993, *La Francophonie, nouvel enjeu mondial.* Paris: Hatier.

GUILLOU, M. and LITTARDI, A. 1988, *La Francophonie s'éveille.* Paris: Berger-Levrault.

HAGEGE, C. 1987, *Le français et les siècles.* Paris: Seuil.

HAGEGE, C. 1992, *Le souffle de la langue.* Paris: Odile Jacob.

HARBI, M. 1994, L'Algérie prise au piège de son histoire. *Le Monde Diplomatique*, May 1994.

HAZAËL-MASSIEUX, M. - C. 1993, *Ecrire en créole: oralité et écriture aux Antilles.* Paris: L'Harmattan.

HDR. (Human Development Report). 1994, *Human Development Report 1994, published for the United Nations Development Programme.* Oxford: Oxford University Press.

HUGON, P. 1993, *L'Economie de l'Afrique.* Paris: La Découverte.

IFA. (Inventaire du Français d'Afrique). 1983, 2nd ed 1988, *Inventaire des particularités lexicales du français en Afrique Noire.* Quebec: ACCT.

JERNUDD, B. H. and SHAPIRO, M. J. (eds) 1989, *The Politics of Language Purism.* Berlin: Mouton de Gruyter.

JOURNAL OFFICIEL (Journal Officiel de la République Française). 1994. *Assemblée Nationale. Débats. Comptes rendus.* 26 A.N. (C.R.) Paris: Journaux Officiels

JUDGE, A. 1993, French, a planned language? In C. SANDERS (ed) *French today.*
Language in its social context (pp. 7-26). Cambridge: Cambridge University Press.
JUILLIARD, C. 1990, Répertoires et actes de communication en situation plurilingue: le
cas de Ziguinchor au Sénégal. *Langage et société* 54, 65 - 82.
KA, O. 1993, Une nouvelle place pour le français au Sénégal? *The French Review* 67, 2,
276-90.
KAZADI, N. 1991, *L'Afrique afro-francophone*. Paris: Didier.
KEATING, M. and HAINSWORTH, P. 1986, *Decentralisation and change in
contemporary France*. Aldershot: Gower.
KEPEL, G. 1994, *A l'Ouest d'Allah*. Paris: Seuil.
KIRK-GREENE, A. (ed) 1995, *State and Society in Francophone Africa since
Independence*. London: Macmillan.
LABRIE, N. 1993, *La construction linguistique de la Communauté Européenne*. Paris:
Honoré Champion.
LACROIX, J.-M. 1993, Le bipartisme en question au Canada. *Le Monde Diplomatique*,
October 1993.
LAFAGE, S. 1985, *Français écrit et parlé en pays éwé (Sud Togo)*. Paris: SELAF.
LAFAGE, S. 1993, French in Africa. In C. SANDERS (ed) *French today. Language in
its social context* (pp. 215-38). Cambridge: Cambridge University Press.
LEGER, J.-M. 1988, *La francophonie: grand dessein, grande ambigüité*. Paris: Nathan.
LEMAIRE, J. (ed) 1989, *Le français et les Belges*. Brussels: Editions de l'Université de
Bruxelles.
LEQUESNE, C. 1993, *Paris-Bruxelles. Comment se fait la politique européenne de la
France*. Paris: Presses de la Fondation Nationale des Sciences Politiques.
LETTRE DE LA FRANCOPHONIE (La Lettre de la Francophonie).
Fortnightly/monthly. Issues from No 1 (September 1990) to No 82 (May 1995).
LIBERATION (La Libération). Daily. Issues of 24.2.1994, 25.7.1994, 27.12.1994,
9.6.1995.
LO BIANCO. J. 1987, *National Policy on Languages*. Canberra: Department of
Education.
LODGE, R. A. 1993, *French: from dialect to standard*. London: Routledge.
LOUVEL, R. 1994, *Quelle Afrique pour quelle coopération? Mythologie de l'aide
française*. Paris: L'Harmattan.
LUDI, G. 1992, French as a pluricentric language. In M. CLYNE (ed) 1992. *Pluricentric
languages. Differing norms in different nations* (pp. 149-78). Berlin: Mouton de
Gruyter.
MADINIER, C. 1993, Les originaires des *DOM. Population* 6, 1855-68.
MANESSY, G. and WALD, P. 1984, *Le Français en Afrique Noire*. Paris: L'Harmattan-
IDERIC.
MARSHALL, D.F. (ed) 1991, *Language planning. Festschrift in honour of Joshua A.
Fishman*. Amsterdam, Philadelphia: John Benjamin Publishing Company.
MARTIN, G. 1989, France and Africa. In R. ALDRICH, R. and J. CONNELL (eds)
France in World Politics (pp. 101-25). London: Routledge.
MARTIN, M. L. 1995, Armies and politics: the 'lifecycle' of military rule in sub-Saharan
Francophone Africa. In A. KIRK-GREENE (ed) *State and Society in Francophone
Africa since Independence* (pp. 78-96). London: Macmillan.
MATHIEU, J.-L. 1988, *Les DOM-TOM*. Paris: Presses Universitaires de France.
MAURAIS, J. 1993, Etat de la recherche sur la description de la francophonie au Québec.
In D. de ROBILLARD and M. BENIAMINO (eds) *Le français dans l'espace
francophone* (Vol 1, pp. 79-99). Paris: Honoré Champion.
MAURAIS, J. (ed). 1985, *La Crise des langues*. Paris/Quebec: Le Robert.

MCKESSON, J.A. 1993, France and Africa: the evolving saga. *French Politics and Society* 11, 2, 55-68.

MCRAE, K. D. 1986. *Conflict and compromise in multilingual societies: Belgium.* Quebec: Wilfrid Laurier University Press.

MEKACHA, R.D.K. 1994, Language death: conceptions and misconceptions. *Journal of Pragmatics* 21, 1, 101-16.

MELLING, P. and ROPER, J. 1991, *America, France and Vietnam: cultural history and ideas of conflict.* Aldershot: Avebury.

MINC, A. 1989, *La Grande Illusion.* Paris: Grasset.

MIROIR, A. 1990, La Belgique et ses clivages: contradictions structurelles et familles politiques. *Pouvoirs* 54, 5-14.

MITTERRAND, F. 1959, *Aux frontières de l'Union française.* Indochine-Tunisie. Paris: Julliard.

MOATTI, G. (ed) 1989, La France dans le monde. *L'Expansion* (6-19.7.1989).

MOATISSIME, A. 1992, *Arabisation et langue française au Maghreb.* Paris: Presses Universitaires de France.

MONDE (Le Monde). Daily. Issues of 2.7.1994, 5.8.1994, 2.9.1994, 8.3.1995.

MONDE DES DEBATS (Le Monde des Débats). Monthly. Issue of July 1993.

MONDE DIPLOMATIQUE (Le Monde Diplomatique). Monthly. Issues of April 1993, May 1993, January 1994, April 1994, May 1994, July 1994, November 1994.

MONTAGNON, P. 1989 (Vol 1), 1990 (Vol 2), *La France Coloniale. Vol 1: La Gloire de l'Empire. Vol 2: Retour à l'hexagone.* Paris: Pygmalion.

MOUGEON, R. 1994, Interventions gouvernementales en faveur du français au Québec et en Ontario. *Langage et société* (March 1994), 37-52.

NISS, H. 1994, European Cultural Diversity and its implications for pan-European advertising. In S. ZETTERHOLM *National cultures and European integration. Exploratory essays on cultural diversity and common policies* (pp. 161-72). Oxford: Berg.

NOGUEZ, D. 1991, *La colonisation douce.* Paris: Editions du Rocher.

NORTH, D. 1994, Why Mauritius is so successful. *Pacific Islands Monthly* (May 1994), 27-9.

NOTE D'INFORMATION. 1992 and 1994, Note d'Information du Ministère de l'Education nationale 92-42 and 94-11.

NOTES BLEUES. 1994. Les Notes Bleues du Ministère des Finances 94-1.

NOUVEL ECONOMISTE (Le Nouvel Economiste). Weekly. Issue of 17.6.1994.

NOUVELLES CALEDONIENNES (Les Nouvelles Calédoniennes). Daily. Issue of 21.6.1994.

OBSERVER. (The Observer). Weekly. Issues of 9.9.1994, 9.10.1994.

OFFORD, M. 1993, Protecting the French language- the role of private organizations. *French Cultural Studies* 4, 2, 11, 167-84.

OZOLINS, U. 1993, *The politics of language in Australia.* Cambridge: Cambridge University Press.

PALARD, J. 1993, Décentralisation et démocratie locale. *Problèmes politiques et sociaux* 708 (30 juillet 1993).

PARRY, M. M., DAVIES, W. V. and TEMPLE, R. A. M. 1994, *The changing voices of Europe. Social and political changes and their linguistic repercussions past, present and future.* Cardiff: University of Wales Press.

PERGNIER, M. 1989, *Les anglicismes.* Paris: Presses Universitaires de France.

POLYNESIE FRANÇAISE. 1993, *La Polynésie Française.* Paris: Institut d'Emission d'Outre-Mer.

POOL, J. 1972, National development and language diversity. In J. A. FISHMAN (ed) *Advances in the Sociology of Language* (Vol 1, pp. 213-30). Den Haag: Mouton.

POSNER, R. 1994, Romania within a wider Europe: conflict or cohesion? In M. PARRY, W. V. DAVIES and R. A. M. TEMPLE (eds) *The changing voices of Europe*. *Social and political changes and their linguistic repercussions past, present and future* (pp. 23-33). Cardiff: University of Wales Press.

PREMDAS, R. R. and STEEVES, J. S. 1994, Vanuatu: the politics of Anglo-French cooperation in the post-Lini era. *Journal of Commonwealth and Comparative Politics* 32, 1, 68-86.

RAPAPORT, M. 1994, French Polynesia. *The Contemporary Pacific* 6, 1, 179-81.

RAYMOND, G. 1991, French culture and the politics of self-esteem: the Vietnam experience. In P. MELLING and J. ROPER (eds) *America, France and Vietnam: cultural history and ideas of conflict* (pp. 56-70). Aldershot: Avebury.

REGNAULT, J.-M. 1994, Gaston Flosse, adversaire et champion de l'autonomie en Polynésie française. *Tahiti-Pacifique* 38, 31-36.

ROBILLARD, D. de. 1992, L'aménagement linguistique du français à l'île Maurice: un exemple de réconciliation de la théorie et de la pratique? *Présence Francophone* 40, 121-34.

ROBILLARD, D. de 1993, L'expansion du français à l'île Maurice: dynamisme stratificatoire, inhibitions ethniques. In D. de ROBILLARD and M. BENIAMINO (eds) *Le français dans l'espace francophone* (Vol 1, pp. 129-50). Paris: Honoré Champion.

ROBILLARD, D. de and BENIAMINO, M. (eds) 1993. *Le français dans l'espace francophone*. 2 vols. Paris: Honoré Champion

RUHLEN, M. 1987, *A Guide to the World's Languages*. Stanford, California: Stanford University Press.

SANDERS, C. (ed) 1993, *French today. Language in its social context*. Cambridge: Cambridge University Press.

SCHNEPEL, E. M. and PRUDENT, L.-F. 1993, Créole Movements in the Francophone Orbit. *International Journal of the Sociology of Language*, Vol 102.

SERRE, F. de la, LERUEZ, J. and WALLACE, H. 1990, *Les politiques étrangères de la France et de la Grande-Bretagne depuis 1945: l'inévitable ajustement*. Paris: Presses de la Fondation Nationale des Sciences Politiques.

SILVERMAN, M. 1992, *Deconstructing the nation: immigration, racism and citizenship in modern France*. London: Routledge.

SLOWE, P. 1991, Colonialism and the African Nation: the case of Guinea. In C. DIXON and M. HEFFERNAN (eds) *Colonialism and development in the modern world* (pp. 106-20). London: Mansell.

STEEVES, J. S. 1992, Vanuatu: the 1991 national elections and their aftermath. *The Journal of Pacific History* 27, 2, 217-28.

TETU, M. 1987, (Third edition 1992), *La Francophonie: histoire, problématique, perspectives*. Paris: Guérin/Hachette.

THERIEN, J.-P. 1993, Cooperation and conflict in la Francophonie. *International Journal* (Canadian Institute of International Affairs) 48, 3, 492-526.

THOMAS, G. 1991, *Linguistic purism*. London: Longman.

TIMES (The Times). Daily. Issue of 6.8.1994.

TOYE, R. 1994, Le Commonwealth. *Afrique Contemporaine* 171, 53-71.

TRESCASES, P. 1982, *Le franglais, vingt ans après*. Montréal: Guérin.

TRUCHOT, C. (ed) 1994, *Le Plurilinguisme européen*. Paris: Champion.

VALDMAN, A. (ed) 1979, *Le Français hors de France*. Paris: Champion.

VERDOODT, A.F. and SONNTAG, S.K. (eds) 1993, The Sociology of Language in Belgium (revisited). *International Journal of the Sociology of Language* Vol 104

VERGES, P. 1993, *D'une île au monde*. Paris: L'Harmattan.

VIGH, A. (ed). 1989, *L'identité culturelle dans les littératures de langue française. Actes du colloque de Pecs*. Pecs: Presses de l'Université de Pecs.
WEINSTEIN, B. 1989, Francophonie: purism at the international level. In B. H. JERNUDD and M. J. SHAPIRO (eds) *The Politics of Language Purism* (pp. 53-80). Berlin: Mouton de Gruyter.
WILCOX, L. 1994, Coup de langue. The amendment to Article 2 of the Constitution: an equivocal interpretation of linguistic pluralism? *Modern and Contemporary France* NS2, 3, 269-78.
ZETTERHOLM, S. 1994, *National cultures and European integration. Exploratory essays on cultural diversity and common policies*. Oxford: Berg.

INDEX